CarTech®

Tommy Lee Byrd

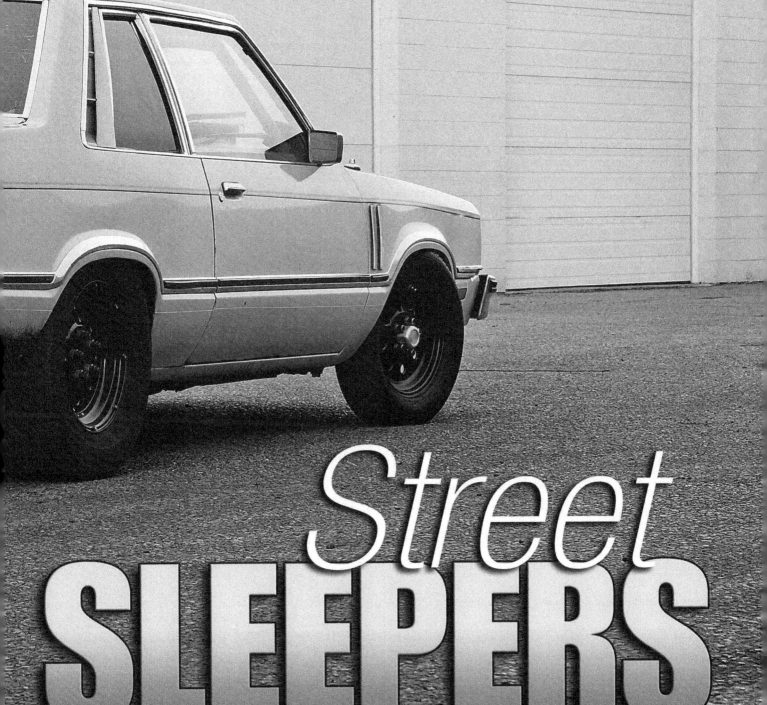

Street SLEEPERS

The art of the deceptively fast car

CarTech®

CarTech®, Inc.
39966 Grand Avenue
North Branch, MN 55056
Phone: 651-277-1200 or 800-551-4754
Fax: 651-277-1203
www.cartechbooks.com

Edit by Scott Parkhurst
Layout by Monica Seiberlich

ISBN 978-1-61325-200-0
Item No. CT498P

Library of Congress Cataloging-in-Publication Data

Byrd, Tommy Lee.
  Street sleepers : the art of the deceptively fast car / by Tommy Lee Byrd.
     p. cm.
  ISBN 978-1-934709-58-0
1. Automobiles, Racing. 2. Automobiles–Performance. I. Title.

TL236.B97 2011
629.228--dc22

2011008788

Printed in U.S.A.

Front Cover:
It may look like a worn and weathered car that reached its prime more than 30 years ago, but this Chevy Nova is one of the most sophisticated cars out there. Extensive chassis strengthening and a well-crafted engine setup make this flawless piece of engineering genius one of the best sleepers around. (Photo courtesy Dominick Damato)

Title Page:
It's old and outdated, so the Zephyr doesn't get much attention, until on-lookers catch a glimpse of it in action. With more than 1,000 hp at the rear wheels, the Mickey Thompson 275/60R15 drag radials fight for traction, while the Sportsman front runner tires skim across the pavement en route to an 8-second pass. (Photo courtesy Kevin Stachniak)

Frontispiece:
While the engine proved its potential by cranking out 435 hp on the dyno, all motor passes have only produced times in the mid-12s for this 4,100-pound sedan. The NOS Big Shot plate nitrous system really wakes up the LT1-based small-block, giving it enough power to gain two full seconds in the quarter-mile. (Photo courtesy Mike Thompson)

Back Cover Photos:

Top:
This is the engine powering the old 1972 Chevy Nova on the front cover. It might look like a car ready for the scrapyard, but it can travel a quarter-mile from a standing start in just over 9 seconds. That's quicker than any new car, or motorcycle, on the planet.

Left:
Twin superchargers force air and fuel into the engine, propelling the car from 0 to 148 mph in 9.25 seconds. The boost can be turned up higher, if necessary, making the car even faster. This setup is completely legal, and the car is driven on the street regularly. Would you even notice it?

Right:
The 1,160-hp engine powering the Nova requires an advanced fuel system to feed it. Would you ever expect to see this hiding under the rusty decklid?

CONTENTS

Introduction

Before you can successfully build a sleeper, you need to understand the ins and outs of the term *sleeper*. An Internet search may provide a lot of information and a few good videos of the sleepy variety, but everyone's opinion of a sleeper is different. Many people think that a sleeper can be most any car, but only a certain breed of cars really fit the bill. A sleeper is a car that is surprisingly fast, but it's not quite as simple as it seems. Real car guys pick up on minor details and put the pieces together in record time. This is especially true if they have a chance to look the car over, because there's only so much you can do to hide serious speed parts.

Some owners are exceptionally crafty when it comes to hiding horsepower, and those are the ones who take home the cash when the dust settles. Winning is also about attitude. You don't want to seem too confident, but you can't expect someone to run unless you let them know you're serious. The idea is to appear as though you're not an expert, but think you really stand a chance against the opponent.

Sometimes, the pre-race activities are just as important as the racing itself.

If you're not concerned with competing in high-dollar drag races, then the point of a sleeper is to simply surprise a street-light jockey with a quick burst of speed or to simply have a good time at the drag strip. The goal is the same either way. A totally average-looking car with a high-horsepower secret under the hood is the ideal sleeper. Without a doubt, your secret won't last long, as one good pass will spill the beans. That's when you have to get creative and up the ante and continue being "sleepy."

Picking the right vehicle is the key. Corvettes, exotic sports cars, and most Mustangs are not good choices, as these makes and models generally have a reputation for great performance right out of the box. However, there are a few bone-stock sports cars that might normally pass under the radar. And just because you have a sleeper doesn't give you immunity from other secretive cars. Never assume a stock-looking

This book is all about sleepers, be it factory-style street sleepers or a purpose-built drag car that looks like a stocker. From cars like this no-frills Buick Skylark to stock-appearing economy cars from the 1980s, you'll see every form of sleeper known to exist and a few you'd never expect.

car is an easy kill, because you might cross paths with another fellow of your kind. Sleeper versus sleeper doesn't happen too often on the street, but the recent grudge race scene has certainly rejuvenated the sneaky side of drag racers.

Although sports cars and most muscle cars are out of the question, you're still left with a wide range of sleeper candidates. The perfect platform is a lightweight, rear-wheel-drive car that would never garner attention from a car guy. Uglier is usually better, and you'd better not have an ego, because a sleeper definitely doesn't provide the same glory as a shiny new Camaro or the like. You might not catch the eye of many ladies or get thumbs up from the car enthusiast crowd, but you'll prove a point when the time is right.

In these twelve chapters, you will see every type of sleeper out there, and some of the tricks and tips to building one of your own. Cool tricks are sprinkled throughout the chapters, as are a number of car and truck profiles that qualify as the best sleepers in the nation. You'll learn about hiding necessary safety equipment, concealing power adders, and hooking up on street radials, along with many more speed secrets.

You're likely to be fooled by some of the cars in this book, but that's the whole idea, isn't it? So, who's to say I'm not just sticking photos of stock vehicles in here and passing them off as scary fast machines? That strategy would have certainly made this book easier to assemble, but there are lots of on-track shots and elapsed times from this collection of sleeper profiles to prove the performance. Some folks didn't want to share their secrets or elapsed times (ETs), and that was to be expected with this tight-lipped group of individuals. In these cases, you just have to take the photos as evidence.

When it comes down to it, building a sleeper is as simple as you make it: You want a non-descript vehicle that has minimal clues to the car's real potential, and you want it to be fast. There are many ways to get bigger and better results. In this book you'll see simple combinations and you'll see extravagant and wildly creative treatments. Each sleeper profile has a Sleepy Factor rating ranging from 1 to 10 with 10 being the best possible sleeper. This way of rating the profiles allows me to share the nature of each car and what makes it special. You're bound to learn a few new tricks but if you already have the sleeper game figured out, you'll at least see some of the coolest examples in the country.

Hiding horsepower is a big part of building a quality sleeper, and the owner of this Camaro did a great job fitting the turbo system under a stock hood. The car makes 1,000 hp to the rear wheels, thanks to a long list of products that no one will ever see.

Okay, so it has a fancy set of wheels on it, but would you really expect to see this Volvo wagon haze the tires from a 60-mph roll, or outrun crotch rockets on a regular basis? Thanks to a twin-turbo LS1, this wagon is a great example of a heavily modified car that still qualifies as a sleeper. *(Photo courtesy Dan Jenkins)*

Without a doubt, Diesel trucks are the hottest sleepers out there right now, and these machines maintain a sneaky status, even with lift kits or big wheels and tires. With a turbo swap, or a compound system like this Dodge pickup features, you can easily produce 1,000 ft-lbs of torque and drive it daily.

Chapter 1

Definition of a Sleeper

To thoroughly enjoy a good sleeper, you have to know what makes it good. A simple definition of the term *sleeper* is a car that is significantly faster than it looks, but it usually isn't that easy. As an example, you've probably seen stickered-up race cars that struggle to get into the 12s in the quarter-mile, even with enormous slicks and a host of other race-ready details. Don't take that the wrong way—12 seconds in the quarter-mile sprint is plenty fast, but a full-on race car can certainly do better.

A sleeper is a car that is significantly faster than it looks, and this Thunderbird Super Coupe is a prime example. It's a 1995 model, which came from the factory with a 230-hp, supercharged V-6. It now has more boost, reworked heads, and a host of other modifications to boast 400 hp at the rear wheels, but it still looks bone stock. *(Photo courtesy Will Smith)*

Making horsepower isn't always easy when you want to keep it a secret, so power adders are generally used on sleeper applications. Nitrous oxide, superchargers, and turbochargers create lots of power without the need for radical camshaft profiles, high-compression ratios, or high-dollar cylinder heads. Turbochargers are definitely a hot item right now.

Since this Ford sedan already had a fuel-injected small-block Chevy the owner decided to up the ante by installing two turbochargers. The turbo system doesn't feature an intercooler, so that limits boost pressure, and ultimately horsepower. However, it's plenty for this mild combination and you'd never see it coming when the hood is closed.

A surefire way to sneak up on the competition is to do it with a car no one expects to perform. Street rods are a nice platform, as most gear heads see these cars as trailer queens. This one looks like your average 1940 Ford sedan, but packs a serious punch, even with two fairly small turbochargers.

If you're not afraid to do some cutting, welding, and fabricating, you can always convert a front-wheel-drive vehicle to rear-wheel drive, and stuff a big engine under the hood. This Ford Focus doesn't look completely stock, but you'd never expect to see a 331-ci small-block Ford under the hood. *(Photo courtesy Will Smith)*

Now, should you pull up to the starting line in a 1976 Oldsmobile four-door station wagon that looks like a run-of-the-mill "grandma" car and bust off a 12-second pass, your Sleepy Factor is high, as you have run significantly faster than the car appears to be capable of.

In that same train of thought, imagine a stock-appearing 1985 Mustang. These Fox-Body rides are quite popular and very effective as drag cars, so if you see one that looks bone stock, you can still safely assume that the owner has something up his sleeve. However, the Sleepy Factor can be greatly increased with a turbocharger, nitrous oxide, or other type of power adder. With this approach, the engine doesn't have to boast an insane compression ratio or feature a radical camshaft, so the exhaust note can be kept relatively tame if the right measures are taken. Take that stock-appearing Mustang and cram a turbocharged mill under the factory hood and you can have an 8-second quarter-mile car if you go through the effort of hiding a roll cage, retaining the stock wheels, and hiding any other major modifications.

Items like a big fuel pump hanging down at the back of the car, or a massive cowl induction hood are dead giveaways and they're quite common on Mustangs and other popular models, even with a stock engine. The whole idea of building a sleeper is to under promise and over deliver. You don't find many sleepers that have external modifications, but sometimes that can work to the owner's advantage. If you have a tricked out Honda Civic, complete with a body kit, a big wing, and any other kind of goofy accessory you can throw on it, that can be a perfectly fine sleeper, since no one really takes those cars seriously on the street or at the track. Put a serious powerplant under the hood and you'll certainly surprise a few folks. Consider it reverse psychology.

Another way to catch car guys off guard is to make big power with a car that's generally viewed as a show car or a trailer queen. This often works with the street rod crowd, because rodders normally use relatively low-power crate engines for the sake of dependability. Though the original purpose of a street rod leaned more toward drag racing, the trend these days is to make the cars easy to drive under any condition. The advantage here is that low horsepower crate engines usually have a low compression ratio, which is perfect for boost. Stick a couple of turbos on a street rod, and you can add at least 100 hp without losing any dependability (or fuel mileage for that matter).

Sleepers have been around for decades, and the look caught on in the 1960s when car buyers could pick and choose any option they wanted. While this Ford could've originally come with the FE big-block, and held its own among other cars of the era, it now has a 427-ci single overhead cam (SOHC) engine producing 615 hp in stock form.

Today, car guys are good at picking out a sleeper, but if you built a 1955 Chevy with this setup in the 1960s, many would assume that it's a stocker. The ride height is close to stock, and the lack of trim leads most to believe it's a lesser-optioned six-cylinder car, when it's really powered by a healthy big-block.

In the end, it's all about owner preference, as you'll hear a thousand different definitions of the term sleeper. Some think that a base model Corvette with a Z06 engine is a sleeper, which is correct, if you consider a sleeper *any* car that is surprisingly fast. If that's the case, then sleepers aren't all that uncommon because there are millions of cars out there that are slightly faster than they look. On the other side of the coin is the true sleeper, which is a vehicle that would never catch a car guy's interest, but has lots of power. Something like a 1980s-era Chevy Cavalier with a late-model Ecotec engine swap, or maybe a Ford Focus with the Kugel Komponents V-8-swap kit would keep the real car guys guessing until it's far too late and they get a good view of your taillights.

No matter how you define the term sleeper, there's no shortage of these cars on the street, and they've become a big sensation at the drag strip as well. Years ago, sleepers were only used for street racing, and lots of money changed hands because of cars that looked and sounded slow, but carried the mail when it was go-time. Now that law enforcement has seriously cracked down on street racing, the original purpose of building a street sleeper is all but gone. However, sleepers still get tons of attention at cruise nights and the local drag strip, and big-time grudge racers still use lots of tricks to throw off the competition when it comes to negotiating a race.

So where did sleepers actually originate? You can safely assume that folks have been racing automobiles since they were considered new inventions, and winning has always been the goal. So, what's the harm in hopping up your car and keeping it a secret? It happened all the time, long before the cars were defined as sleepers and the trend really took off in the moonshine days, especially in the Southeast United States.

During the Prohibition era, moonshine runners built their early V-8-powered Fords to look stock, even when loaded with moonshine. To do this, they experimented with heavy-duty springs to keep the rear end of the car from squatting under the additional weight of the alcohol in the trunk. Depending on how much money they made, and how serious they were with the business, 'shine runners equipped their original flathead V-8 engines with aluminum cylinder heads, multiple carburetors, and a larger camshaft to outrun the law. Fast forward a few decades, and you find a plethora of unmarked police cars throughout the country that catch unknowing traffic violators—wonder where they got the idea? And while unmarked police cars aren't exceptionally fast by nature, you can bet they'll catch you by surprise, and that's the real goal for any sleeper owner.

Factory Sleepers

When you think about fast cars, be it bone stock or highly modified, it's hard not to think about the muscle car era. In the mid 1960s there were a number of options from nearly all of the popular makes when it came to horsepower. General Motors had a good handle on things, in terms of power, and had a certain way of packaging it that pleased the eye. General Motors also had a nice strategy when it came to factory-built sleepers in the muscle car era. Minimal accessories, simplistic looks, and major power under the hood created some very sneaky machines.

Let's use the Camaro as an example. Cars like the 1969 Z-28 are well known, but you wouldn't have much luck finding a race back in the day. Equipped with racing stripes, a bulging cowl induction hood, and plentiful accessories, this car

First-generation Camaros are known as potent muscle cars, so good luck fooling anyone with a sleeper build. However, a plain Jane Camaro, rolling on base-model wheels and skinny whitewall tires, could do the trick. This is another car that could've easily been a sleeper when it was new.

Chevrolet had a good thing going with its full-size cars in the mid 1960s. And while the Super Sport Impalas were very popular, the sleeper enthusiast would've ordered his car as a Bel Air, and had the L72 big-block installed. During the height of the muscle car era, these Chevys definitely looked like grandma cars.

didn't hide any of its potential, so most savvy car guys would know better than to tangle with it. That's the beauty of the ZL-1 Camaro, or any of the COPO (Central Office Production Order—basically a backdoor factory program through the fleet sales department) cars, as most of these models had a short list of creature comforts or accessories, and a long list of performance parts. Body-color steel wheels and dog-dish hubcaps made for a modest appearance, especially compared to the Rally Sport and Super Sport packages of the time.

Some of GM's offerings looked like a base-model six-cylinder car from the outside, but packed a big-block in the neighborhood of 400 horses. This tactic worked years ago for street racing, but it didn't take very long for folks to become wise to the no-frills look. A great example of a true factory-built sleeper would be the 1966 Chevy Bel Air L72, as it represented the quintessential grandma car with its very basic looks, except granny had 425 hp under her right foot. These two-door post sedans are rare, but you could easily pull off the same effect with a junky four-door car or even a station wagon. There's plenty of room in the engine bay, so a turbocharged big-block wouldn't be out of the question either.

Other car manufacturers produced successful sleepers, but you can count Mopar out of that group, at least in the muscle car era. With vivid colors, countless stripe packages, and hood scoops on just about every model, it was hard to miss a Mopar from 1968 to 1974. However, Mopar stepped it up in the 1980s with its front-wheel-drive cars like the Omni GLH and other models that came with the rather potent 2.2-liter, turbocharged, four-cylinder engine. Part of the equation was that turbo, which helped push these little screamers into V-8 territory when it came to horsepower and torque numbers. Combine that with several compact lightweight plat-

forms (such as the Plymouth Reliant or Dodge Shadow) and you have a surprisingly fast street car that gets 34 mpg on the highway. You can bet thousands of Mustang owners were embarrassed by these econo-boxes, and that was before turning up the boost! With the boost cranked up to the maximum safe limit and a few modifications (like a better air intake system and less restrictive exhaust), it was one fun ride.

Mopar kept this theme going for a while using the turbocharged four-cylinder approach and brought it back in 2003 with the Dodge Neon SRT-4. This, however, is far from a sleeper, with its standout and brash SRT-specific wheels, body kit, and wing. If you want a modern-day sleeper from Mopar, find yourself a PT Cruiser GT, which features 220 or 230 hp, depending on the model year. This gives you SRT-4 power in an unsuspecting package. Make it even better by trading the premium wheels for a set of base-model steelies and hubcaps.

Not to be left out, Ford built several sleeper candidates, but its most recent offering, the re-release of the Taurus SHO, can be an all-time best if it ends up in the right hands. The early Taurus SHO packed more power than the standard version, but it wasn't a record-breaking sedan by any means. The new SHO proves to be a killer platform to build upon, with 12-second quarter-mile potential, with just the addition of a cold-air intake and moderate tuning. That's a four-door, 4,200-pound car by the way. The only problem with the new SHO is the very noticeable appearance package that goes along with the model. Imagine the SHO drivetrain in a standard Taurus. It's yet to be done, but you can bet someone will try it.

An honorable mention for factory sleepers goes to Pontiac with its GTO and G8 GXP. With 400 hp on tap from the get-go, and a plenty strong drivetrain behind it, there's lots of fun to be had in either of these unsuspecting vehicles. The

The L72 engine option was a great one, as it featured a 427-ci big-block Chevy, pushing out an advertised 425 hp. The L72 big-block was used in several applications during GM's muscle car days, but the 1966 Bel Air and Biscayne models were certainly the sneakiest.

In the 1980s, Chrysler built several cool economy cars that featured turbocharged four-cylinder engines. One of them was the Dodge Omni, a tame-looking four-door with a 2.2-liter engine. These cars were exceptionally light, and even though the Shelby GLHS edition (pictured) had a few model-specific features, it was still a mighty sleeper. *(Photo courtesy Jim Knights)*

GTO has a famous name, but it tends to blend in with all of the other cars on the road, and the G8 GXP has all sorts of fancy equipment compared to its base-model counterparts, but it's a four-door and folks generally don't expect much out of a family car. Both cars use LS-based V-8 engines, which make for a very sturdy platform to build upon. Add a camshaft and some decent bolt-ons and you have a rather plain-looking Pontiac with more than 400 hp at the rear wheels. The only drawback with these modern muscle cars is weight—the GTO comes in at 3,700 pounds and the G8 is over the 4,000-pound mark.

There's no doubt that Detroit has built some cool sleepers over the years, but imports have been known to hurt the ego of many muscle car enthusiasts. The idea of getting beat by a four-cylinder car brings a tear to most muscle car owners, but

it happens often. A throaty exhaust and the tendency to spin the tires easily make domestic performance cars hard to resist, but the lighter weight and higher revving capabilities of most imports make them great candidates for sleepers.

Mitsubishi had a great product with its Eclipse line, as these cars were available with all-wheel drive and turbochargers from 1990 to 1999. The Eclipse GSX, the lightweight coupe, featured a 2.0-liter, four-cylinder engine that produced anywhere from 180 to 210 hp, depending on the production year. Obviously, the later-model cars are the more powerful. Keep in mind that Eagle produced a sister car to the Eclipse, the Talon, and the TSI models featured the same turbocharged engine and all-wheel-drive package. Another sister car to this was the Plymouth Laser RS, which was built from 1990 to 1994.

There aren't many car guys that would take a Ford Taurus seriously, especially when it's a station wagon model. And while this one isn't exceptionally fast, its original engine has been swapped for the 32-valve Yamaha-Cosworth V-8, which was available in the 1996–1999 Taurus SHO. *(Photo courtesy Will Smith)*

A performance car that blends into society is usually a good thing for sleeper enthusiasts, but that doesn't often equate to great sales overall. Pontiac built the GTO from the Australian-based Holden platform, and it certainly doesn't stand out as a 400-hp muscle car. This one features a camshaft upgrade and makes more than 400 hp at the wheels.

Diamond-Star Motors (DSM) is known in the import world for its all-wheel-drive, turbocharged economy cars, which prove to be awesome sleeper candidates. The cars have excellent traction from a dead stop, making them a Corvette killer with very few modifications. This Mitsubishi Eclipse looks stock, but launches hard at the track. *(Photo courtesy Jim Knights)*

General Motors had a grand idea when it developed the Chevy TrailBlazer SS, and managed to make an attractive SUV with lots of power and plenty of room for upgrades. Using the 395-hp LS2 engine, General Motorsoffered the TrailBlazer in all-wheel drive, which is great for launching. These trucks hook up great on the street and on the track.

The Goal for Sleeper Owners

So why do sleeper freaks go through so much trouble to hide the potential of their machine, when they should pound their chests like all the other car guys? If you've ever been around a group of performance junkies, you've heard plenty of folks brag about horsepower numbers, elapsed times, and street races. The owner of a street sleeper gets a kick out of simply watching as the exaggerations elevate to astronomical levels. That's where the sleeper owner has his fun—by toasting the self-proclaimed fastest car in town with something that looks as if it doesn't belong on the drag strip in the first place. It could be a generic truck, an old economy car, or perhaps a huge wagon from the late 1970s or early 1980s. As long as it looks plain and has plenty of horsepower, they put those braggers in their place without breaking a sweat.

Some owners build a sleeper merely for the fun of it. The owner may not be trying to prove a point or take part in any kind of late-night street racing, instead he's building the car to please himself and amuse others. Maybe it's the challenge of seeing how fast he can go on regular street radials, or finding out the limits of the original suspension that puts a smile on the face of an owner. What about the joy of being asked to leave the local drag strip because of the lack of safety equipment? Sleeper owners know all about that, and they also know all the tricks to hiding the necessary equipment when it comes time to going even faster. Ultimately, the goal for the owner is to build the car to his liking, not anyone else's, because these cars generally don't have a high resale value and they definitely don't provide the head-turning qualities of a new sports car.

Since sleepers never seem to sell at top dollar, the goal for most owners is to build it on the cheap and have fun. It's common to see race shops build a sleeper out of used and left-over parts, giving them a cheap toy that isn't all that important. It won't have a slick paint job, so there are no worries about scratching or leaning too hard against the body, and the pressure to make the car perform at its highest potential is out the door. Customer cars have deadlines and, of course, the owner has high expectations, so the shops are under the gun when it comes to making the car run like it should. With a sleeper, race shops can be carefree and simply have a good time. Now, for the average individual building a sleeper, the situation is a little different, but the goal for most is to build it for an affordable cost.

Some of the cars in this book are high-dollar machines but sometimes the sleeper look is a secondary byproduct of a low-budget build. Maybe the owner didn't want to shell out a couple thousand dollars on a set of lightweight race wheels, or mess with installing fiberglass panels on his street-based car. These features are to be considered when looking at certain sleepers, but be aware that a seemingly low-budget car can have some high-tech secrets hidden within. It's all part of the game.

The sleeper thing is a little different mindset than the average car-guy has. A sleeper owner rarely builds a car because he likes the styling or always wanted the particular make or model, since most sleepers are built from nondescript cars, such as Ford Fairmonts, Chrysler minivans, and boring vehicles of that nature. Most of the time, a car guy wants to relive the past with a car like he had (or one that he wanted) while he was in high school, so it's easy to see how

For a successful muscle car sleeper, make sure to pick a color that is unpopular and a platform mostly used for base-model cars. This 1965 Chevelle 300 Deluxe is a two-door post with tan paint, tan interior, and tan wheels, making for a bland overall appearance, while a dual-quad big-block rests under the hood.

If a car guy finds your attempted sleeper questionable, he'll look inside for further inspection. A base-model interior, consisting of rubber mat flooring, bench seats, and minimal accessories is a good start for a muscle car. It's hard to hide a floor shifter and third pedal, but an automatic car would need a column shifter to complete the look.

this differs from the mindset of a sleeper enthusiast. You don't see many folks working hard to scrape up enough money to buy a minivan just like the one they wanted as a teenager, so it's easy to understand why many people take a desirable car and dial it down a notch.

Some guys want to turn their fairly common muscle cars into sleepers, and that's not always an easy task. Really, it goes against the sleeper mindset, since car guys are supposed to know that a Mustang or a Camaro has the potential to be fast. For these types of builds, it's important to remember how the lesser-known base-model cars looked when they came from the factory and stick to the no-frills appearance of every aspect. Details like a measly, single exhaust, a column-mounted shifter, and a set of stock hubcaps certainly helps the matter, but sometimes there's no hope in calming down an already-aggressive car, like a 1969 Mustang fastback, or

any of the early Camaros. Even with all the cool tricks, you'll still have a hard time fooling everyone, but at least it'll be an attractive car with a potential for value, unlike some of the more dedicated street sleepers out there. Let's face it—you're not going to get much money out of a mid-1980s Chrysler at this time, so if you plan to profit on the investment, a muscle car–era sleeper is the way to go.

The key to building a believable muscle car sleeper is to pick an unpopular year or body style; so think about four-doors, station wagons, or some of the full-size family cars. Another important aspect to remember when building a fairly popular car as a sleeper is paint color. Bright red is great, but not on a sleeper—try the least popular colors, like the various greens, golds, or browns of the 1970s. White is also an acceptable color, especially on modern muscle cars. (See Chapter 2 for more about car choice and modifications to consider.)

The Ford Maverick was available during the muscle car era, but it was an economy car with very few options for performance, even if you ordered the Grabber package. This 1973 Grabber actually makes double the horsepower of the original V-8 with a turbocharged four-cylinder from a 1988 Thunderbird Turbo Coupe.

When Ford introduced the Fox platform in 1978, car enthusiasts didn't realize how big of an impact it would have on drag racing, and performance cars in general. The Ford Fairmont shares the same suspension mounting points and basic platform as the wildly popular 1979–1993 Mustang, making it easy to build a Fairmont sleeper.

Early 1970s Chevelles are not sleepy by any means, but give it the right color combination and the right rolling stock and you have a grandma-fresh sleeper. An LT1 engine with lots of nitrous powers this one, allowing it to easily run in the 10s and still be perfectly tame on the street.

Another option for building a sneaky muscle car is to build it from an unlikely platform. This 1967 Chevelle has billet wheels, but car guy logic prevents the thought of performance when you see the extra pair of doors. This four-door is powered by a big-block, but you'd never know it by its simple cruiser look.

Where are the Limits?

There are lots of places to slip up when building a sleeper, so it's rare to see a car that truly embodies the theme in every possible characteristic. Whether it's an outward detail like a cowl-induction hood, or an interior detail like racing seats and some sort of fancy shifter, mistakes are common. A cowl hood can potentially ruin a great sleeper, but sometimes it's necessary to clear an engine with a tall intake manifold, or one that's installed in a compact car that originally came with a much smaller unit. Either way, a big scoop on the hood is generally a sign of speed, as shallow as that sounds. Sure, there are bone-stock Mustangs running around with 6-inch cowl hoods, so it shouldn't necessarily mean that the car is fast, but building a quality sleeper is all about making the car look stock. Exterior modifications should be non-existent, but engine bay and interior details can sometimes go under the radar.

With all of this in mind, you have to consider the environment where the car is most commonly used and judge its limits accordingly. If your sleeper spends most of its time on the street, slicks are unacceptable, and every visible speed part takes you further away from the sneaky status. Roll cages are a dead giveaway, so if your street car has a jungle gym inside, most folks know that NHRA (National Hot Rod Association) rules specify at least an eight-point roll cage for cars faster than 9.99 seconds in the quarter-mile. The goal for a true street sleeper is to have the most generic-looking and completely stock car out there, and since you have no real rules on the street, you don't have to worry about the safety equipment required at most tracks. Of course, you may be sacrificing your safety by leaving some of these components out of

the car, but everyone plays at their own risk when it comes to racing on the street.

If you plan to campaign your car on the drag strip, then some of the minute details can be skimmed over for the sake of actually being able to race legally. The trick is to hide the safety equipment in the most efficient manner. Another detail that helps hide a sleeper at the drag strip is smaller-width rear tires, even though the outlaw street car crowd knows that a small tire can put down some serious numbers. Just about anyone can buy or borrow a set of slicks and get into the track, so having slicks at the drag strip isn't necessarily a tip-off to unsuspecting racers. In fact, if you frequent the drag strip, you've probably seen late-model Mustangs run very disappointing times, even with full-race slicks out back. Lightweight aftermarket drag racing wheels are generally a sign of speed, but large-diameter aftermarket wheels give your late-model car a little extra sleepiness at the strip. The street custom look isn't taken seriously at the track, so you can definitely fool a few folks with a car that has a set of 17- or 18-inch-diameter wheels. Making a car hook on the low-profile drag radials may not be easy, but be aware that cars have run deep into the 8s on Mickey Thompson's excellent drag radials mounted to 17-inch wheels.

If you're not against putting slicks on your sleeper, the next step to sliding under the radar is a stock hood and quiet exhaust system. Drag racers are accustomed to fast cars being loud, so a car with a full exhaust system (complete with mufflers and tailpipes) certainly keeps the attention to a minimum. Loud exhaust is one of those drag strip limits that you can sometimes get away with, but it absolutely does not fly on the street. On the subject of noise, many of the greatest sleepers out there feature a turbocharger or some kind of supercharger,

If you want simplicity and a low-budget build, then a Fox-Body Mustang is the right choice. However, it's hard to hide performance when dealing with this body style. The lack of a roll cage or lightweight race wheels certainly helps, but details like a flat hood and a full, quiet exhaust system seal the deal.

Most racetracks enforce the roll bar rule to any car running quicker than 11.49 in the quarter-mile, or 7.49 in the eighth-mile. If you want to risk it without a six-point roll bar you can, but the best option is to tuck the roll bar as close to the body as you can.

but power adders such as these make lots of racket in most cases. If you're worried about that, pick a supercharger with a helical gear set (the straighter the gear set, the more noise it makes) to keep whine to a minimum, and if you're running a turbo, make sure to put a small blow-off valve on it to help muffle the whoosh-effect when you let off the throttle. (See Chapter 4 for more about hiding horsepower.)

One of the best sleeper platforms out there is the four-wheel-drive pickup truck, simply because the limits are very broad. When most folks see a full-size truck, speed generally isn't a normal accusation. Even if your truck is outfitted with tons of modifications, like a lift kit, big wheels and tires, or custom paintwork, no one expects it to perform. The four-wheel-drive feature allows the truck to launch without much tire spin, even on street radials, but there's definitely a limit as to how much horsepower and torque the original transmission, transfer case, and differentials can handle before bad stuff starts happening. The advantage here is that you don't have to be so careful about your modifications, yet the performance aspect remains hidden to the uninformed. Combine this with the constantly evolving Diesel and turbo technology, and you have a work truck that doubles as an outstanding sleeper when you crank up the boost. The competition generally has a major weight advantage, but with stock-appearing pickups making well over 1,000 ft-lbs of torque, it takes a pretty serious street car to stand a chance.

Followers of outlaw street car racing know the potential of drag radial tires, but most of them use 15-inch wheels. Many tire companies make drag radials for large-diameter wheels, like these 17s, but they haven't proven to work extremely well in all cases. However, with the right suspension setup, these tires have been in the 8s with no problem.

The key to building a sleeper with forced induction is keeping it quiet. Some blowers have straight-cut gears, which produce a lot of noise, so pick a supercharger with helical gears and it will blend into the exhaust note nicely. For turbo applications, a smaller blow-off valve will help keep the noise level down.

It's hard to deny the sleeper status of modern Diesel trucks, as an average-looking work truck could produce well over 1,000 ft-lbs of torque without major engine work. Even with multiple modifications, like lift kits, big tires, or a wild paint job, no one expects a big heavy truck to run 11s in the quarter but it's quite common these days.

Finding the Right Car

If you're planning to build a sleeper, there isn't a more important step than picking the right platform to build upon. Sometimes it comes down to budget and other times it's personal preference, but choosing the right vehicle makes all the difference in the world. The decision revolves around surprising the opposition, so the scale of difficulty greatly increases with more noticeable or performance-minded cars. In other words, you have to work much harder to make a Mustang surprisingly fast than if you spent the same amount of money and time on a ragged-out station wagon from the 1980s. With that said, there are most certainly sleepers built from cars like Corvettes and other sports cars, but it's much harder to fool anyone with a car that's presumably fast from the factory.

While the Chevy Vega is already a favorite at the drag strip, it's also a great candidate for a sleeper. It might be hard to find a stocker, but that's the key to making it work. It has to be stock with stock-style wheels and tires to pull off the look.

There are many decisions to be made when building a sleeper, but finding a good platform points you in the right direction. The key for a simple build is parts availability, in terms of suspension upgrades or engine modifications, if you plan to use the original mill. Some folks opt for more exotic platforms, which result in more fabrication time and, ultimately, more money. No matter which route you go, it costs money to build a fast car, but there are definitely ways to save a few bucks along the way. Junkyard parts are a must if you're on a budget, but don't expect them to last forever, even though some guys have good luck with well-worn parts. Some engines last several hundred thousand miles in stock form, but expecting one to survive through nitrous or some form of boost is pushing the limit. Be realistic and the car should easily reflect your efforts.

If you're trying to fool the general public, and not the car guy crowd, building a sleeper isn't nearly as difficult because the general public doesn't know any of the tricks to making horsepower or putting it to the ground. The general public knows only what it sees in advertisements and the occasional television show; so typical performance cars are easily identified as *fast cars*, while others aren't given a second look. However, the intended goal of a sleeper is to fool someone into racing, and take their money, or at least their pride, so you'll probably be dealing with gear heads most of the time. This opens the door to all sorts of platforms, and choosing your modifications becomes the next challenge. Even if you simply plan to take your sleeper to cruise nights, you'll have a better finished product if it's undetectable, even by car guy standards.

Even though lots of them were dogs back in the late 1970s and early 1980s, Corvettes still have go-fast appeal, making it very difficult to fool anyone with the sleeper approach. This one barely slips under the radar, but that's only because it makes 1,000 hp, thanks to a twin turbo LT5 engine.

It's possible to build a successful muscle car sleeper, but the level of difficulty is greatly increased. Paint color has to be plain and ordinary, wheels have to be base-model attire, and a quiet exhaust system is a must. Any hints to the car's potential will be exposed unless you go the extra mile.

A keen eye might spot the larger-than-normal rear tires on this once luxurious Lincoln Town Car, but suspecting that it makes more than 500 hp at the wheels would be pushing it. However, this Lincoln does just that with its supercharged small-block Ford, and it would certainly surprise a street racer.

Sometimes muscle cars make great sleepers, but it's never by accident. It's a difficult process to hide the potential of a car that has horsepower written all over it, so it's usually necessary to remove certain emblems, give it a base-model appearance, and paint it a color that no one wants—like green or brown. Or, if you're not really concerned with looks at all, you can give it a rattle-can paint job, or just leave the random dents, dings, and rusty spots to give it the "barn fresh" look. There are a number of ways to keep folks guessing, even with a difficult sleeper subject, like muscle cars, but it all comes down to picking the right body style and sticking with the rough-and-junky theme. Even a little reverse psychology (like a big hood scoop and lots of stickers) works wonders on a street car since most car guys see that as *poser material*, instead of true performance modifications.

Econo-Sleepers

Other ways to take the poser approach is to jump on the import bandwagon and build a Honda or any of the other popular makes or models. As long as you don't mind being called a ricer, you can certainly pull off the sleeper look. Having the right attitude helps, so acting the part gives you the right dimwit attitude that real car guys love to take advantage of. At this point, you can actually tell someone how fast your car is, because it's common to hear a ricer come out and say his car runs 10s because he's trying to be a cool guy with a fast car. If you roll up in a Honda that has a body kit, vinyl graphics, and a huge exhaust tip, the last guy who takes you seriously is the one in the *built* Camaro. That's exactly what you want. Make a ridiculous wager that your car is faster than

his, and he'll quickly respond one way or the other, but it's important to know that your car actually *is* faster than his. When it's time to race, put the hammer down and watch all of his buddies cringe as you pull away from the high-horsepower muscle car.

Though Hondas and various imports are expensive to build if you buy name-brand parts, these cars respond to boost very well, so you can scratch-build a turbo system and save a ton of money. Engine swaps are also common in the import world, so it's easy to swap a great engine (like the H22 Honda) into an unsuspecting body (such as an early CRX), which is known for its extremely lightweight structure. Also keep in mind that many Honda enthusiasts swap the B20 engine out of the 1996–2000 Honda CRV (compact SUV platform) into flyweight Civics, as these engines respond exceptionally well to turbo systems. But, for someone building a sleeper, wouldn't it be easier to leave the B20 engine in the CRV, install a turbo, and take advantage of the all-wheel drive? You might be sacrificing in the weight department, but a quicker launch and a huge sleepy factor makes the CRV a great candidate.

If front-wheel drive is your thing, you can also concentrate on the lesser-known cars of the 1980s and step away from the full-on ricer mindset. You definitely have to let go of any insecurities concerning your self image, as driving a junky economy car from the 1980s doesn't do much for a car guy's ego. It does, however, feel pretty good to beat a muscle car, or a late-model sports car, so pick your priority and go with it.

As mentioned in Chapter 1, Chrysler Corporation had a decent platform with its tendency to turbocharge just about anything that rolled out of the factory from 1984 to 1994. From K-cars to Caravans, you could get a turbocharged

The sleeper game can get a little tricky with reverse psychology. Most car guys would never take this Mustang seriously because of the wing, the scoop, and the stickers, among other poser qualities. This car may not apply, but if you had some serious power under the hood, it could be a killer on the street.

You have no worries of someone suspecting big (or even marginal) power out of an Escort station wagon, but just about any engine comes alive with the addition of boost. This one has a sizable turbo on the otherwise stock 1.9-liter engine, making it a surprisingly fast economy car. *(Photo courtesy Will Smith)*

four-cylinder in many Chrysler products, making them an outstanding sleeper platform today.

Any way you look at it, the easiest way to build a budget-friendly, low-maintenance sleeper is to choose a rear-wheel-drive platform. Front-wheel-drive vehicles are a little sneakier, but you'll be shredding axles, CV joints, and transmissions constantly if you're launching hard with anything over 200 hp. The parts just aren't made for that type of abuse, and if you buy the good stuff, you pay dearly for it. That's why most folks resort to some sort of rear-wheel-drive vehicle that is firmly out of style, or maybe something that was never *really* in style, like a Volvo station wagon. Again, muscle cars are an option, but the details have to be hidden well, and you're not likely to fool everyone 100 percent of the time.

Quick, Like a Fox

On the subject of muscle cars, you can't deny the potent platform known as the Fox Body, which was a Ford design that made its debut in the late 1970s. It was first developed for the 1978 Ford Fairmont and its sister car, the Mercury Zephyr, but later boomed in popularity when the new Mustang made its debut in 1979. The Fox platform was rear-wheel driven, and it was a fairly lightweight, unibody design that proved to withstand lots of abuse. Another great feature of the Fox platform is the roomy engine bay that can hold just about any small-block or big-block V-8 engine, be it a Ford or Chevy design.

Now, if you try to get away with building a 1979–1993 Mustang, you'll have a hard time fooling anyone, but pick

Chrysler produced a great number of factory turbo-charged cars in the 1980s and early 1990s, but they never garnered much attention from the performance-minded crowd. Cars like this Daytona looked sporty at the time, but it's quite outdated these days, even though the potential for power is ever present.

When building a sleeper that would never turn a car guy's head, it's okay to slip up and give the car a few exterior modifications. This Volvo wagon is a prime example. Even with a lowered stance and custom wheels, would you expect a twin-turbo LS1 under the hood? *(Photo courtesy Dan Jenkins)*

The Fox platform was a great way for Ford to make a comeback in the late 1970s. And while the car pictured isn't a sleeper, these Fox cars are easy to find, cheap to build, and work amazing well on the street and at the track. Small-block Ford and nitrous makes this one fly.

The list of forgotten Foxes is a long one, but that's great if you want a sleeper. The Fairmont is a prime candidate with its ordinary appearance, yet every Fox-Body Mustang performance part bolts directly into place. The bright red paint and five-spoke wheels don't help the sleeper status on this example, but it's still sneaky.

one of the other Fox-Body designs, and pulling off the sleeper look might be a little easier. Take the Fairmont for example: None of these cars were performance-based, and they're not too pretty, but every aftermarket part from a Fox Mustang bolts directly into place. Taking that into consideration, you can outfit the car with custom Mustang suspension parts, a tubular K-member, and countless other go-fast parts to create one killer drag car with the looks of an old clunker.

You should also consider the vast interchangeability of Mustangs in general, as suspension parts from a 2004 car bolt up to a 1979 model, giving you the option for large brakes, five-lug wheels, and the very strong 8.8-inch rear axle, which wasn't available until 1986. Another great aspect of building from the Fox platform is the affordability of the parts and the availability of the car. Millions of Fox-bodied cars were on the road, so if you look hard enough you can find one very cheap. Pick up an old body for a few hundred bucks, shell out a few more hundred, and you have a fine platform for sneaking up on the competition. Throw in any engine you can think of, and hit the road with a chassis that hooks up better than most sleeper candidates, and fool just about anyone if you keep the stock wheels on all four corners.

Fox-Body Quick Tech

The Fox-Body platform was used by Ford from 1978 to 1993, and lived through many models, including those from the Mercury and Lincoln camps. The lightweight, affordable design makes the Fox platform a no-brainer when it comes to budget builds, but some of the lesser-known models prove to be great sleepers as well. The different models had varying wheelbases and curb weights but you can count on Mustang being the lightest, as it features the shortest wheelbase. Here's a quick breakdown of the makes and models built on the Fox platform:

1978–1983	Ford Fairmont		1981–1982	Ford Granada
1978–1983	Mercury Zephyr		1982–1987	Lincoln Continental
1979–1993	Ford Mustang		1983–1986	Ford LTD
1979–1986	Mercury Capri		1983–1986	Mercury Marquis
1980–1988	Ford Thunderbird		1984–1992	Lincoln Mark VII
1980–1988	Mercury Cougar			

During the 1980s, Ford produced many models with its 2.3-liter, four-cylinder engine. Outfitting this engine with a turbocharger made for a responsive and fuel-efficient powerplant that actually made more power than its V-8 counterparts. This is a rare and highly desirable Mustang SVO, which produced anywhere from 175 to 205 hp.

More Power or Less Weight?

From compact cars to massive oversized station wagons, choosing your sleeper platform is a matter of preference, but the larger you go, the more power you have to make to compensate for the additional weight. However, the larger automobiles from the 1970s and early 1980s offer vast amounts of space under the hood, so big blocks are an easy fit, and that's certainly the easiest way to make reliable horsepower without the need for power adders. Another advantage of the larger platform is traction, as the lighter cars always struggle with hooking up, whether you're on the street or at the drag strip. The additional weight of the large vehicle transfers to the rear wheels easily, as the shocks and springs are likely to be worn

This car isn't all that fast, but the potential is there, and it makes for a good laugh. It's an exact replica of the Family Truckster, which was featured in the movie, *National Lampoon's Summer Vacation*. The car is very well done, and features a GM Vortec engine, which is essentially an LS1 in tamer clothing.

out and softer than they were 30 (or more) years ago. It's a balance of pros and cons, but it all depends on what you want out of your sleeper.

If it's all about performance with little regard to the Sleepy Factor of large family sedans and station wagons, go for the lightweight approach. This allows for less stress in the drivetrain, and little need for excessive horsepower because of the lighter platform—not that car guys can ever have too much horsepower, but less power generally leads to a more dependable setup. The biggest disadvantage with lightweight cars is finding the right one. You want a car that has the necessary room for a larger engine, the proper suspension, and an overall appearance that is unsuspecting, which isn't always easy. One very popular make that fits the bill is the Opel brand. And while the most popular model is the GT, a sporty two-seater that many folks refer to as a mini-Corvette, there are other more simple models, such as the Kadet, that would slip under most car guys' radar. The advantage here is the fact that you have a sneaky platform that shares the same rear-wheel drive and very lightweight qualities as the GT without the sporty looks.

Another great option for a lightweight, rear-wheel-drive sleeper is the Dodge Conquest, or its sister car the Mitsubishi Starion. These compact cars were available with turbocharged four-cylinder engines, manual transmissions, and a sturdy rear end so the potential for speed is definitely there. The cars have a unique appearance that isn't shared with any makes or models of the time, so they don't exactly blend in with society, but they're not the pictures of performance in most folks' eyes either. And since fooling the opposition is always the goal, making one of these cars into the average-looking clunker is a good way to go.

One sleeper platform that is gaining notoriety is the Mazda RX-7. The first-generation cars are especially sneaky, even though the body design was sporty for its era. Granny's Speed Shop makes kits that allow you to bolt nearly any engine between the fenders of one of these very lightweight cars—this one has a small-block Ford.

Heavy cars can pack quite a punch, but it takes a lot of power to make it worth the effort. This ragged full-size wagon definitely has the beater look going with its dented, rusty, and faded body, while an aluminum-headed big-block Chevy rests under the hood.

However, a junky-looking car isn't the only way to achieve ultimate sleeper status. Sometimes, it's all about making a car look like a perfectly restored stocker. When this is performed on a car that normally wouldn't be restored, like a 1976 Ford Pinto wagon, it gives your opposition one of two mental pictures. One is that someone found a low-mileage Pinto in a relative's garage, and gave it a wash job just to have something to drive. The other scenario is that someone simply had too much time on their hands to restore that type of car. Either way, a freshly restored Pinto will not be considered a performance car and you're likely to fool a sizable percentage of car guys.

If you're considering a larger family sedan or station wagon as your sleeper project, the actual buildup isn't nearly as difficult. Find any mid 1970s to late 1980s full-size car and stuff the biggest engine available under the hood. It's that easy. However, keep in mind that a 200-hp car that weighs 2,000 pounds likely outperforms a 400-hp car that weighs more than 2 tons, so the engine that powers a heavyweight needs to be up to the task.

Big-blocks are generally a rule of thumb when it comes to these builds, and power adders help, but it all depends on how fast you want to go. When turbochargers, superchargers, or nitrous are thrown in the mix the potential for power is greatly increased, but so is the chance for parts breakage. If you put aside the fear of breaking parts or wasting horsepower by toting around an extra thousand pounds or so, a full-size sleeper is the way to go. Besides, who expects your family-size wagon to boast a 1,000-hp twin-turbo big-block?

Sleeper Trucks

Another platform that has immense sleeper potential is full-size pickup trucks. You'll see plenty of Diesel truck sleepers in Chapter 9, but just a regular old pickup certainly gets the job done. There are lots of trucks on the road, so fooling car guys is easy with a stock-appearing pickup. The easiest of all platforms seems to be the GM brands, as they come from the factory with the Vortec series V-8 engine, which is essentially an LS1 in different clothing. Simply swap the original camshaft, which is made for towing power, for a custom piece from one of the many manufacturers, or install a factory LS6 camshaft for a cheaper, easier alternative.

The Vortec engines are easy to modify and respond well to large amounts of boost, so a simple turbo system is a no-brainer for one of these trucks. Jim Neuenfeldt was the first to really capitalize on the sleeper truck idea, and did so with a 2003 Chevy Silverado (see page 122), which featured a turbocharged 6.0-liter Vortec engine with four-wheel drive. That truck roamed the streets of Omaha, Nebraska, for quite some time, picking on anything and everything in its path. It was the ultimate stoplight street racer. Unfortunately, the owner got a little more serious with the truck, installing a roll cage and a set of race wheels and tires, so its sleeper status was slightly downgraded.

Other options for sleeper trucks are plentiful, as most auto manufacturers are producing full-size trucks with V-8 power. Whether it's a Nissan Titan, a Toyota Tundra, or any of the Big Three offerings, adding a nitrous system or a

Pulling alongside this Silverado wouldn't spark any ideas that it might be fast, but it was a superb street-racing machine a few years ago. With a turbocharged Vortec engine and the original four-wheel-drive system, the truck launched well, and left many so-called fast cars in the dust. *(Photo courtesy Kyle Loftis)*

turbocharger to one of these trucks increases the horsepower and puts the truck into sleeper territory. If you're really serious about fooling your car guy brethren, choose one of the compact trucks from the 1980s, as these generally have a beater look from the get-go. Another advantage of the compact truck approach is weight—you're looking at a difference of at least 1,000 pounds, depending on the application.

All trucks are rear-wheel drive, so fitting a V-8 to your original driveline is easy, as long as you're not afraid to do some cutting to make it fit. Even better would be a turbocharged four-cylinder engine (like a 2.3-liter Ford) in a small truck.

One of the drawbacks of using a truck for a sleeper is traction. If you're using a two-wheel-drive pickup, the front-heavy weight distribution results in tire spin, unless you figure out a way to soften the suspension and plant the tires. However, trucks that feature four-wheel drive have a major advantage in terms of traction.

The only problem with four-wheel drive is breakage, as the transfer case, driveshafts, and differentials aren't made for high-horsepower applications. Many drivers launch in four-wheel drive, and switch to two-wheel drive on the fly to reduce drag in the drivetrain when the additional traction isn't needed.

These folks seem to have found something interesting under the hood of this Ford F-100. It has the patina of a traditional hot rod, and the whitewalls to match, but what could cause a constant crowd around the engine bay and the status of a legendary sleeper?

All that attention comes from a Dodge Viper V-10 that makes 500 hp in stock form. It's truly an odd combination, but that's what makes it such a cool sleeper. No one would ever assume this truck is fast, and even if they had a hunch—a Viper V-10? Really?

If you had to pick a winner without any prior background knowledge on either truck, would you bet on Whitley's *Farm Truck* in the far lane? It's one of the most popular sleepers in the country, and it's run a best of 10.43 at 129 mph, thanks to a nitrous-fed, 502-ci big-block Chevy that cranks out 837 hp. *(Photo courtesy Kyle Loftis)*

Chapter 3

Engine Swaps

A good horsepower-to-weight ratio is the name of the game when it comes to going fast, be it in drag racing or any other motorsport. The more weight you have to pull, the more horsepower you need, so it makes sense to build a lighter car that doesn't require as much effort in terms of power. That's why folks generally opt for a small or mid-size car to start out in the lightest possible configuration without gutting the body and interior. Shedding weight is a great way to make your car faster. Professional race teams have been dealing with minimum weight requirements for years, and while it's a great way to keep the field even, it's one of the toughest parts of a race team's setup. With a sleeper, you have no weight requirements or any other limitations for that matter, so the sky is the limit when it comes to reducing your car's weight, and thus increasing its horsepower-to-weight ratio.

A good horsepower-to-weight ratio is a key element of going fast, and drag racers have been using this logic for years. One very popular platform is the Opel GT, which is a very light, rear-wheel-drive car. An engine swap is essential for a build of this nature.

With that said, it pays to start with a fairly lightweight car, and that usually leads enthusiasts to a number of compact-car platforms. Whether you plan to swap in a V-8, or simply swap in a bigger version of the car's existing engine design, you'll face a few challenges along the way. Stuffing a big engine between the fenders of a compact or mid-size car is never easy, but it's hard to rely on the stock engine, because in most cases, you're using a platform that never had any major performance capabilities. Keep in mind that you don't want a car that originally had going fast on its agenda—you want an unsuspecting candidate with plenty of room for a more powerful engine.

With engine swaps, fabrication is almost always required, and it's important to know your limits from the start. It's not smart to stuff a big-block Chevy under the hood of a Cavalier (not to say it can't be done), so get creative and figure out your expectations and the most realistic swap for your

budget. Instead of spending hundreds of hours converting a front-wheel-drive car to rear-wheel drive; think about swapping in an engine that shares the same basic attributes. Continuing with the Cavalier example, junking the original engine in favor of a supercharged Ecotec piece from a late-model Cobalt SS would be the easiest route. The car would remain in its original front-wheel-drive configuration, and reap the benefits of a much more efficient and powerful engine. That's not to say the later model engine is a direct bolt in, but it's certainly easier than many other engine swap alternatives. However, some folks see the miles of wiring as a much bigger obstacle than the fabrication aspect, so see where your skills stack up, and base your choice on that.

If you're more comfortable cutting, welding, and grinding on your project car, go for the biggest possible engine, as long as you can keep it hidden. And if you'd rather spend less time

When considering an engine swap for your sleeper, the first thing to think about is the new engine's physical size in relation to the car's engine bay. For this 1969 Mustang the shock towers are long gone and the suspension has been redesigned to accommodate the massive 427-ci SOHC engine.

A car with narrow shock towers, like early Ford Mustangs and Mavericks, can't fit much more than your basic small-block Ford engine, so if you want to keep the original suspension design, you'll have to get creative. The owner of this example slid a 2.3-liter turbocharged four-cylinder into the tight confines with ease.

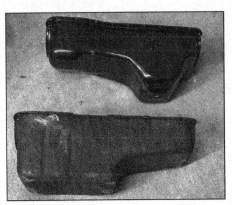

Another aspect to remember when considering an engine swap is oil pan clearance. Some engines were offered in different applications with a unique oil pan, but others have very limited choices. These two pans are from a big-block Ford, and the new one requires a longer oil pickup tube to fit the rear sump.

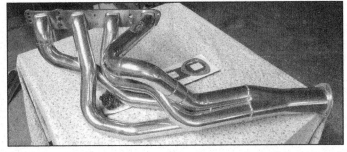

Header clearance is another huge obstacle when it comes to engine swaps. Various companies make headers for specific applications, but some of the more obscure swaps require a set of fabricated headers. However, if you don't mind compromising on horsepower, stock exhaust manifolds are an easier option.

building custom mounts and more time figuring out the wiring diagram, try an upgrade in technology by installing a modern engine. In the end, it's all about preference, but swapping in a different engine is a challenge any way you go about it. Also, consider choosing a platform that has available parts to make the job easier. For instance, the Fox-Body platform has a laundry list of available aftermarket parts, such as tubular K-members made for specific engine swaps. However, if your plan calls for a low budget, you need the basics on making your own engine mounts, transmission mount, and other necessary fabrication, because that certainly saves some dough.

It's important not to be fooled by the physical size of a particular engine. Just because it physically fits within the confines of your car's engine bay doesn't mean it works. You must first take oil pan clearance into consideration and change your combination accordingly. Sometimes, it's as easy as an oil pan swap, which also involves changing the oil pump pickup and pickup tube. In extreme cases, a custom oil pan is necessary, and there have been more than a few cases that a lack of oil pan clearance prevented the engine swap altogether. Do your homework before you start hacking away at your project car, or you could be wasting lots of time and effort.

Another area of focus when swapping in a new engine is the exhaust system, and most specifically, headers. Not everyone can handle the task of building a set of headers from scratch, but sometimes it's the only way to make it work. In some instances, you can take a set of existing headers and change flanges, or reconfigure only a few of the tubes. When looking at a potential sleeper project car, get a grasp on steering box and shaft location, as well as shock towers and general width of the frame rails. Yet another advantage of the Fox platform is the availability of small-block Chevy and LS1 headers to fit—it doesn't get much easier than that. However, engine swap parts can be a little pricier than the regular components, so prepare for that in advance. If you're on a budget, you better brush up on your cutting, grinding, and welding skills.

Swapping Transmissions

One of the major aspects of swapping a larger or more powerful engine into your sleeper is installing a transmission to withstand the increased torque. Whether you're making a drastic change in the car's configuration, or simply swapping in a new engine, the transmission needs some attention. For front-wheel-drive cars, the transmission is a little harder to deal with, as these drivetrains are generally specific to each car. Most front-wheel-drive engine swaps require an entire drivetrain swap, including the differential, axles, and all the related parts to go with it. For these builds, the entire cradle from the donor car is used, and it can sometimes be a compli-

cated process. Unless you're simply stepping up to a slightly better engine (such as from a Honda D16 to a B18), it's a lot of work. Even then, you're looking at a potential problem with your transmission, thanks to the increased power output.

If you're installing an engine and transmission into a car built by a different manufacturer, take note of the original transmission dimensions and shape. This determines how much real estate you're working with beneath the car, and indicates if any cutting is required. Sometimes the transmission tunnel is simply too small or misshapen for the specific transmission. Reshaping a car's transmission tunnel is no easy task, but building a transmission mount from scratch is easier than you think. In most cases, you attach the engine with solid mounts, so you also attach the transmission with a solid mount, which means you bolt the transmission directly to the homemade crossmember. It's very important to remember that you can never use regular rubber engine mounts with a solid transmission mount—the combination of flex from the motor mounts and rigidity of the solid transmission mount results in a broken bell housing, or the entire transmission case if it's an automatic.

In most cases, a piece of square tubing suffices as a transmission crossmember, but many cars need a 4- to 6-inch drop in the crossmember, to correctly position the mounting pad. That's why many owners opt for round tubing, as it's easy to bend, and a little more appealing to the eye. When the main crossmember is complete, all that's left is a flat steel mounting pad with gussets to support it. Building a transmission crossmember that includes a rubber mount isn't much more difficult, and it certainly helps reduce the amount of vibration in your car.

While some engine swaps require drastic changes in a car's drivetrain, cars like this Mustang II are a little less difficult. If you simply want to update the car's engine, you can keep the original C4 transmission and retain the 8-inch rear end, until you reach the point of breakage on the stock components.

Mixing an engine and transmission from two different applications can sometimes give you the necessary power and strength, but it can also present a few problems when it comes to matching the components. Bellhousing bolt patterns, flywheel backspacing, and many other factors go into swapping transmissions, but it's all part of the process. Also, be prepared to cut a new hole for the shifter if you're swapping in a new transmission, because you're not likely to get lucky enough to choose an engine and transmission that puts the shifter in the stock location. It's rarely that easy.

You should also consider the driveshaft and universal joints before making a decision on your transmission. Again, you might get lucky and find a driveshaft that's the perfect length and size, but it's not likely without some serious studying. The slip yoke needs to fit the transmission, and it also needs to match up with your driveshaft, in terms of its universal joints. If you can't find a good match, various companies manufacture U-joints with different-size cups on each side—

one size to fit in the driveshaft and another to fit on the slip yoke or rear end side. These are commonly known as conversion U-joints, and they're used often by off roaders with 4x4 trucks when they replace the stock housings with bigger units.

As horsepower levels increase, the odds of breaking transmission and driveline parts also increase. It's part of the never-ending process of going fast, but a good transmission is invaluable to the success of your vehicle. If it's an automatic transmission, then you're relying heavily on your torque converter to match the engine's power band, and if you're dealing with a manual transmission, the clutch and shifter are your points of interest. You won't put all the power to the ground if the clutch has the least bit of slip, and you certainly won't stay ahead of the opposition if you can't shift gears quickly. Consistently fast shifts with a manual transmission are generally a product of an aftermarket shifter, but abusing your stock transmission may not end well. Shifting forks and synchronizers are usually the first parts to fail, so make sure

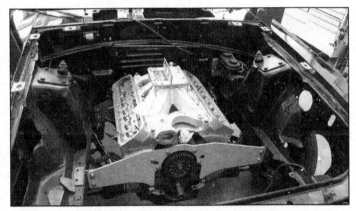

Options for engine and transmission mounting are wide open, and most race-inspired cars use an engine plate and a mid plate to simplify the process. The mid plate bolts between the engine and the transmission to eliminate flex between the engine mount and transmission crossmember.

The great thing about modifying your transmission to withhold lots of power and torque is the fact that no one will ever notice. As long as you select a torque converter that has a moderate stall speed, no one will suspect the car can put some serious horsepower to the ground.

If you're building a sleeper, you're probably not dealing with a car that came from the factory with a floor-mounted shifter, so cutting a hole in the floor might be necessary. Column shifters are sneaky for automatics, but it's hard to hide a shifter for a manual transmission.

Sometimes transmission crossmembers can be as simple as cutting up a trailer hitch. This hitch is going under the knife to mount a T-5 manual transmission in a Ford Maverick. It will be cut and drilled to mount to the existing crossmember mounting holes and then bolt directly to the transmission.

your application is up to the task. Drivetrain breakage almost always leaves you stranded, and it bruises your ego if you're in the middle of a race when it happens.

Old Car, New Engine

Whether it's a full-on sleeper build, or just a regular street machine, engine swaps are often performed to update the drivetrain. The hot trend is to install a modern powerplant in an old car, making it more reliable and powerful. For example, many car guys have installed one of the engines from the GM LS V-8 family in a first-generation Camaro. The car still keeps its vintage look, but you have a very dependable engine with fuel injection and a distributor-less ignition under the hood. If you're building a sleeper, the LS engines are the go-to choice, as they're easy to obtain, and rather affordable. Hunting down one of the more desirable and pricey engines, such as an LS7 or LS9, isn't absolutely necessary, since you can modify a basic LS1 or even a Vortec truck engine to perform at the same level.

The Vortec series of engines originally powered GM trucks and SUVs, but many engine builders firmly believe in the engines and their ability to hold up to big-time power. Nearly all of the Vortec engines feature an iron block, and a very strong crankshaft, but the heads and camshaft are the biggest differences among the various sizes. These Vortec engines are dirt cheap and feature a great amount of interchangeability among the entire LS family. This makes for a dramatically cheaper alternative to a high-dollar race engine.

For the Blue Oval camp, modern engine swap candidates are fairly limited, as the only modern engines are based on the "modular" engine platform. While these engines make great power, especially when supercharged, they're rather large in size, and present a problem when it comes to fitting them into older mid-size or compact cars. Full-size cars easily have enough real estate for a mod motor, so keep that in mind when choosing your sleeper platform. Depending on the year, and the original application, these engines feature either a single overhead cam (SOHC) or a dual overhead cam (DOHC) design for a very efficient valvetrain. Modular engines fetch a little more money than the GM Vortec series, but they're still a great platform to build upon.

Mod motors were introduced in the 1991 Lincoln Town Car. The 4.6-liter, SOHC engine was no powerhouse, but it proved to be a great start for the new engine series. A few years later, Ford gave its Mustang a 4.6-liter mod motor for power, and that started an interest in trying to make these engines perform well. From there, it was proven that big displacement wasn't necessary for big power, as these 281-ci engines were cranking out 390 hp in stock form. Keep in mind, that horsepower rating is due in part to an Eaton Roots-style supercharger. The common swap candidate for these engines is the Fox-Body Mustang, which has enough room for the sizable engine, but that also means the engine fits within the confines of a Ford Fairmont, or any other Fox-Body Ford.

Modern Mopar performance offers a limited number of choices for engine swaps, but the new Hemi certainly holds its own among its two major competitors—LS engines and modular engines. With the right modifications, the new Hemi works well, but a cheap one is virtually non-existent. Two sizes are currently available (5.7 and 6.1 liters) and Chrysler plans to unveil its latest rendition, the 6.4-liter Hemi in the near future. The new engine pumps out more than 500 hp in an effort to keep pace with GM and Ford offerings.

Aside from the initial cost, swapping in a modern Hemi isn't a huge challenge. You have to fabricate the mounts, but these engines aren't as large as their predecessors, or the Ford

The enormous family of LS engines is a popular choice for engine swaps because General Motors did a great job packing lots of power into a small package. These engines fit where other engines won't, and the Vortec truck engines are very affordable, if you don't mind buying them used from a salvage yard. *(Photo courtesy General Motors)*

Ford introduced the modular engine in 1991, and still produces a great number of these engines today. The latest and greatest edition is the Coyote engine, which is an all-aluminum, 5.0-liter DOHC engine that started life in 2011 Mustangs. Horsepower is rated at 415, and there's plenty of room to improve. *(Photo courtesy Ford)*

The four-letter word that every Mopar fan knows about is Hemi. It's a legendary moniker, and it appeared back in 2003 in many of Chrysler's production vehicles. Horsepower levels are moderate compared to GM and Ford offerings, but a new 6.2-liter engine boasts nearly 500 hp. *(Photo courtesy Mopar Performance)*

mod motor. As with any of the Big Three engine swap candidates, wiring may cause a problem, but many companies are willing and able to create a custom harness for your application. Just tell them what you want and fork over the cash.

Sparks Will Fly

If you have a problem with cutting, grinding, or welding steel, step away from the engine swap idea and lean toward something a little simpler. Moderate metal-working skills can make any engine fit in any car, but keep safety in mind. If you don't think your welding equipment is up to the task, don't risk sticking the car together to keep from updating your equipment or paying someone else to do it. Neglecting this topic could result in major breakage and a potential hazard if the welds don't hold, or if the metal isn't strong enough to support the weight and torque of the drivetrain. Cutting up a car in order to go fast is what hot rodding is all about, but don't get too brave if you can't back it up with quality workmanship—it's an accident waiting to happen.

For general fabrication, like engine mounts, transmission crossmembers, and headers, a good MIG welder is a sufficient choice, as long as you have a full tank of argon. A MIG welder with no gas can do the job, but it's much easier for a novice welder to get started with the assistance of argon. It makes for a much cleaner weld, and that's always a good thing. You need to know a little about welding before you jump into a big project, because the heat and wire speed settings make the difference between a good weld and a bad one.

You've probably seen TV shows where the guys use a TIG welder on every conceivable part of the build. While that's nice for TV and it results in a beautiful weld if you know what you're doing, TIG welding isn't necessary if

you're bonding two pieces of steel. It's rather time consuming, and some builders consider it a waste of time and effort, as a MIG welder can produce the same strength if the settings are correct. On the other side of the coin, arc (stick) welding used to be the standard for thick steel, as it was known for its strength, but it's becoming a lost art within the automotive crowd. Today's MIG machines can weld pretty much anything you want, so an arc welder is really out of the question, unless it's all you have.

For cutting and grinding, there are lots of options that are affordable and easy to use, even at a beginner's level of skill. If you don't have access to an air compressor, most cutting and grinding can be handled with electric tools if they have the correct attachments. Building a sleeper on your own saves a ton of money compared to having a professional shop perform the work, but you should consider the cost of the tools and materials into the budget. You'll be surprised how much you can spend on grinding discs, cut-off wheels, and "Sawzall" blades. While some engine swaps may not require major fabrication, you'll likely run into a situation that only a grinder can fix, so it's important to keep the necessary tools within arm's reach. Also keep a big hammer on hand for similar occasions.

Any time you consider an engine swap, you should also consider the amount of time you'll spend cutting, grinding, and welding to make it all fit. Sometimes a torch is the only way to get the job done, and it certainly cuts through double-wall panels, like these shock towers, much easier.

Application Guide

The following information is organized by size within each manufacturer.

GM LS-Based Engines

LS4
5.3-liter, aluminum block, aluminum heads, 303 hp
2006–2009 Chevy Impala SS
2006 & 2007 Chevy Monte Carlo SS
2005–2008 Pontiac Grand Prix GXP
2008 Buick LaCrosse Super

LS1
5.7-liter, aluminum block, aluminum heads, 305 to 350 hp
1997–2004 Corvette (non Z06)
1998–2002 Chevy Camaro Z28 or SS
1998–2002 Pontiac Trans Am or Firebird Formula
2004 Pontiac GTO
Various Holden models in Australia

LS6
5.7-liter, aluminum block, aluminum heads, 385 hp (2001),
    405 hp (2002-2005)
2001–2004 Corvette Z06
2004 & 2005 Cadillac CTS-V

LS2
6.0-liter, aluminum block, aluminum heads, 390 to 400 hp
2005 & 2006 Pontiac GTO
2005–2007 Corvette (non Z06)
2006–2009 Chevy TrailBlazer SS
2006 & 2007 Cadillac CTS-V

LS3
6.2-liter, aluminum block, aluminum heads, 424 to 436 hp
2008–Present Corvette (non Z06)
2009 Pontiac GT GXP
2010–Present Chevy Camaro
Various Holden models in Australia

LSA
6.2-liter, aluminum block, aluminum heads, supercharged, 556 hp
2009–Present Cadillac CTS-V

LS9
6.2-liter, aluminum block, aluminum heads, supercharged, 638 hp
2009 Corvette ZR1

LS7
7.0-liter, aluminum block, aluminum heads, 505 hp
2006–Present Corvette Z06

Vortec Engines
Multiple versions of the Vortec engine powered GM trucks and SUVs, with displacements of 4.8, 5.3, 6.0, and 6.2 liters. From 1999 to current production, General Motors has used these engines in everything from full-size pickup trucks to large conversion vans. Power output ranges anywhere from 285 to 395 hp, depending on the model, but your best bet for performance is the later model 6.2-liter engines from 2009 and newer GM SUVs. Vortec engines in general share the relatively small dimensions of the LS family of V-8s, making them great for engine swaps into compact cars.

LS engine swaps are quite popular because of the vast availability of these V-8 engines. This Corvair is not an easy engine swap candidate as it originally featured a rear-engine design. That means the owner of this car had to install a solid rear axle, driveshaft, and transmission from another car to accommodate the LS engine.

From a quick look at the aluminum block, this appears to be a true LS engine, rather than a Vortec engine from a truck or SUV. Obviously, there aren't any companies making LS-swap headers for a Chevy Corvair, but the generic shorty headers seem to work nicely.

Ford Modular Engines

4.6-Liter SOHC Two-Valve
Iron block, aluminum heads, 190 to 260 hp
1991–2004 Lincoln Town Car
1992–Present Ford Crown Victoria
1994–1997 Ford Thunderbird
1994–1997 Mercury Cougar
1997–2010 F-series pickup
1997–Present E-series Van
1996–2004 Mustang (non Cobra)
2002–2005 Ford Explorer

4.6-Liter SOHC Three-Valve
Iron or aluminum block, aluminum heads, 292 to 315 hp
2005–2010 Ford Mustang (aluminum block)
2006–Present Explorer (cast-iron block)
2007–Present Explorer Sport Trac (cast-iron block)
2009 Ford F-series pickup (cast-iron block)

4.6-Liter DOHC Four-Valve
Iron or aluminum block, aluminum heads, 260 to 390 hp
1993–1998 Lincoln Mark VIII
1995–2002 Lincoln Continental
1996–2001 Mustang SVT Cobra
2003 & 2004 Mustang SVT Cobra (cast-iron block)

2003 & 2004 Mustang Mach 1
2003 & 2004 Mercury Marauder
2003–2005 Lincoln Aviator

5.0-Liter "Coyote" DOHC Four-Valve
Aluminum block, aluminum heads, 412 hp
2011 Mustang GT

5.4-Liter SOHC Two-Valve
Iron block, aluminum heads, 255 to 380 hp
1997–2004 Ford F-series pickup
1997–2004 Ford Expedition
1997–Present Ford E-series Van
1999–2004 Ford SVT Lightning (supercharged)

5.4-Liter SOHC Three-Valve
Iron block, aluminum heads, 300 to 320 hp
2004–2010 Ford F-series pickup
2005–Present Ford Expedition
2005–Present Lincoln Navigator

5.4-Liter DOHC Four-Valve
Iron or aluminum block, aluminum heads, 300 to 550 hp
1999–2004 Lincoln Navigator
2000 Mustang SVT Cobra
2005 & 2006 Ford GT
2007–2011 Mustang GT500

This 1967 Ford Fairlane originally had shock towers like many mid-size cars of the 1960s and 1970s. To fit a larger engine, it requires cutting out the shock towers and replacing them with flat steel. In the case of this car (and most others for the matter), the original suspension has been replaced with Mustang II equipment. *(Photo courtesy Will Smith)*

The engine of choice for the Fairlane is a Ford modular engine. This particular combination is a 4.6-liter, SOHC (two valves per cylinder) design, which powered many Fords from the 1990s. Horsepower levels varied greatly throughout the production run, with 260 hp being the highest available in stock form. *(Photo courtesy Will Smith)*

Application Guide CONTINUED

Modern Hemi Engines

5.7-Liter
Iron block, aluminum heads, 340 to 399 hp
2003–Present Dodge Ram
2004–2009 Dodge Durango
2005–Present Chrysler 300C
2005–2008 Dodge Magnum R/T
2006–Present Dodge Charger R/T
2005–Present Jeep Grand Cherokee
2006–Present Jeep Commander

2007–2009 Chrysler Aspen
2009–Present Dodge Challenger R/T

6.1-Liter
Iron block, aluminum heads, 425 hp
2005–Present Chrysler 300C SRT-8
2005–2008 Dodge Magnum SRT-8
2006–Present Dodge Charger SRT-8
2006–Present Jeep Grand Cherokee SRT-8
2008–Present Dodge Challenger SRT-8

Most folks wouldn't expect much out of an old beater like this mid-1950s Chrysler New Yorker, but it features a modern Hemi for power. And while it's a heavy platform for a bone-stock engine to motivate, the engine has plenty of room for improvement.

The modern Hemi is a standard pushrod V-8, and this example is the more common 5.7-liter version. These engines made their debut in 2003, and they've been extremely popular ever since. The physical size is much smaller than the original Hemi, making engine swaps much easier to perform.

For most jobs, a MIG welder suffices on steel, as long as you're confident in your welding skills. Metal preparation and welder setup are important aspects, so try a few test welds before diving into the real thing. Here, a set of solid motor mounts is being fabricated.

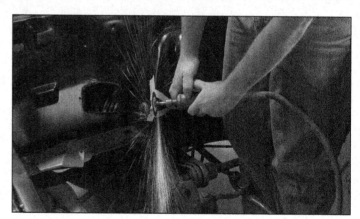

Sometimes a big powerplant physically fits within your engine bay, but accessing the important parts like spark plugs becomes a problem when real estate is limited. Don't be afraid to make an access hole through an inner fender, or simply cut a relief to make room for a ratchet and socket.

Engine Swap Kits

Though it limits the options for your sleeper's body style, you should consider an engine swap kit available through the aftermarket. An engine swap kit greatly simplifies the process, and some companies offer every component necessary to make it happen with minimal fabrication. While this option is convenient, it's not cheap, so be sure to weigh the pros and cons to see what's better for your sleeper buildup. If you're confident in your abilities and plan to do all the fabricating, the swap kit is a waste of money, but if you plan to hire someone to do the work, you're certainly better off to pick up the phone and order a kit. Depending on your application, you can buy the engine mounts, headers, and oil pan made for a specific engine swap.

One very popular car that can be outfitted with a full-on conversion kit is the first-generation (1979–1985) Mazda RX-7. While these cars generally aren't built with the sleeper theme in mind, they are ideal sleeper candidates. Lightweight, rear-wheel-drive platforms handle horsepower well. The cars were sporty for the early 1980s, but they don't garner much attention from performance-minded enthusiasts these days, so you'll easily slip under the radar as long as you keep the stock wheels and hide the V-8 power.

Granny's Speed Shop builds engine swap kits for all years of the RX-7, along with many other applications. Whether you want a small-block Chevy, small-block Ford, or LS-series engine, Granny's has it covered, and has proven examples all over the country. First-generation RX-7s can be gutted to weigh just over 2,000 pounds—with that light of a car, you don't need a ton of power to make it insanely fast on the street. The cars also have a fairly good rear suspension, but the tiny 7-inch rear end won't hold up to much abuse. The go-to rear-end swap is an 8.8-inch rear axle from a late 1980s Mustang.

Second- and third-generation RX-7s are still considered "fast cars" by enthusiasts, so it would be tough to build a sleeper from one of the later model examples. However, if that's the car you want, Granny's Speed Shop and Hinson Super Cars build conversion kits for them. Other engine swap kits come from companies like Muscle Rods, which special-

Bolt-in swap kits are absolutely the most convenient way to perform an engine swap. Companies like Muscle Rods build kits for all sorts of GM applications to adapt a new LS-style engine. The basic kit comes with engine mounts and a transmission crossmember, while more advanced kits come with an oil pan and headers. *(Photo courtesy Muscle Rods)*

izes in mostly LS1 swaps for older GM cars and trucks. These companies take the guesswork out of engine mounts, transmission mounts, oil pans, headers, driveshafts, and other variables that go into an engine swap, so they're a good option if you have the cash.

Another bolt-in swap candidate that fits the sleeper theme is the Pontiac Fiero. It's possible to swap in a great number of GM V-6 engines, any small-block Chevy, or any of the GM LS-series V-8 engines into this tiny platform, which has great traction capabilities with its mid-engine configuration. Upgraded transmissions are also available for these cars, making them much stronger, but other driveline parts can't hold up to the stress of hard launches, so extreme drag strip abuse isn't advised with the Fiero platform.

Between Granny's Speed Shop and Hinson Super Cars, you can get an engine swap kit for any of the three generations of Mazda RX-7. This one is the sporty third-generation model, which isn't necessarily a sleeper, but it features a healthy LS engine. The earlier cars are definitely good sleeper candidates.

Car guys rarely take any Pontiac Fiero seriously, so building a successful sleeper out of these mid-engine compact cars is rather easy with the available engine-swap kits. This one features a conventional small-block Chevy, but kits are also made for modern LS engines, which could create all sorts of go-fast possibilities.

Chapter 4

Sneaky Horsepower

Years ago, hot rodders wanted high-compression engines with radical camshaft profiles to make big horsepower. And while there were sleepers back then, it was certainly difficult to hide a snarling big-block in terms of noise. Even with a quiet exhaust note, the use of solid-lift camshafts resulted in the well-known clatter that most folks immediately recognize as a performance component. Keeping your engine quiet is usually the main goal in making sneaky horsepower, and the parts your competition can't see is where you should focus. Hidden nitrous systems, disguised aftermarket cylinder heads, and stock-appearing exhaust manifolds are common features on a genuine sleeper, but creativity usually prevails in these cases.

Normally, disguising your engine as a big-block Chevy isn't the right approach, but it works for this application. This is inside a 1967 Chevy C-10 pickup. The faux valve covers and factory air cleaner hide an LS3, but look like a restored original truck big-block, which would've had around 300 hp, compared to this particular engine's 480 hp.

When it comes to hiding horsepower, it's downright difficult to disguise a big-block Chevy, so think about your engine options and go for something a little tamer if you ever plan to open the hood of your sleeper. Some owners simply keep the hood closed and disclose very little about their combination, but that generally doesn't fly in a grudge-racing environment. Street racers rarely agree to race someone who outright refuses to show the engine. So even if your car looks completely stock on the outside, you don't want to immediately give away your horsepower secret when the hood is opened. That's why many sleeper enthusiasts spend lots of time under the hood, disguising speed parts, and giving the engine an unsuspecting appearance. It's one of the more difficult aspects of taking the sleeper theme to the extreme, but it pays off when you shock the opposition, and all of his buddies.

Like any performance engine, a good sleeper combination starts with a healthy bottom end. If the block and internals can't handle the power, you're wasting time, and taking a chance on crashing your car if it happens to puke out a bunch of oil or coolant during the engine failure. When you push a stock or a mildly modified engine to the limit, things are bound to break, and that rarely ends well. Carnage is a part of racing, even in its simplest form, but it's rather expensive and

a good thing to avoid altogether. Do some research on your block and rotating assembly before boosting it or turning too many RPMs and you'll be glad you did.

Cylinder heads are an easy place to score more horsepower without giving away your secret. A stock set of heads can be professionally ported to flow lots of air, and keep the original appearance, so that's a no-brainer for most sleeper builds. You won't be able to get the flow numbers that a set of aftermarket heads can produce, but you will keep a low profile when it comes to the engine's appearance.

Camshaft selection is another major choice, as it plays a role in the car's exhaust note, so mild grinds are suggested to retain the stock sound. Many camshafts designed for nitrous and forced induction offer little difference in the idle quality from a stock setup but provide great power increases when the power adder is in full force. If you've ever heard a turbocharged outlaw street car idle, then you've heard the rather tame exhaust note.

Many sleepers rely on power adders for their sneak attack, and they have proven to be a most effective way of making horsepower without showing it off to the world. Be it nitrous oxide, superchargers, or turbochargers, installing a power adder seems to be the go-to engine modification for

Porting is an easy way to gain horsepower without changing the engine's outward appearance. This intake manifold is for a 2.3-liter Ford engine, and originally had four small holes leading to the intake ports. Now, the holes have been blended together to create a much smoother path.

Camshaft selection is another area for compromise in a sleeper build. One nice option for older engines is upgrading to a full roller setup, as you can still select a mild grind to keep a fairly tame idle quality, while reaping the benefits of a roller valvetrain.

Cylinder heads are an important part of any engine, be it a full race engine or a sleeper buildup. The key for sleeper builds is to retain a production-style head rather than opting for an aftermarket piece. Stock-style heads can be ported to perform well, and it gives your engine a much lower profile. (Photo courtesy GM Performance Parts)

The owner of this 1966 Chevelle 300 Deluxe made a nice effort when it came to engine bay cleanliness. This may look like a stock 396 or even a 427, but it's really a 496-ci stroker with a set of Pro Comp cylinder heads, which resemble stock castings.

sleepers. In terms of keeping the components hidden, nitrous is the easiest, but it's possible to mount turbochargers at the rear of a vehicle. It's much harder to relocate a supercharger, but the instantaneous boost and big horsepower numbers make the advantages of superchargers hard to dispute.

A sleeper's engine needs to blend in with its surrounding, so taking the extra step to make it look stock gives your car the right attitude. A stock, drop-base style air cleaner is a must if you plan on hiding an aftermarket carburetor or if you're attempting to conceal a nitrous system. If the car had air conditioning and power steering, keep all of it hooked up, as these are generally known as power robbers, and the first step for a hot rodder is to remove factory equipment that is unnecessary, heavy, and causes a drag on the engine. A stripped-down engine (with no accessories) will more than likely tip off the knowledgeable car guy. All aftermarket aluminum components should be painted engine color, and you could even leave the gunk on the outside of the engine for added effect. Making your engine pass under the car guy's radar isn't always easy, but it definitely adds to the cool factor of your car when you finally reveal the secret, whether that means verbally telling someone about it, or simply showing him when you hit the throttle.

You Can't See Air...

If there's one thing every car guy knows it is that airflow is the answer to all horsepower-related questions. If your engine can't flow the air, you're doing no good by piling boost on top of it, so a good-flowing set of heads and an equally well designed intake manifold are very important. The advantage for sleeper owners is the fact you can't see airflow,

which means an engine could look completely stock and have a much smoother path for the air and fuel mixture to travel. This frees up tons of possibilities for horsepower, and helps a power adder do the job to its full potential.

The key to good engine flow is a set of aftermarket cylinder heads, but you can get close to the same performance with a set of ported stock castings. That's where a lot of owners look for performance, but bigger ports aren't always better. Airflow doesn't increase by simply increasing the size of the ports—you must direct the air into the combustion chamber in the most efficient manner possible, and that's not always easy. Be aware that porting a set of stock heads can sometimes do more harm than good if the guy holding the grinder

Professional head porting isn't cheap; so many budget builds involve a little at-home port work. However, many folks do more harm than good by simply enlarging the ports. The pros are paid well for a reason—they know their stuff, and have plenty of tricks up their sleeve.

doesn't know his stuff. If you don't have much porting experience, you're better off to leave the heads alone and turn your focus elsewhere, saving a lot of time and effort. Your best bet is to find the best-flowing set of stock heads for your specific engine and simply bolt them on.

Some folks still think a set of camel-hump heads are the best thing you can put on a small-block Chevy, but the majority of gear heads know better. In reality, the best stock cast-iron head for the small-block Chevy is the Vortec design, as it offers a great port design and appropriately sized valves for mild street engines. With that said, it can sometimes pay off to dig a little deeper into the novice car guy mindset, and play dumb when it comes to engine specs. Telling someone you have a full race motor, then lifting the hood to show them a

small-block Chevy with a set of camel-hump heads, instantly removes all doubt that you're either way behind the times or clueless about speed parts. This results in a boost of confidence in your opponent, which convinces him that he's about to take your money and win the race. If you get your opposition to this point, you've already won the race because he never sees it coming.

Brzezinski Racing modifies GM cast-iron exhaust manifolds and complete exhaust systems that have been known to create big power gains. Brzezinski also modifies stock intake manifolds and cylinder heads for racers in the F.A.S.T. (Factory Appearing Stock Tire) drag racing series, which is composed of stock-looking muscle cars that run deep into the 10s in the quarter-mile. Brzezinski is definitely a good source for hidden horsepower, as the crew expertly modifies stock parts to create much more power and look completely stock, even when the engines are disassembled for inspection. There's a lot to be learned from these crafty folks.

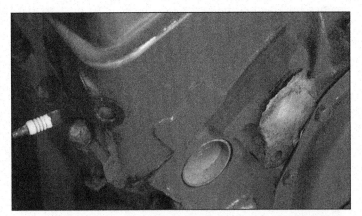

If an up-to-date gear head sees a set of camel-hump heads on your small-block Chevy, he'll be convinced that you're either behind the times or totally clueless about making horsepower. This elevates your opponent's confidence, as he thinks it'll be an easy win. Mind games are a big part of the sleeper theme.

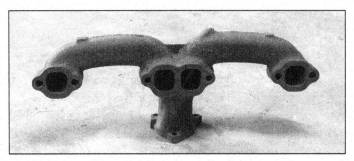

It's hard to take an engine seriously if it sports a set of cast-iron exhaust manifolds, but Brzezinski Racing takes stock manifolds like this one, and ports them out to flow more air. Its manifolds have made up to 10 hp in some cases and even more with one of its 2-into-1 collectors.

Roller rocker arms are nice, but if you want to run stock-style valve covers, they're not an option. You can always grab a set of stamped steel rockers with roller tips to upgrade your valvetrain and keep it all under the stock covers. Double nuts on the rocker arm studs offer the "poly lock" effect.

GM's LT1 engine was used in a variety of platforms, and it's great for a sleeper build. It's outdated, compared to the LS1, so knowledgeable car guys sometimes overlook it. Most LT1s came with aluminum heads, so it's easy to upgrade without anyone noticing.

Another way to throw off the competition when you show them your engine is to retain stock valve covers. Most conventional V-8 engines require a taller valve cover when running roller rockers, and most enthusiasts know that. So if your engine has a set of stock short valve covers, it's yet another step in the right direction. You can get shims to elevate the valve covers enough to clear the rockers, but that's easily noticeable, so to take it a step further, you can ditch the roller rockers and go with a set of stamped steel rocker arms with roller tips. They don't give you the lighter weight and various operating ratios of aluminum roller rockers, but they fit under stock valve covers.

If you want the clamping power of poly locks on your stock rocker arms, simply adjust your valves to spec and then install another rocker arm nut to act as a jam nut. This trick doesn't apply to every powerplant, but it works well on small-block Chevys and allows you to run stock valve covers.

There's little doubt that modern engines are highly desirable for sleeper applications, but if someone spots an LS1 under the hood of your car, it may lead him to believe your car is fast. The point of swapping in a modern engine is to take advantage of the great airflow and efficiency of the engine. Though it's hard to consider them modern, engines from the late 1980s and early 1990s are great candidates for sleepers, because these engines are considered outdated by most performance-minded individuals. The GM LT1 is a prime example, as it has the same features of a conventional small-block Chevy, which accepts a great number of aftermarket cylinder head choices, while also featuring fuel injection.

Generally, when a gear head sees an LT1 engine he doesn't immediately think about a killer powerplant, as these mills

originally produced less than 300 hp in most applications. Many of these engines came with aluminum heads, so a set of aftermarket heads won't stand out quite as much, and allow the engine to breathe much deeper. The original fuel injection system and intake manifold prove to be the limiting factor on the LT1, but you can still build a surprisingly powerful engine without spending nearly as much as you would on an LSX buildup.

While General Motors has a number of options for modern powerplants, Ford has its share as well, (See Chapter 3 for the breakdown of Ford modular engine production). The nice thing about mod motors is the fact that cylinder heads and camshafts generally aren't the corks in the system when it comes to horsepower. Mod motors are small-cubic-inch engines, but they respond exceptionally well to boost, so that's where most enthusiasts seek additional power. There are many car owners with mod motors that have never had the valve covers removed but run 9-second elapsed times on a regular basis. While most guys go with a Roots-style or a twin-screw supercharger on mod motors, these forms of boost are extremely hard to hide, so it's not exactly sleeper material. However, a rear-mount turbo system on one of these engines might just be the hot ticket to big power and reveal very few clues to its potential. Airflow is definitely the strong point of Ford's modular engine, so consider that when building your sleeper.

The Bottom End

To build any performance engine, you need to do some research on its bottom end before piling lots of power on it. Some engines hold up well under the additional forces, but

The Ford DOHC, four-valve modular engine has a great cylinder head design, which makes these small-cube engines respond very well to boost. This one features a Whipple supercharger, and runs 9s in a 2004 Ford Mustang Cobra, which tips the scales at 3,600 pounds. Quite a feat for a 281-ci engine with stock heads.

Internals are very important if you plan on installing any kind of power adder. Most V-8 engine platforms have a block strong enough for 500 hp, but the connecting rods and cast pistons are usually the weak points. Forged pistons and forged H-beam rods hold up nicely in a strong street motor.

some aren't so strong. No matter where your engine stacks up, in terms of cylinders or cubic inches, you should consider beefing up the bottom end before installing a power adder. Most original engines feature cast aluminum pistons, which have been known to fail when nitrous oxide or forced induction is thrown into the mix. However, some engines came from the factory with forged pistons, making it easier to apply the power adder. If you're planning on big boost numbers, or a lot of nitrous, a set of aftermarket pistons is a must either way.

Connecting rods also take a beating, as most original units are an I-beam design. A good set of H-beam forged rods is plenty strong, but they can be pricey. The same can be said for forged crankshafts, but it's sometimes the only way to make an engine hold up to the power adder. One way to get a little more bang for your buck from a crankshaft purchase is to utilize a longer stroke. Without question, stroker motors are very popular with sleepers, because the opposition can't physically see that your engine has more cubic inches. A better bore-to-stroke ratio can make the engine operate much smoother in high-RPM situations, while the additional displacement can provide more low-end torque. If your stock block is up to the task, you can keep the bottom-end modifications a secret.

Most stock V-8 blocks are capable of withstanding well over 500 hp but there are ways to make a bottom end stronger. Simply using aftermarket studs, rather than bolts to hold the main caps, rod caps, and cylinder heads, has proven to provide stronger and better-distributed clamping force than stock fasteners. And if you've been around cars you've heard the debate about two-bolt and four-bolt mains. The average street car small-block Chevy will not overpower a two-bolt main block if the engine is built well, but you can install a main girdle to give it additional strength. To install the girdle, you need to use longer main studs and torque the fasteners to the suggested specs. Then the girdle bolts atop the main caps to tie the system together rather than relying on each main cap to work on its own.

When building an engine there's always a battle of compromises—you can either spend a bunch of money and have a bulletproof bottom end, or spend the money elsewhere and take your chances. Most street racers take the risk, since their cars are generally built on a budget, while professional racers spend big money and have a little more trust in their powerplant. If you're pushing the limits of your stock block and bottom end, it's a ticking time bomb, and it won't be pretty when it lets go. Weigh the options for your particular build, but if you plan to spray lots of nitrous, or make large amounts of boost, engine failure is inevitable with a stock bottom end.

Nitrous Oxide

One of the most popular forms of sneaky horsepower is nitrous oxide. It's been a very effective engine modification since the 1970s and it's common to see multiple stages of nitrous on a full-on race application. One of the first racing classes to use nitrous oxide in extreme quantities was the IHRA Pro Modified class, which began in the late 1980s. These cars featured big-inch big-blocks with swoopy bodies that allowed them to run deep into the 6-second zone in

If you're planning for big-time power (more than 1,000 hp), then carnage is inevitable if you're still using a stock block. For the LS1 crowd, the hot item is GM Performance Parts' LSX block, which is a cast-iron piece that feature lots of extra webbing for additional strength. *(Photo courtesy GM Performance Parts)*

Aftermarket blocks generally have some sort of strengthening feature in the main cap area. This Dart aluminum big-block has splayed main caps, while others have splayed and cross-bolted main caps to keep the crankshaft snug. For stock two-bolt main blocks, a main girdle works well to strengthen the mains.

the quarter-mile. In the early days, most Pro Mods relied on horsepower from supercharged engines, similar to those in a Top Alcohol Funny Car. This combination of extremely high horsepower in a door car with suspension gave spectators some exciting action. Modern-day Pro Mods are equally as exciting to watch, but many teams use nitrous oxide for their power adder. These cars are now dipping into the 5s in the quarter, thanks to more than 1,000 hp worth of nitrous being fogged into the big-block engines.

Outlaw street car racers are also firm believers in nitrous and have been using it since the early 1990s when the Fastest

Street Car Shootout began. It's easy to see why nitrous oxide is so popular with these high-dollar race engines, but it's also a great way to make a sleeper even faster. There are two ways to inject nitrous into your engine, and your choice depends on how big of a "shot" you plan to spray.

If you're using a small shot (50 to 100 hp), you can safely use what's known as a dry kit. A dry system only injects nitrous oxide into the engine, while a wet kit injects both nitrous and a dose of fuel to keep the engine from leaning out. Without the addition of fuel, you run the risk of creating too much heat in the combustion chamber, which could result in a damaged

Nitrous oxide is a potent way of adding power to an engine, whether you're dealing with a bone-stock 5.0-liter Mustang engine or a full-on race mill. Nitrous is used in two major forms—dry and wet. Dry kits are nitrous only, while wet kits have a dose of fuel thrown into the mix. *(Photo courtesy Zex Performance)*

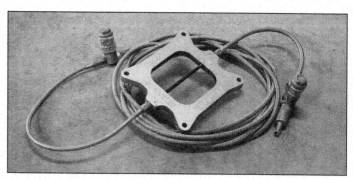

For wet kits, you can choose between two ways to distribute the nitrous: a plate or a fogger. Shown is a plate kit, which bolts beneath a 4150-style carburetor and sprays a mix of nitrous and fuel into the intake manifold. Most street kits top out at a 150-hp shot, but upgrades are available for much bigger gains.

A fogger is used in high-end applications, giving the nitrous the most direct path to the combustion chambers. NOS makes a fogger kit that mounts beneath the intake manifold for the ultimate sleeper nitrous system. Hide the lines and the solenoids and you have one sneaky setup.

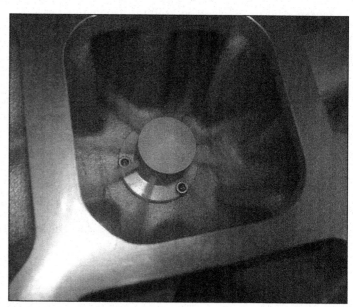

Street racers have been hiding nitrous for years, and Nightmare Motorsports actually sells a Stealth Nozzle to make the task a little easier. The sprayer module mounts in a single-plane intake just below the carburetor and sprays nitrous directly into the runners. It's efficient and it makes lots of power. *(Photo courtesy Nightmare Motorsports)*

piston. Rings are also susceptible to damage under these situations, so consider that when deciding on your nitrous system.

That's not to say a wet kit doesn't have disadvantages, especially to the sleeper enthusiast, as the additional lines and solenoid add to the list of things to hide. It's also important to note that a wet nitrous system isn't faultless—it can toast an engine just as quickly as a dry kit. Without the right bottom end modifications, carburetor adjustments, and ignition timing, even a professionally plumbed nitrous system eventually results in engine failure.

A wet nitrous system can be applied in two ways—a plate kit or a fogger. A plate nitrous kit consists of a plate that mounts between the intake manifold and carburetor, and features an inlet for nitrous oxide and an inlet for fuel. It's a very simple installation, and it's the most common for street cars. For more serious applications, a fogger system is used, and consists of direct-port nozzles that are threaded into the runners of an intake manifold. This is obviously a more effective way of sending nitrous into the heads, but it's also more complicated to tune and extremely hard to hide.

The easiest nitrous system to hide is a dry system, as it only requires one additional line, and a nozzle that you can place pretty much anywhere, as long as it makes it into the engine somehow. On late-model applications it's as simple as threading a single nozzle into the air intake pipe so it sprays toward the throttle body. For carbureted applications, NOS (Nitrous Oxide Systems) makes a wet nitrous kit that can be hidden within a standard round air cleaner. The "Top Shot" nitrous system mounts on top of the carburetor, rather than beneath it like a conventional plate kit. According to NOS, it's super easy to install and it can be jetted for 75- to 150-hp gains. It fits 4150-style Holley carburetors, and it's a very savvy way to increase your sleeper's horsepower. Another option for a hidden nitrous system is the "Stealth Nozzle" from Nightmare Motorsports. It mounts in the plenum of a single-plane intake manifold and sprays nitrous directly into the intake runners.

NOS' dry nitrous system, "Sneaky Pete," consists of a very small and easily concealable bottle and all of the components to make it work. Horsepower gains aren't nearly as high as with the Top Shot system, but NOS has another offering that is quite sneaky and packs a big punch. It's a fogger system that mounts on the bottom side of the intake, instead of the top. The nitrous/fuel distribution block mounts beneath the intake and all of the hard lines are plumbed to fogger nozzles in a compact manner. The kit requires drilling and fabrication, but it offers many options for hiding solenoids and inlet hoses. This kit is designed for V-8 engines, and it offers horsepower gains from 100 to 250 hp depending on jet size. This is sneaky horsepower at its finest!

Pros

- Easy to hide, thanks to pre-made hidden kits
- Use it only when you need it to save parts
- Adaptable to *any* engine and easy to install
- It's *cheap*

Cons

- Empty bottle
- It's not street legal if the line is hooked up to the bottle
- Nitrous backfire and parts breakage

Superchargers

Superchargers have been used as power adders for much longer than nitrous oxide, and they're a more reliable source of horsepower, since they are belt-driven by the engine itself. They're used on countless factory-built models where horsepower levels are moderate, and they're used in extreme applications, like Top Fuel dragsters and Funny Cars. In its simplest form, a supercharger is an air compressor. The supercharger multiplies air at varying pressures, depending on internal gearing and pulley size. Using a different set of pulleys can change boost pressures, as this causes the supercharger unit to spin faster or slower. There are two basic forms of supercharging used in the automotive industry—Roots and centrifugal. Neither is easy to hide on a sleeper build, but they certainly make huge gains in horsepower and torque, even on a stock engine.

Both centrifugal and Roots-style superchargers have been used on many factory performance cars. Ford, General Motors, and even Studebaker have used superchargers in production vehicles, with Ford being the most recognizable in the

Superchargers have been involved in drag racing for many decades, and most applications have featured Roots-style blowers, like this one. This style of blower is still used in many forms of racing, but there are more efficient ways of making boost these days. Good luck hiding one of these things.

industry because of its plentiful usage of boost. Ford has used superchargers on several models, including the 2003 and 2004 Mustang SVT Cobra, the second generation SVT Lightning, the GT, and many others.

In terms of drag racing, and superchargers, the trend started in the 1950s as crafty racers configured GMC Roots superchargers to work on their V-8 engines. The workmanship may have suffered, but these guys made it work, and quickly realized the potential of forced induction. As the cars continued to get faster many companies began producing superchargers specifically for racing and then manufactured a manifold to easily adapt it to any engine. It was the

hot rodder's dream, and Roots blowers ended up on drag cars, street cars, and just about everything in between. The 1970s and 1980s saw a huge Pro Street craze, and the most popular combination proved to be a polished 6-71 blower topped with two 4-barrel carburetors. Stack all that on top of a big-block Chevy and you had a real eye-catcher.

Since a Roots blower sits atop the engine, it provides a big wow factor, but that's not exactly what the sleeper enthusiast wants. That's where the centrifugal supercharger comes into the picture. These superchargers mount to the side of the engine, but feature the same basic principles of forcing air into the engine with a belt-driven compressor. To run a centrifugal

Many modern superchargers use the Roots design, but manufacturers have definitely upped the game in terms of technology. This one is a MagnaCharger, and it bolts atop the LS6 engine in a Cadillac CTS-V. This system gave the stock CTS-V 440 hp at the rear wheels—about 100 hp more than stock.

Centrifugal superchargers offer a different approach to building boost, and generally produce a cooler intake charge, which allows them to make more boost. Pro-Charger is a strong force in outlaw street car racing, and it makes many kits for regular street cars, too. You can expect a 50-percent increase in horsepower from one of its street kits.

Since superchargers are driven from a belt-and-pulley system, changing boost pressure involves changing pulleys. A smaller blower-pulley spins the unit faster, which creates more boost. As you increase boost, you also increase intake temperatures, but an intercooler solves that problem and allows for much more boost.

In the 1980s, Roots blowers were hot stuff, so B&M designed what was known as "underhood" superchargers, which were basically smaller versions of the popular 6-71 and 8-71 units. The smaller housing meant you'd need to spin the blower much faster to build boost, but that also makes for a heated intake charge.

supercharger you can utilize a regular intake manifold, which greatly simplifies many aspects of the build. You will, however, need to modify the carburetor to withstand the boost pressure, which is being fed through it instead of drawn from beneath like a Roots-blown application.

Centrifugal superchargers are also tough to hide, but most at least fit under a stock hood, as compared to a Roots blower, which generally requires a large hood scoop, or simply a hole in the hood. Again, that was a popular look a few decades ago, but it doesn't help your sleeper status in the least.

If you're determined to completely hide a supercharger, your only option is mounting it in the rear of the vehicle. This requires a shaft-drive setup, which runs from the front of the engine to the rear of the car, parallel with the driveshaft. It's a complex system, similar to a PTO (power take-off) on farm equipment, but totally worth it if you can hide the supercharger and its tubing beneath the car.

Finding the right pulley combination isn't always easy because boost pressure is often determined by a number of things. The physical size of the supercharger plays a big role, as a larger blower doesn't need to spin quite as fast as a smaller blower to produce the same amount of boost. It should also be noted that swapping to a more efficient set of cylinder heads nets a lower boost reading, even if the pulley sizes remain the same. This is caused by the engine's ability to consume the forced induction at a higher rate, thus making more power with less boost pressure. Camshaft selection can also affect boost readings, but it's usually anything related to airflow that causes the biggest change. On a typical street engine, 10 pounds of boost is the average on an un-intercooled application.

Many companies are jumping on the supercharger bandwagon, and the twin-screw design is very popular. It's a more efficient way to force the air into the engine, but these supercharger kits are very pricey, compared to the standard Roots or centrifugal setups. This Techco supercharger is made for a modern Hemi.

A small Roots-style blower is susceptible to overheating the intake charge if it spins too fast, so many owners resort to a blower that allows more airflow at a lower drive speed. If intake air temperatures are still a problem, intercooling is always an option for centrifugal superchargers, while the same process is generally referred to as "aftercooling" on a Roots-blown application, as the cooler is mounted between the blower and the intake manifold. Studies and thousands of hours of dyno time have proven that centrifugal superchargers create far less heat than a Roots style, and those figures are multiplied when you install an intercooler, be it a simple air-to-air core or a race-ready air-to-water unit. Superchargers are a great way to give your machine much more power with instantaneous boost and incredible power gains if all of the components match up right. If you don't mind giving up your secret when the hood is raised then a supercharger is a very potent option in terms of power adders.

Pros
- Instant boost—no lag and it's always there
- Easy installation for most engines
- Increase horsepower 50 percent on low boost
- Most superchargers have self contained oiling systems

Cons
- Expensive
- Changing pulleys to change boost levels
- Nearly impossible to hide

Turbochargers

These days, the ultimate power adder in many forms of drag racing is the turbocharger. This form of forced induction is so efficient that it's created a huge boom in the automotive industry, and continues to grow in popularity. Turbochargers are not simple to install and they create plenty of tuning issues, but they are absolutely the best way to make horsepower in a street engine. Many enthusiasts are more than doubling the output of their engines by installing a turbocharger, and reaping the benefits of a mild engine setup, as compared to a radical race engine that makes the same amount of power. You can get good fuel mileage, keep the engine relatively stock, and make big power—what could be better than that?

Turbochargers work in the same way a supercharger operates, by forcing air into the engine at a high rate of speed via the engine itself. The difference is a supercharger is driven directly from the engine's crankshaft, while a turbocharger uses the engine's exhaust gas to build boost pressure. This method of forced induction robs very little power, while the slight drag of the supercharger has been known to rob a significant amount of power, depending on the size, and the configuration. Much like superchargers, turbochargers have been around for years, and racers have experimented with them quite a bit over the past few decades. Somewhere along the line, someone figured out how to make a turbocharger perform to its potential, and it's been a blessing for the automotive enthusiast wanting speed and reliability in a low-maintenance package.

For several years, many companies have been producing pre-manufactured turbo kits for all sorts of applications from Hondas to Mustangs, and everything in between. This makes it easy to adapt a powerful component onto an otherwise boring engine, and the trend is expanding to backyard mechanics and average Joes who want to go fast. People are building

This cutaway of a turbocharger provides an interesting view of how the boost is built from the engine's exhaust gases. The front of the turbo is known as the cold side, as it brings in fresh air. The back brings in air from the engine's exhaust and it's called the hot side for obvious reasons.

If you're planning to make 10 to 12 pounds of boost on a V-8 engine with a fairly low compression ratio, then an intercooler may not be necessary. Another non-intercooler option for high-boost applications is to run the engine on alcohol or methanol, as these fuels help cool the intake charge.

their own turbo systems using parts from Diesel trucks, and having incredible results from low-budget builds. It's a matter of getting the combination right before applying the boost, and then making sure the engine stays alive by increasing the fuel delivery or retarding the timing. Obviously, turbochargers are great for sleepers, and even if you don't go to great lengths to hide the system, you will have one killer setup with surprising results.

It's been proven that stock, low-compression engines respond very well to turbochargers, and that's great news for sleeper owners, as well as budget-conscious gear heads in general. If you're crafty and have the knowhow to build the turbo system yourself, the setup can be assembled for less than $1,000, and you could have well over 500 hp with a completely stock engine! Keep in mind that this theory is based on the most basic of engines, the small-block Chevy, which is a perfect platform for such a build. Other engines apply, but the small-block Chevy engine is one of the most expendable engines out there, so hurting parts won't hurt your wallet quite as much.

Exhaust gases drive turbochargers, so it doesn't take much studying to realize additional heat enters your engine without the assistance of an intercooler. In most cases, intercoolers are a very important aspect of a turbocharged engine, and if you choose not to run one, you're looking at a serious horsepower limitation. Potential boost levels are greatly increased with an intercooler, even though it requires a little more fabrication to run the piping to and from the unit.

A budget-friendly tip is to scour junkyards for a suitable intercooler from a factory-built turbo car, rather than buying an aftermarket piece. Even if it's damaged and you have to make some repairs to it, the monetary difference is substantial.

A peek under the hood of this late-model Dodge Challenger displays an aftermarket air intake system on an otherwise stock Hemi. The piping that appears to be a cold-air intake is actually ductwork for the STS system, which features a rear-mounted turbocharger.

Since the intercooler rides up front, usually in the lower grille opening to get clean air, hiding it is important for a sleeper build. However, that's an easy fix, as you can simply install a piece of mesh in the grille opening and paint the intercooler black. It'll blend in and get the job done.

Many turbocharged applications do not utilize a muffler, because the turbo offers a cool sound and actually does a great job of keeping the engine quiet. Some guys run a short down pipe and still keep a pretty low profile, but the ultimate sleeper setup is a down pipe that leads to a muffler and then a stock-appearing exhaust tip. For the four-cylinder crowd, you always have the option of leaving the open down pipe and going for the "muffler rusted off" sound. The Ford 2.3-liter four-cylinder is a perfect candidate for said treatment as it doesn't have to try very hard to sound like a piece of junk and car guys rarely take a four-cylinder car seriously. These engines are amazing platforms for boost though, and they handle lots of abuse, so a light car with a turbo 2.3 is a recipe for a great sleeper.

Pros

- Double your car's horsepower
- Can be rear-mounted to keep it hidden
- Works well on a stock, or highly modified engine
- Relatively inexpensive if you buy used parts

Cons

- Turbo lag if you're setup isn't dialed in
- Lots of fabrication involved
- Running oil supply lines to the turbo

Mounted just before the tailpipe, the hidden turbocharger is more susceptible to picking up debris, but it would certainly fool the average car enthusiast. Some folks fear turbo lag as a potential issue with rear-mounted systems because of the expanse of tubing, but STS promises almost instantaneous spool with its kits.

A lot goes into choosing the right turbocharger for your application. Generally speaking, a small exhaust wheel and A/R offers quicker turbo spool, but can suffer on top end power. The size and pitch (trim) of the intake wheel also affect power spool time. Do your homework and find the right one for your engine.

If you have a tight budget, but want an intercooler, you can scour junkyards to find a factory unit to suffice. This one is from a Ford Super Duty truck, and it's massive, but the owner painted it black to help it blend in with its surroundings once the grille is installed.

Chapter 5

HOOK It Up

You can build a 1,500-hp race engine for your sleeper, but all that effort doesn't do much good if the result is a plume of tire smoke and a couple of squirrely black marks. Long, rolling burnouts are certainly fun, but if you're planning to get serious with racing, you need to make your car hook on street tires unless you have a crafty way of disguising a set of drag radials or slicks. It's no secret that small slicks and drag radials can get the job done on a fast car, as Outlaw Street Car racers have proven over the past 10 years or so. If you were building a sleeper 20 (or more) years ago, you could get away with putting a set of 8-inch-wide slicks on your stock suspension street car and have a valid argument, when it comes to setting up a race. Back then if it didn't have big tires, most folks didn't think it would hook. Many street races were won with this approach, but it just doesn't fly these days, with Outlaw 10.5 cars running faster than NHRA Pro Stock cars on a slick that was once considered small.

Drag racers have been concerned with traction since the early days, but it's become a serious area for tuning with the introduction of 10.5-inch-tire racing. This truck is hitting the tires hard, and the track is holding it, meaning the suspension tune-up perfectly matches the track conditions.

If you're building a sleeper strictly to cruise on the street, then tire size may not be your biggest concern. With this example of a sleeper, your biggest competition is at the traffic light. Even then, it doesn't really matter if your car dead hooks when the light turns green, as you're generally lined up against a guy who thinks his new Mustang is fast. As long as it doesn't get too wild and swap lanes, or something of that nature, making a basic cruising sleeper hook up isn't at the top of the list. However, if you're planning to do some serious street racing, the car needs to hook and stay hooked for the endurance of the race. A lot of races are lost due to tire spin, and it certainly adds a high level of inconsistency if your car loses traction at the slightest blip of the throttle. At the track, it's a similar story, because a good launch is key to winning the

Rear suspension upgrades are common to help with traction, and most racers rely on a multi-link suspension system with coilover shocks. Even with stock suspension setups, like this Fox-Body Mustang, coilovers are in place to offer vast adjustability to perfectly dial in the launch, but they're not easy to hide.

For cars with a factory link-style suspension, a set of control arms help transfer weight and keep it over the rear tires. It also offers a stiffer platform to keep the rear end stable. This square tube control arm is strong and light, but simply boxing the original control arms can have the same benefits.

Street racing still happens, regardless of how hard law enforcement cracks down on it, but organizations like the Flashlight Drags put on events with a strong street racing feel. Usually held on abandoned airstrips, there is no track prep, but this twin-turbo Pontiac Tempest is hooking up nicely. *(Photo courtesy Rich Chenet)*

race in most cases. Some cars have enough horsepower to run down the opponent on the top end, but it's never advised to rely on that to win races.

Making a car hook up at the track takes a combination of efforts involving the tires, suspension, and weight balance, but making a car hook on the street is a whole different ball game. While it still requires all three of those factors to be tuned perfectly, it takes a lot of trial and error to make a car hook up on un-prepped asphalt. It is possible to pull the front wheels on the street if the setup is just right, but traction compound is almost always necessary, as it greatly increases traction on un-prepped surfaces. The results of a wheelstand on the street aren't quite as dramatic as those you've probably seen in the Fast and Furious movie series, but it's still something to see. However, the average street car, or sleeper for that matter, isn't going to do a wheelstand on the street, and your efforts should be focused on keeping the car hooked up and straight all the way down the track. Obviously, driving technique is part of the equation, but if you don't have the right suspension setup, the majority of your passes will leave you feathering the gas and fighting the wheel to keep it between the lines.

On the subject of sleepers, there's always talk of street racing, and while it's illegal and unsafe at times, it still happens. The street-racing scene isn't nearly what it used to be, but any back-road straightaway can offer the temptation to race. Just so you know, there are organizations that promote safe drag racing with the feel of street racing. One series of events is the Flashlight Drags, held mainly in Pennsylvania—its motto is "Street Racing Without the Jailtime!" These events take place on abandoned airstrips, which are not prepped for drag racing. That means your car reacts just as it does on the street, and you can have some serious fun without the risk of getting caught. As law enforcement cracks down on street racing and fast cars in general, it's only a matter of time until you see more of these races pop up around the country.

Rolling Stock

Since the 1950s drag racers have used slicks to hook up at the track, and while a lot has changed over the years, slicks are still the norm for drag cars. Back when slicks first hit the market, the only form of manufacturing was to take an existing tire and recap it with a slick tread. After a few years of fighting these hard-compound and inconsistent tires, many companies began manufacturing purpose-built drag racing tires. M&H was the first, with many others to follow. But as the years went on drag racing tires grew in terms of popularity and physical size. By the 1970s drag slicks for dragsters measured at least 32 inches tall and no less than 14 inches wide with various compounds for different applications. Street cars followed suit with Pro Street builds that involved monstrous meats tucked under everything from Impalas to Chevettes.

For the past 15 years or so drag racers seem to be reverting to small tires, as the outlaw drag racing scene explodes into a big industry. For a while, the go-to tire for outlaw racing was the 29.5x10.5-inch size, but now folks are testing the waters with 26x8.5-inch tires to see exactly how fast they can go. It's all about suspension setup, as these "Outlaw 8.5" cars consistently run 5.20s in the eighth-mile with stock suspension. Another huge breakthrough in outlaw drag racing has been the development of drag radials, and the knowhow to make a car with stock suspension hook up on street legal radials that are less than 10 inches wide.

As drag racing evolved, rear tires kept getting bigger, so racers began narrowing the rear end and enlarging the wheel tubs in their cars to fit the larger rubber. This increases traction greatly, but a massive set of slicks instantly give away your car's secret. Finding a way to hook up on small tires is the goal.

This stock-suspension Chevy Malibu relies on 28x10.5-inch slicks for traction and it seems to be hooking up nicely on this pass. Any savvy car guy knows that small-tire cars are capable of fast times, so you're not fooling anyone with a set of slicks that would've been considered small a couple of decades ago.

Outlaw drag racing came from street racing, so these racers know a thing or two about making a car hook, whether it's on a fully prepped track or a back road in the middle of nowhere. While tire technology has come a long way since the introduction of purpose-built drag slicks, traction is a complicated process of weight transfer and power application. There are a number of good-hooking street radials out there, but slicks are definitely faster on pretty much every combination. Drag radials and cheater slicks split the difference and work well, but they're a dead giveaway to your big secret, unless you get creative. If you think whitewalls give your car the extra *grandma* look, then painting them onto your rear tires could be the key to hiding the race-ready rubber. From a distance, the rear tires blend into the stock appearance, but curious car guys quickly spot the drag radials or slicks. If you want to bypass that whole scenario, and stick to regular street radials, then you have to adopt a new driving style to make them hook.

Concerning the burnout, you hear all sorts of advice on the best strategy, but a moderate burnout is really all you need for a street car. In fact, for a car on hard street radials, the burnout should be nothing more than a quick spin of the tires to sling any water or debris from the tires without putting too much heat in the rubber. This concept is the exact opposite of most drag racing principles, as racing slicks tend to work better with heat, but street tires do not benefit from a big burnout in the least. Testing has shown that big, smoky burnouts on hard street radials actually hurts elapsed time, so save your tires and keep it simple in the burnout box if you're running a real street car.

When it comes to hooking up on street tires you won't find too many tips simply because most folks haven't figured it out yet. Hard radials just aren't made for high horsepower applications, and they have trouble hooking on any surface imaginable. Even a fully prepped drag strip doesn't help, but driving style is key. Obviously, you can't go out there with intentions of leaving the line under full power, so dialing back the throttle input helps, but items like programmable boost or nitrous controllers help cars with a power adder. This allows you to leave the line at minimal boost and slowly ramp it up as you go down the track.

The biggest mistake many sleeper enthusiasts make when building their car is installing large slicks, since that's the first thing a car guy looks for when he's the least bit suspicious. Generally, a big set of tires requires the car to be mini-tubbed, which is a very obvious modification in most cases. However, it can be pulled off if you retain the original rear end width, and order the rear wheels with plenty of backspacing, so the wheels look stock from the outside. For a basic street car that is mini-tubbed, you would more than likely run a 10-inch-wide wheel, so you'd want about 7 of those inches to be backspacing, leaving the stock look of a 3-inch lip on the front side of the rim. This applies mainly to steel wheels, but you can pull off the same look with aluminum.

Rolling stock is very important when building a car that could possibly show some signs of speed, so don't give in to the temptation of putting lighter drag wheels and tires on your sleeper. A car like a Chevy Vega or a Ford Pinto can virtually transform from a junky stocker to an all-out drag car with a simple swap of wheels and tires, so it's important to keep it stock, even if you're losing out on performance. Most of the 1970s economy cars had 13-inch wheels with four-lug bolt patterns, so finding appropriate wheels and tires is never easy, but it is part of completing the look. One option for

To disguise a set of slicks or drag radials, you need to get creative with the sidewall treatment. This crafty sleeper enthusiast painted a whitewall on his Mickey Thompson 215/60R14 drag radials. These tires happen to be smaller than stock, so they definitely do not stand out as racing rubber.

Progressive timing advance can be controlled with an ignition unit, such as this MSD box, known commonly as the 7531. It can work to the advantage of a sleeper builder by increasing timing as the car goes down the track. Similar controllers are available for nitrous and turbocharged applications.

Sleeper Tire Possibilities

Bias-Ply Street Tire

This is an ancient form of tire production, but it's still a safe option for cars produced before 1976, prior to the big switch to radial tires. The tires are constructed using nylon or polyester cord that is layered in a crisscross pattern at a 45-degree angle from the tire's centerline. Most passenger car bias-ply tires feature four plies, and a very simple tread pattern. If you're building a car from the 1950s to the mid 1970s and want a totally stock appearance, bias ply tires are the way to go, but they don't offer much in the way of traction. This is mainly because of rubber compound, not necessarily the tire's construction.

Polyglas tires were common during the late 1960s and early 1970s and provided limited traction to muscle cars of nearly every make and model. These days, you can still get these Goodyear tires or Firestone Wide Oval tires, from specialty tire dealers like Universal Vintage Tire. *(Photo courtesy Universal Vintage Tire)*

Radial Street Tire

A basic street radial doesn't offer much more traction than its bias-ply ancestors, but modern tire construction and rubber compounds have certainly helped hard street radials hook up. The radial's cord runs 90 degrees to the tire's centerline, which allows the tire to conform to the road. Getting a car to hook on hard street radials is no easy task, but with the right driving style, it's a possibility. Traction compound has been known to help radials hook on the street and at the track, and some sneaky racers have been known to soak the tread in a special mix of ingredients to soften the rubber. Although there isn't an official study on the subject don't be fooled by expensive tires with the mindset that they hook better than cheap tires. Many fast street cars rely on budget-friendly tires to get the job done.

Regular street radials are available in a wide variety of sizes and brands. The BFGoodrich Radial T/A is a popular choice with muscle car enthusiasts, and they're a decent choice for a sleeper, as long as you can keep them glued to the racing surface. Suspension setup is part of the battle, but driving style is key. *(Photo courtesy Coker Tire Company)*

Drag Radial

When the outlaw street car scene exploded in the 1990s, racers wanted a street-legal tire that would hook up like a slick. The result was the drag radial tire, first made by BFGoodrich in 1995. The tire's main casing is very similar to a regular street radial, but the compound used is a happy medium between a slick and a regular radial. This makes for an interesting mix, as the tire's stiff sidewalls react differently than slicks, making suspension tuning tricky. Then Mickey Thompson, M&H, and Goodyear stepped into the game, and now there are well-prepped radial-tire cars running 4.30s in the eighth-mile. Car guys are catching on, so putting a set of drag radials on your sleeper might not hide its potential.

Drag radials are widely accepted as good-hooking tires these days, with stock-suspension cars running mid-4-second passes in the eighth-mile. These tires work well and offer great street driving manners, but most folks know the potential of these soft-compound, street-legal tires and can spot them from a distance.

Cheater Slick

The cheater slick has been around for just about as long as the full-on racing slick, but its biggest advantage has always been the fact that it's street legal. Its main casing is the same as a bias-ply slick, which means a flimsy sidewall that most certainly wrinkles during a hard launch. This is great for the track, but street driving is rarely pleasant with a tire of this nature. At highway speeds the tires aren't very stable so a quick lane change could result in a scary ride. These tires are great for traction, but you won't stand a chance of keeping your sleeper's performance a secret. You'd be just as well off running a set of real slicks.

While a pair of cheater slicks will not help you stay off the radar, it is street legal thanks to the tiny grooves in the contact patch. These tires are of bias-ply construction and they are nothing more than a street-legal slick. These are difficult to hide, but hook very well. *(Photo courtesy Coker Tire Company)*

Drag Slick

Generally, a regular drag slick is a bias-ply tire with very soft rubber compounds, and absolutely no tread. This is the optimal tire for drag racing, but it's a common assumption that a car with slicks is probably fast, even though it's not always true. Slicks offer the most traction for your sleeper, but finding a way to hide them is the toughest aspect of this tire selection. Painted-on whitewalls is a step in the right direction, but you're not going to fool everyone with that trick. If you're running slicks on the street, keep in mind that traction is still limited unless you have traction compound on hand.

Full-on slicks are not street legal and they're extremely hard to hide, but some guys can pull it off. This Buick Skylark has a pair of Buick mud flaps to take attention away from the Mickey Thompson slicks. The owner says mud flaps are only cool if your car runs 10s or faster!

Many cars from the 1960s had small wheel tubs that are limited to 7-inch-wide wheels and accompanying tires. To fit larger meats without being too obvious, many enthusiasts mini-tub a car by widening the wheel tubs by a couple of inches. This is especially true with early Nova platforms.

When it comes to hiding wide rear wheels, it's nearly impossible, but you can fool the eye with a set of stock-appearing wheels. Even if the wheel measures 10 inches wide, the backspacing should be 7 inches, leaving a stock-looking 3-inch lip. This is purely for a drive-by appeal—a closer look reveals the wide meats. *(Photo courtesy Rich Chenet)*

late-model cars that came from the factory with aluminum wheels is to have the front wheels narrowed significantly. This sheds approximately 20 pounds per side on average when you consider the lighter front tires that are mounted.

Hubcaps are the ticket for most cars, as it's not a natural car guy tendency to believe that a car with hubcaps is fast. First, hubcaps aren't allowed on most drag strips, and second, most hubcaps are ugly. Stick a set of caps on your sleeper and you certainly offer a surprise to anyone paying attention.

Even popular muscle cars like Chevelles and Torinos take on the grandma-fresh appearance when you install a set of stock caps and whitewalls. It may not fool everyone, but it's certainly a good place to start.

A good way to sum up the subject of tires and wheels is to keep it as stock-appearing as possible. The hardcore racers who participate in F.A.S.T. drag racing have the tire and wheel situation figured out, so that's a great place to learn about traction on a street tire. It was impressive enough when the majority of these muscle cars ran in the 12s with stock Polyglas tires, but now there are a few guys running deep into the 10s and pulling the front wheels when they leave the line. Some of the fastest cars in the class are amazing sleepers, as they look completely stock even under the hood, and feature no power adders or anything that wouldn't have been a factory option. Lane Carey's 1971 Ford Mustang is the record holder with a 9.84 at 138 mph on Goodyear Polyglas tires. These guys know a thing or two about hooking up.

A popular trend among modern muscle car enthusiasts is having the original aluminum front wheels narrowed. This sheds lots of unneeded weight from the front of your car, while providing the appearance of a stock wheel. This Mercury Marauder looks stock from the side profile, but runs 9s in the quarter.

Ed Cook campaigns this 1969 Plymouth Roadrunner in the F.A.S.T. racing series, and pulls the wheels off the line, using Polyglas street tires. While this 440-powered Mopar is fast, the current record holder is Lane Carey in his 1971 Mustang. The record is currently 9.84 at 139 mph, with a completely stock-appearing muscle car. *(Photo courtesy Jim Knights)*

Power Application

Getting a sleeper down the track without tire spin isn't simply about tires, chassis setup, or suspension—there's more to it. Having the right torque converter is a big part of hooking up on any kind of tire, and going fast in general. If the converter isn't set up specifically for the application, the results won't be optimal. If it's set up too *tight*, then the risk of spinning the tires is even greater as a *tight* converter is very similar to an aggressive clutch. It tries to send every ounce of available power through the transmission, and that's a recipe for disaster on street tires. However, a *loose* converter eats up horsepower and helps in the traction department, but the slipping effect can sometimes affect power application farther down the track, where you want as little slip as possible. This slipping effect of a loose converter is even greater on a heavy car. It's not always easy to pick the right converter, but if you're not happy with it, lots of manufacturers and shops cut it apart

F.A.S.T. racers often try to soften the 1-2 shift to reduce tire spin as the car goes down the track, and there are several ways to accomplish it. You can modify the valve body to cushion the shifts, or in the case of a Chrysler 727, you can swap the kickdown levers to regulate how firmly it shifts.

For sleepers with an automatic transmission, the torque converter plays a huge role in making the car hook, be it on street tires or slicks. A "loose" converter won't shock the tires quite as hard, but it certainly eats up some horsepower, while a "tight" converter results in tire spin if you're going for a hard launch.

Manual transmissions are great for the street, and this Tremec TKO-600 is a prime example of what most folks utilize in a modern street car. In stock form, these transmissions aren't the best for super-fast shifts, but they're strong and they can be modified for quick, high-RPM shifts.

Shannon Medley, owner of this green Chevelle, says he brings the car up on the converter (3,000 rpm in his case) and simply lets off the brakes when it's go time. He lets the car settle, then goes full throttle, and then sprays a 175-hp shot of nitrous about 50 feet out.

and adjust it to fit your application. If your car will see lots of track time, a good converter plays a huge role in your success, especially on small tires.

Launching is one thing, but making the car stick all the way down the track is another tricky detail of hooking up on small tires. Many F.A.S.T. racers have perfected the launch, but it took a while to get the cars to hook past the 60-foot beams. Custom internal work was the answer, as these crafty racers manipulated the transmissions to provide softer shifts. Normally, you want a firm shift, but the cars were experiencing tire spin on the 1-2 shift and this modification resulted in gains of more than half a second in the quarter-mile.

If you're dealing with a manual transmission, the clutch setup is of similar concern. It determines how hard the car "shocks the tires" on the launch, but there's a very fine line between tire spin and clutch slippage when it comes to manual transmission cars. If you're planning to build a bulletproof clutch and transmission that you can really thrash on, you need a rear suspension that can handle the shock of a hard-hitting, high-RPM launch. At least with an automatic, you can put a load on the car with the torque converter to prepare the suspension for launch. With a manual, the transition between no suspension load and 100-percent wide-open power application is nearly instantaneous. It's common to see racers struggle with a manual transmission setup at the track, but it's proven to be the best route for street use, especially in the case of roll races.

Modern manual transmissions are prone to breakage with high-horsepower applications, but with the right equipment, you can row the gears hard and know the transmission will stand up to the abuse. With turbocharged cars, it's easy to lose boost between gears, so most enthusiasts choose to shift as quickly as possible without letting off the gas. This is obviously hard on the transmission and driveline parts, as well as the engine, as a sluggish shift could result in too many RPM if your right foot stays pinned to the floor. Some guys can perfect it, but you'll never be able to see the true potential of a turbo car if the engine is backed by a manual transmission. A similarly prepared car with an automatic transmission outruns it every time, as long as the torque converter allows the car to build boost off the line, and continue to pull hard on the big end.

With all of these components blended into a nice mix, you must also consider driving technique in the power application department. Being patient with the car, and taking the time to learn what it takes to make it hook makes all the difference, and with enough practice you can learn to launch a car on hard street radials. Restraint is the biggest element because your inner car guy automatically thinks that going fast means wide-open throttle. If you're running an automatic transmission, you want to keep the RPM at 3,000 or lower on the line

(if your torque converter allows), and simply let off the brake when it's go-time. Don't give it any throttle input, just keep the gas pedal in the same position until the rear suspension has enough time to settle and you can safely ease into the throttle. At this point, you can experiment with the ramping of nitrous or boost if you're running a power adder. If not, keep adjusting the launch RPM and throttle input until you find the car's limit. For cars with manual transmissions, launches are a little less consistent, but slipping the clutch is your only option to launch the car without shocking the rear tires. The idea is to let the car settle before going wide open.

If you're running nitrous, timed controllers are available, but it's not entirely necessary with a small-horsepower shot. Most folks want to leave the line with nitrous, but it's not an option if you're running street tires. In this case, it's a game of luck, knowing when to hit the button. It's best to wait until at least 60 feet out to start spraying, but you can make that call depending on track conditions. Different tires and different tracks react differently so you can count on several trial-and-error runs to get the timing just right.

Chassis and Suspension

The first modifications most racers make involves strengthening the chassis, which could consist of subframe connectors or additional bracing, depending on the application. Chassis flex generally isn't a good thing, as it throws off the car's weight transfer during the launch, and it can greatly affect the way your body panels line up if the car is making a good bit of power. Some street racers could care less about those factors, and choose to retain the stock frame or unibody structure to keep the car light. The same can be said for roll cages and safety equipment (See Chapter 6 for more information).

Next is the rear suspension, and it seems to be the most obvious area of focus for any high-horsepower build. It's important to build the rear end and rear suspension to be strong, but making the car hook involves placing the weight of the car on the rear tires, and keeping it there during the entire race. If a car squats hard off the line, but rebounds too quickly, the rear suspension unloads, which means the weight shifts to the front of the car and allows the rear tires to spin. This is a common problem with leaf-spring rear suspensions—hooking at the line isn't a problem, but the rebound in the spring causes it to spin just after the launch. To help with this problem, many sleeper builders use a softer leaf-spring setup, and place additional weight in the trunk, or install a set of Cal-Trac bars to reduce axle wrap. Cars with factory four-link-style rear suspensions have problems of their own, but they are usually cured with a set of aftermarket control arms and adjustable-drag shocks.

The disadvantage to a leaf-spring rear suspension is the lack of tuning ability, as compared to a multi-link setup with coil springs or coilover shocks. This Nova transferred weight at the hit of the throttle, but the rebound in the rear suspension allowed the weight to shift to the nose, which resulted in tire spin.

For leaf-spring cars, you can help weight transfer by changing spring rates, but the key to hooking is usually a set of CalTrac bars. These bars are adjustable and help control axle wrap, which is a major cause of rear suspension recoil. CalTrac bars also keep the pinion angle consistent.

Whether you're racing on the street or at the track, people are going to sneak a peek under your car to see if they can spot any performance parts. Suspension parts are hard to hide, but leaf spring cars definitely have the advantage in this regard, because a leaf is a leaf in terms of appearance. (Photo courtesy Rich Chenet)

It makes sense to rework the rear suspension to better plant the tires, but many car guys overlook the importance of a good front suspension. Without the correct front spring and shock setup, ideal weight transfer to the rear wheels is impossible, and the car ultimately suffers from traction issues, or poor launches in general. Most owners go with an aftermarket 90/10 racing shock to help transfer weight, and these can generally be hidden with some flat-black spray paint. Without question, the goal is to make the front of the car as light as possible, so many racers resort to lightweight, tubular components. Lightweight brakes are another popular addition, and it's a great way to reduce the weight on your sleeper, as stock wheels usually keep the brakes hidden well.

Subframe connecters are a great way to stiffen a unibody car, but many of the generic kits do not go through the floorpan. Generic subframe connectors sometimes hang down into clear view, while through-the-floor connectors are undetectable without crawling under the car and offer lots more strength.

Lightweight racing brakes are a great way to shed some weight from your sleeper, and they're easy to hide if you're running plain steel wheels. Losing weight from the nose is great for better weight transfer, while losing weight from the rear decreases the amount of rotating mass.

Chapter 6

Safety Features and Interior Details

There's no question that safety is often overlooked on a sleeper buildup, since it's common car guy knowledge that a car with a roll cage must be pretty fast. The same can be said for many other safety features that sometimes get left out, simply to keep the car looking as stock as possible. While this doesn't ease the minds of the girlfriends, wives, and mothers of sleeper builders, it happens all the time. In addition, most of these cars are backyard builds with a tight budget, so the workmanship may not be up to the standards of professional chassis shop owners. Sometimes, a car that seems a little shady can be the most fun to drive, albeit unsafe at times.

This back-road burnout is being performed by a car that many sanctioning bodies would consider unsafe. At this point in the car's buildup, it had run a best of 6.50 seconds at 110 mph in the eighth-mile without any roll bar equipment. That's low-10-second territory in the quarter.

With that said, no one wants to see a fellow car guy crash his car, and potentially hurt himself or others. If an accident happens on the street or at the track, it's never a good thing, so having the right gear to stay safe is a good idea, even if it hinders the authenticity of your sleeper. Some of the cars in this book aren't fast enough to necessitate a full roll cage, but if you're running 11.49 or faster in the quarter, most track rules require you to have at least a five-point roll cage. Add to that a set of racing harnesses and you've converted your sneaky sleeper into an all out drag car, right? Don't be so sure—some racers keep a low profile and stay safe at the same time. It's not easy, but it's possible and very cool when it's executed correctly.

Any way you go about it, installing safety equipment is going to be hard to hide, but if you craft every safety component so it can be easily removed, it's a step in the right direction. For instance, many sleeper builders put a roll cage in their car, but bolt it in rather than weld it. A bolt-in cage allows you to pass technical inspection ("pass tech") at the track, as long as you follow the NHRA guidelines for bolt-in roll bars, but remove it when you're ready for the full-on sleeper look. A bolt-in cage is common for five- or six-point setups, but the more labor intensive cages, like 8- or 10-points, are in there for good because of the amount of cutting and fitting involved in the fabrication process. In this case you compromise a little of your sleeper ingenuity for the sake of safety, which isn't necessarily a bad thing when you're talking about a car with elevated levels of horsepower and possibly a different powertrain altogether.

Another important aspect of driving a fast car is having the appropriate gauges to watch the engine's vital signs. However, a bunch of auxiliary gauges isn't exactly sleeper material,

so hide them in a place that's easy to access when you really need them. Various switches can also blow the sleeper look, so tuck them away inside the console, ashtray, or glove box. There's a multitude of objects to hide when you want to go all out on building a genuine sleeper, but it's certainly worth the effort when your opponent looks in your car to find a stock-appearing interior.

Passing Tech

According to the NHRA Rulebook, any car quicker than 11.49 in the quarter-mile must use a five-point roll bar. This means, the roll cage needs to mount to the chassis structure in five areas—two points for the main roll bar, two points for the support bars to the rear, and one point for the driver's door bar. This roll bar tubing must consist of no less than 1¾-inch-diameter tubing, with .118-inch wall thickness on mild steel, and .083-inch wall thickness on chrome-moly tubing. It also states that roll bars in full frame cars must attach directly to the frame, not the floorpan.

Unibody cars must use 6-inch-square 1/8-inch-thick plates as a mounting surface on the car's floorpan. If you're bolting the cage into place, these plates mount to the top and the bottom side of the floorpan and bolt together with no smaller than 3/8-inch hardware. Weld-in cages mount to a single 6-inch-square plate, which is welded to the floorpan.

The five-point roll bar is good to 10.00 seconds, as long as the floorpan and firewall are not modified—widened wheel tubs are not considered a floorpan modification. A full 10- or 12-point roll cage is required for any vehicle faster than 9.99 seconds in the quarter-mile, or a trap speed of 135 mph, whichever comes first.

With a Roots-blown LS engine under its worn and weathered hood, this early-1950s Dodge has plenty of power. While the owner was concerned with general safety, the car would more than likely run fast enough to require a roll bar at a big-time track.

Hiding your car's potential means tucking away auxiliary gauges and toggle switches to keep the bone stock flavor, but this is much easier with classic and spacious cars from the 1960s. This Detroit Speed and Engineering 1965 Chevelle Test Car features a tach, an oil pressure gauge, and a water temperature gauge inside the glove box.

Keep in mind that most eighth-mile tracks mandate a five- or six-point cage at 7.50 seconds or faster, but there are lots of outlaw tracks that don't give cars a second look, and allow much faster vehicles to run without any real safety equipment besides a helmet and a lap belt. The problem with most outlaw tracks is the fact that they're not prepped well, so you're doubling the risk of hurting yourself, by running with no safety gear on a track that doesn't hook.

While NHRA has its set of rules, a separate organization, the SFI Foundation, has created lots of guidelines when it comes to safety. Countless rules and requirements make it tough to sneak by with a rough-and-rugged sleeper, but if you plan to go faster than 8.49 seconds with your sleeper, prepare for some serious requirements. Granted, 8.49 is very quick for any street car, but it's possible to see some very sneaky suspects running deep into the 8s.

Pretty much the only SFI chassis certification that remotely applies to sleepers is the 25.5 specification. This is mandated for cars 3,600 pounds or lighter and running in the 7.50 to 8.49 range. The 25.5 spec means the subject is a full-bodied car with an OEM (original equipment manufacturer) floorpan (stock or modified). The roll-cage tubing can be mild steel or chrome-moly, (you need to purchase the SFI handbook to see the accepted roll cage designs for this spec). To build a 25.5-spec cage, you start with a standard 10-point cage. Then, additional tubing is to be added to create what's known as a Funny Car cage, which wraps completely around the driver to better contain head and neck movement in the event of a crash.

As stock-appearing cars continue to get faster, roll cages become more and more important, as these cars become increasingly dangerous because of the limits of stock suspension systems, small tires, and other elements. The Outlaw

Street Car scene has brought lots of safety innovations into the drag racing hobby, and roll cage designs have changed drastically over the past couple of decades. Years ago, a roll cage, even in a 7-second quarter-mile car, consisted of multiple points, but there was no designation for additional driver protection, like today's SFI-spec cages, which feature a Funny Car-style driver compartment.

Hidden Cage

Incredibly fast or not, a sleeper needs safety equipment just like any other performance car, so the real challenge at hand is hiding the roll cage tubing, or at least doing something to draw attention away from it. One of the easiest ways to keep people from noticing your roll cage is to use dark

According to NHRA rules, a car that runs faster than 11.49 seconds in the quarter-mile is required to have at least a five-point roll bar. At 9.99, a car with a stock firewall and floorpan is required to run a full cage, which is generally considered an eight- or a ten-point design.

Outlaw tracks are usually eighth-mile tracks that offer very little, if any, technical inspection. Vehicles like this rat rod pickup resort to outlaw tracks to keep from installing the correct safety equipment. This truck does have a roll cage, but it wouldn't pass at a big track, as it runs well into the 5-second zone.

NHRA Tech and Safety Rules

You may not actually compete in NHRA events with your sleeper, but many big-name tracks go by NHRA rules when it comes time for technical and safety inspection. It's best to be prepared for this situation, as it keeps you safe and keeps the track personnel happy. There are plenty more regulations and guidelines in the NHRA Rulebook, but here are some quick tips to help you pass tech in most cases.

General NHRA Rules
12 inches maximum rubber fuel line—supply line must be metallic
One pint overflow container for coolant
No hubcaps on drive wheels
Any vehicle using a spool must use aftermarket axles and C-clip eliminators

13.99 and Quicker
Driveshaft loop (if running slicks—11.49 or quicker if running street tires)
Snell or SFI-approved helmet

11.99 and Quicker
Metal, screw-in valve stems

11.49 and Quicker
Five-point roll bar
Five-point, 3-inch-wide safety harnesses

10.99 and Quicker
SFI-approved harmonic balancer (bolted, not pressed on)
SFI-approved transmission shield or blanket (if automatic)
Complete roll cage if floorpan is modified
Aftermarket axles and C-clip eliminators

150 mph and Faster
Single parachute

9.99 and Quicker
Master power shut-off switch at rear of vehicle
Complete roll cage if floorpan and firewall is stock
Window net

You can configure your roll cage to be bolted in, as long as you follow NHRA's guidelines for mounting it. This allows you to remove the cage, and the accompanying 3-inch safety harnesses. This savvy racer retained the stock seats so the car could easily be switched over to sneaky street duty.

If you've relocated your battery, an external master kill switch is required to pass technical inspection. If you're planning to run 9.99 or faster, the external kill switch needs to look something like this. Unfortunately, these are difficult to hide, because the point of it is easy viewing and easy access in case of an emergency.

According to NHRA rules, any vehicle running a spool needs to have C-clip eliminators and aftermarket axles. It also requires the wheel studs to extend into the hex portion of the lug nut as much as the stud's diameter. So if it's a 5/8-inch stud, it needs to reach 5/8 inch into the hex portion of the nut.

window tint. It sounds too good to be true, and extremely dark tint is illegal in many states, but it definitely does a good job of keeping them from seeing inside your car. Tinted windows sometimes give a car a more aggressive look, which isn't what you're going for, but look at it this way—a guy who sees a car with tinted windows and no visible cage isn't going to think it's as fast as a car with a completely noticeable cage.

If your sleeper is in need of a roll cage, and you want to make sure it's hidden well, it's best to stay away from pre-fab kits. Even though they're configured for specific makes and models, pre-fab kits are always generous on tubing-to-body tolerances, which make the cage easier to install, but it also makes it easier to spot because it isn't extremely tight against the body. The main goal with a custom-bent cage is to tuck the tubing as close to the inner body structure as possible. If you can get the main hoop to rest less than an inch away from the roof and surrounding structure, that's a great place to start. Then, try to keep the rear support bars very close to the rear roof panels and the front bars (if using an eight-point or larger cage) close to the A-pillars, so that it seems to blend in with the original appearance. It may not work on all makes and models, but tightly tucked roll cages can sometimes fool the savviest of car guys.

Custom-bent roll cages allow you to make sure the tubing stays out of clear view at the most obvious angles. Whether you're able to do the work yourself or hire a fabrication shop, you can mock-up the tubing in the desired location and take a good look before welding it into place. If something doesn't look exactly the way you want it, this is the time to make a change.

Some chassis or fabrication shops frown on building a roll cage that isn't a standard design, because the generic setup has proven to be plenty strong. Many fabricators don't want to sacrifice structural strength in an effort to keep the roll bar (or cage) hidden, but as long as you don't leave out any attachment points, it should do what you want. Another reason fabrication shops don't necessarily like the idea of a tightly tucked cage is the fact that welding the joints that are closest to the body structure is difficult. If you find a shop that's willing to go to great lengths to hide your roll cage, don't hesitate to go for it—it's a step you won't regret.

Obviously, there's no hiding a Funny Car cage, so if you're legitimately going 8.49 or faster, your safety greatly overrides the authenticity of your sleeper build. However, the majority of genuine sleepers don't need to worry about Funny Car cages, and SFI 25.5 specifications, as 8.49 is pretty darn fast for any street car. The limit for most genuine sleepers is in the low-9-second range, as going any quicker than that requires a dedicated setup that breaks all of the sleeper rules. That's not to say it can't be done, but generally, that's when a stock-appearing car reaches its limit. It's safe to say that most sleepers can get by with a six-point roll cage, unless you're really getting serious.

For the sleeper truck crowd, there isn't much you can do to hide the necessary rear support bars of the roll cage, which ultimately protrudes from the back glass. You can try to hide the tubing that resides inside the cab, but when a car guy sees tubing coming out of the back glass, it's a dead giveaway to a vehicle that runs 11.49 or faster in the quarter—for a full-size truck, that means a pretty serious powerplant, as it has

The SFI Foundation is responsible for all sorts of guidelines, which are closely followed in many racing classes. One advancement in safety equipment is the 25.5 specification, which requires a Funny Car cage, among other safety equipment, in cars that run in the 7.50 to 8.49 range. You can't hide a Funny Car cage.

If you get extremely serious with your car, you'll quickly graduate from sleeper status into full-on race car, but your safety is the most important factor. If you have to drop a few sleeper features, and add a few race car features to improve your odds of surviving a crash, it's usually worth it.

When attempting to hide a roll bar, it's important to tuck the tubing close to the inner body structure, while leaving enough room to install the headliner and interior trim pieces afterward. This Chevelle is a prime example with its tightly tucked cage and bone-stock interior treatment.

Whether you like it or not, people are going to poke their head inside your car and have a look around. This car is actually outfitted with a 10-point cage, 3-inch safety harnesses, and a window net, but you can't see any of it from here. The car runs very low 9s in the quarter and it's legal to do so. *(Photo courtesy Seth Cohen)*

It may sound too simple to be effective, but dark window tint can do wonders for hiding a roll cage. This 2002 Camaro ran low 9s in this configuration and it was completely legal for competition.

For trucks, even the simplest of roll bars is difficult to hide, as the NHRA rules mandate rear support bars on all roll bars. The rear support bars must exit through the back glass of a regular cab pickup, which makes it obvious you're running 11.49 or faster. *(Photo courtesy Kyle Loftis)*

Sean Whitley's *Farm Truck* has the necessary equipment to pass tech and run mid-10s in the quarter, but hides the roll cage rear support bars with a big camper shell. It's the truck's trademark, and it also helps to hide the widened wheel tubs and weight ballast. *(Photo courtesy Kyle Loftis)*

to motivate nearly 5,000 pounds of steel. Just about the only option to cover up roll-cage tubing is a camper shell, like the legendary *Farm Truck.* It has all of the legal requirements to pass tech, but the grandpa-esque camper hides the cage, as well as its widened wheel tubs.

Sleepy Surroundings

When it comes to building a sleeper, hiding the interior details is just as important as the outward appearance. It's not always easy to accomplish a sneaky interior, but if someone pokes their head inside your car to see a full cage, a pair of racing seats, and more gauges and switches than an airliner, he's going to be suspicious of your car's potential. While racing seats are more supportive in a crash situation, and provide better mounting positions for safety harnesses, a pair of racing buckets can ruin a genuine sleeper. For someone attempting to build a sleeper from a muscle car platform, a bench seat is a must—factory buckets usually mean that the car was equipped with some sort of performance package from the factory, and most car guys translate that into speed, even if the car was low on power.

Taking the base-model approach is generally a decent route to achieving a presentable sleeper without working too hard to cover up any performance parts. Many GM cars from the 1960s featured a rubber mat instead of carpet, a simple bench seat, and a column-shifted transmission to save on production costs and offer a cheap alternative to the exciting special editions, like the Super Sport, GS, GTO, etc. The mid-1960s Chevy 300 Deluxe is a good example, as it had all

of these stripped-down qualities, with the option for a big-block engine. This was definitely a factory-built sleeper, but you could recreate this no-frills example and up the game in terms of horsepower. The key would be hiding the necessary gauges, and figuring out a way to conceal anything that might tip off the savvy car guy.

The interior in general is a tough area to stay with the sleeper theme because there are so many ways to slip up. Auxiliary gauges are an instant giveaway, as is a fancy ratchet shifter or a row of toggle switches, so keeping all of the sometimes-necessary components hidden is a great way to fool the competition. The great thing about building an old car as a sleeper is the fact that many classic cars had large glove compartments, and plenty of room to hide stuff in the ashtray. If you're really creative, you can take a factory GM radio and reconfigure the preset buttons to control components like an electric fuel pump, an electric fan, or a nitrous arming switch. You can configure this feature pretty easily and keep the interior barren of any toggle switches. The factory heat and air-conditioning control panel can also be used for various activations in most classic cars.

For modern cars, it's easy to mount auxiliary gauges behind air-conditioning vents, so they're not in the limelight but still visible when you need them. Switches can ride inside a compartment in the console, or under the dash, as long as they're easy to reach. Another trick that works for new or old cars concerns hiding a nitrous system. Most of the time you see a big button and its accompanying wires attached to the shifter or to the steering wheel it's basically a huge flashing light that you have nitrous. To conceal a nitrous system,

Building a sleeper requires vast creativity, and some folks resort to extreme measures to keep their interior free of any toggle switches or auxiliary gauges. You can reconfigure original radios to control components like your electric fan, electric fuel pump, or even cooler stuff like a line lock or trans brake.

Late-model cars have fairly large plastic air conditioning vents, which generally offer a nice hiding spot for a couple of auxiliary gauges. You may not be able to see them well during the day, but at night, they glow nicely through the vent.

you can hide the arming switch in the ashtray or console, and then use a micro-switch on the throttle pedal to activate the solenoids when you hit wide-open throttle.

Another way to hide your nitrous activation—if you don't plan on spraying it for the duration of your race—is to wire it into the horn button. Since a car's horn is a simple wiring setup, you can manipulate the solenoid wiring to make the nitrous activate when you press the horn. You'd also need an additional toggle switch to arm the nitrous system, but that can be hidden elsewhere. Obviously, you'd have your hands full if you are pressing the horn, shifting gears, and keeping the car straight (presuming it spins the tires when the nitrous is activated), so this is mainly for come-from-behind situations when you need a little extra power at the top end.

Hiding a nitrous bottle is never easy, considering the size of most bottles. However, NOS makes nitrous bottles in a wide variety of sizes from 10 ounces to 20 pounds. The small bottles can be hidden pretty much anywhere, as the slim design is perfect for the sneak attack. The only issue with these small bottles is the fact that you are constantly refilling them, and you run the risk of running out midway through the race, which is never good. Yes, it's a lot of work to completely conceal a nitrous system, but it's worth it if your opponent is without a clue to the additional power.

For turbo or supercharged applications that require an air-to-water intercooler, it always pays to have an ice box mounted somewhere in the car to supply the intercooler with the coldest water possible. Most of the time, these are made from aluminum and definitely have a high-dollar race parts look. If you can find a spot to stow the intercooler (between the backseat and a block-off panel in the trunk area) you can keep the ice in a generic, plastic cooler. Modify the cooler to accept the custom plumbing and you're good to go. This is ideal for a rear-mounted turbo setup.

Whether your car is old or new, the horn button is a fairly simple wiring setup that can be manipulated to activate a nitrous system. You can hide the system arming switch in the console and all that's left to do is press the horn if your car needs a little boost.

Hiding a nitrous system within the confines of your car is never easy, but NOS makes a wide variety of bottle sizes for this reason. The Sneeky Pete bottle comes in a mere 10 ounces, but there are larger bottles that require less refilling with the advantage of a small design. Shown from left to right are: 10-ounce, 2-pound, and 10-pound versions. *(Photo courtesy Holley Performance)*

Turbochargers and superchargers respond very well to air-to-water intercoolers, which require a source of cold water. Rob Freyvogel used a generic plastic cooler for his ice box, and although he didn't make an effort to hide the intercooler, a rear closeout panel in the trunk area would be super sneaky if he had a little more trunk space. *(Photo courtesy Rich Chenet)*

Drag Strip Sleepers

Building a good sleeper is all about considering the car's main area of focus, as well as its environment. Some folks build their cars strictly for the street, but others plan for lots of drag strip abuse. For those wanting to drag race, you can easily get by with some of the non-sleeper details that might blow your cover on the street. The point here is that sleepers at the drag strip have a little more leeway in terms of hiding your car's horsepower. If it has a cowl induction hood, or a set of lightweight wheels and slicks, it isn't automatically assumed to be fast at the drag strip, as this is very common equipment. However you go about it, building a sleeper for the drag strip still requires some effort to hide the car's potential, and you must take the necessary safety precautions to pass tech inspection and stay safe.

A car like this 1966 Chevelle might raise a few eyebrows on the street, but at the track, it looks like a stock SS with drag-style wheels. Stock interior, stock badges, and an all-steel body hide the fact that it runs mid 5s in the eighth-mile, thanks to a nitrous-fed SB2.2 engine.

For many drag strip sleepers, the limitations for speed are almost nonexistent, as the minor details that hold most sleepers back can be resolved without too many people noticing. It's truly the most practical sleeper to build, as the car has a dedicated purpose and you can have fun with it legally. Obviously, street racing is a thrill and it still happens all across the country, but it's not a good way to make friends with the local law enforcement agency. Aside from being illegal, street racing it outright dangerous, so a sleeper built for the drag strip means that you can realistically get some use out of your car and leave many of those worries behind. The possibility for mishaps and breakage is still quite high for a drag strip sleeper, but that's just part of drag racing, no matter the car.

Without question, you can turn heads with a drag strip sleeper. People have grown to expect low slung, tube-chassis cars to be fast, so when a fairly original-looking car rolls into the lanes and busts off a 9-second pass, it's a big deal. Even if it has a few stickers here and there, or a 10.5-inch set of slicks under it, a drag strip sleeper needs to be extremely fast to be in the same league as street sleepers.

This concept also works with muscle cars, as these vehicles are generally perceived as "fast" because they were cool in the 1960s and 1970s, but most of them struggled to get into the 14s. Even with lackluster elapsed times in stock form, muscle cars are tough sleeper builds, based solely on perception of the general public. A stock-appearing muscle car doesn't start stepping into sleeper territory until it gets into the 10s, but there are a number of these examples out there already. If you retain the stock wheels and keep body modifications to a minimum, it's a step in the right direction to building a great drag strip sleeper. Add a set of lightweight race wheels, and you'd better step up the horsepower to keep the sleeper theme going. Again, the car's details are relative to how it performs— it works on a sliding scale.

Station wagons are very potent drag strip sleepers, mainly because no matter how many times you see a fast wagon, you never expect the next one to be impressive. Car guys see a station wagon and automatically think about the unnecessary weight, and aerodynamic disadvantage, rarely expecting it to perform well. Even with a cowl-induction hood, sizable slicks, and lightweight wheels, a big wagon from the 1970s just isn't going to gain any notoriety from the car guy crowd. That's not a bad thing when the whole idea of a sleeper is to under promise and over deliver. Imports, Diesel trucks, and four-door sedans fall into the same category, but it's no walk in the park to build a genuine and believable drag strip sleeper.

Hard street radials are a huge factor in making your car a sleeper at the drag strip. This 1964 Corvette, owned by Bobby Russo, doesn't look like much but has run a best of 10.69 at 131 mph on BFGoodrich Radial T/A tires sized at 235/70R15. Power comes from a turbocharged LS1 engine tucked beneath the stock hood. *(Photo courtesy Kyle Loftis)*

This is an instance where the track crew saw a car they didn't expect to perform well, and failed to make the driver wear a helmet. Generally, helmets are required for 8.50 or faster in the eighth-mile, which is quicker than most street rods. However, this one busted off a mid-6-second pass and surprised everyone.

Small-Block Shocker —
Hemi Power isn't Necessary For This 1973 'Cuda

Sleepy Factor: 7 out of 10

Mike's 'Cuda proves to be very dependable, as it has successfully participated in *Hot Rod* magazine's Drag Week event, where fast street cars are driven from track to track over a five-day period. Mike has won the Small-block Naturally Aspirated class multiple times with his sneaky Mopar. *(Photo courtesy Kyle Loftis)*

Pros
- Stock wheels
- All stock body
- Small-block power

Cons
- Legendary muscle car

Part of the definition of a sleeper is a car that is surprisingly fast. That's generally easy to spot with some of the cars featured in this book, but this Plymouth 'Cuda seems to blend into the muscle car crowd. A legendary muscle car status makes it tough to call this one a sleeper, until you find out just how quick it is and the fact that it retains plenty of street-friendly details. It's a full-weight car with complete interior and steel Magnum wheels on all four corners. Sure, it would be a decently quick car from the factory, but what would you expect a small-block, naturally aspirated, stick-shift car to run in the quarter?

While you ponder that, let's learn a little more about what makes it so quick. It's not easy to go fast without a power adder, and it certainly isn't cheap, but Mike Crow does just that in this 3,690-pound muscle car. It looks like a restored stocker, but there's plenty of steam under the shaker hood to take this 'Cuda from everyday muscle car to all-out performer. It starts with a solid foundation, and since these cars featured a unibody construction from the factory, Mike felt the need to strengthen it with braces in the key areas. Up front, he installed a pair of Magnum Force tubular upper control arms to shed a few pounds off the nose, but retained the original lower control arms, so it still looks stock when you peek beneath the car. He also utilized the stock torsion

bars, but upgraded the shocks with a pair of QA1 double-adjustable units. Mike then slid a pair of Wilwood discs over the spindles, and hid them with 15x6-inch Magnum 500 wheels and Goodyear radials.

Out back, another pair of Magnums completes the stock look, but measure 15x10 inches and mount to a pair of Mickey Thompson ET Street 28x12.5-inch tires. The ET Street tires are DOT (Department of Transportation) approved, but feature all of the attributes of a regular slick. Mike relies on leaf springs to plant the rear tires, which is no easy task with a stick-shift car, but the addition of Calvert Racing Split Mono-Leafs, CalTrac bars, and QA1 double-adjustable shocks make it happen. The rear end housing is a Fab 9 unit, packed with bulletproof components, such as a 3.50:1 gear set, a locker, and a pair of 35-spline Moser axles. Just ahead of the 9-inch rear end is a Mark Williams 3-inch driveshaft, which hooks up to a G-Force GF-5R manual transmission. This transmission is built for abuse and features five forward gears, with fifth gear being 1:1, rather than overdrive like most 5-speed transmissions. A McLeod clutch applies the horsepower, while a QuickTime bell housing keeps it contained and connects the transmission to the engine.

Mike's small-block Mopar would've normally started life at 340 ci, but after some machine work at S&K Engine Specialists and a new BRC crankshaft, the final displacement is much larger. The Mopar R3 race block features a 4.155-inch bore and the BRC crankshaft has a 3.875-inch stroke to create 420 ci. A set of Oliver 6.3-inch connecting rods ride on Clevite bearings and send the JE forged pistons into motion. Final compression is 11.67:1, in relation to the Mopar Performance W9 cylinder heads. The aluminum castings are generally used in high-end stock car applications, so they work well right out of the box, but this pair of W9s is Chapman-ported and modified by Dean Steward for maximum performance. The heads are fit with Ferrea valves, measuring 2.18 inches on the intake side and 1.65 inches on the exhaust. An Elgin camshaft features 274 degrees of duration on the intake and 279 degrees on the exhaust, measured at .050-inch lift, while max lift comes in at .640 inch on the intake and .670 inch on the exhaust.

With street driving and all-out performance in mind, Mike decided to use EFI (electronic fuel injection), rather than a carburetor. The setup he uses is a Mopar Performance single-plane intake manifold with custom fuel rails and 48-pound injectors. Atop the intake manifold is a 1,550-cfm Accel throttle body, which bolts to a regular 4150-style flange and is controlled by a F.A.S.T. ECU (electronic control unit). Fuel delivery consists of an Aeromotive A1000 pump, while an MSD Digital 6 box controls the ignition. Spent fumes travel through a pair of owner-built headers that feature a step from 1.875-inch tubing to 2.125-inch tubing before they merge into a 3.5-inch collector. From there, an expanse of 3.5-inch piping leads to a pair of Flowmaster two-chamber mufflers and then out to the original tailpipe cutouts in the rear valance. Mike doesn't have an official figure on horsepower, but according to the times and weight of the car, you're looking at close to 700 hp of raw small-block power—no nitrous, no blower, no turbos. Oh yeah, and it runs on pump gas, and gets 16 mpg!

The exterior on Mike's 'Cuda is all stock, and wears a slick coat of the stock Rally Red hue. Leo Connors of Topeka, Kansas, did the paint and body work. Inside, it's all stock, aside from a six-point roll cage and RJS safety harnesses. Stock bucket seats and the original console are intact, and a pistol-grip shifter handle rides atop the long H-pattern G-Force shifter. Mike has a few Auto Meter gauges to keep him posted on the small-block's vital signs, and a Pioneer stereo, complete with an Alpine amplifier to keep him and his wife, Vicki, occupied on long trips, such as *Hot Rod* magazine's Drag Week event. Mike has competed more than once in the 1,000-plus-mile tour to multiple drag strips, and he's always a strong force in the Small-block Naturally Aspirated class. Mike and his 'Cuda even graced the cover of *Hot Rod* magazine's December 2009 issue, which was surely a proud moment.

Though most of the car was built in Mike's home shop, he received help from many individuals, such as Leo Connors, Brian High, Danny Dodds, and Bob Weakland to name a few. He says the car is never finished, as he'll always be updating to bigger and better components, in search of quicker elapsed times. For now, he's content with 10.36 at 132.67 mph in the quarter, and continues to drive his 'Cuda frequently, banging gears along the way.

TOP: Although Plymouth 'Cudas are generally considered fast from the factory, Mike's Mopar exceeds most folks' expectations on the drag strip. With 700 naturally aspirated horsepower, the small-block gives the G-Force transmission, and its operator, a workout. A pair of Mickey Thompson 28x12.5-inch ET street tires manages the traction department. *(Photo courtesy Kyle Loftis)* MIDDLE: The stroked small-block isn't assisted by any kind of power adder, so it works hard, and is very dependable. The heads are W9 castings, which are heavily ported and fit with a laundry list of lightweight valvetrain components. The end result is 700 hp on pump gas with an average of 16 mpg. *(Photo courtesy Kyle Loftis)* BOTTOM: Inside, Mike's 'Cuda is mostly stock, aside from the roll cage. A pistol-grip shifter pokes out of the console to operate the G-Force 5-speed manual transmission, while stock bucket seats keep the sleeper look alive and well. Notice the packed backseat—Drag Week doesn't allow tow vehicles, so Mike stuffed the backseat and trunk. *(Photo courtesy Kyle Loftis)*

Big Car Blues—
Nitrous and a Big Pontiac Make For 9-Second ETs

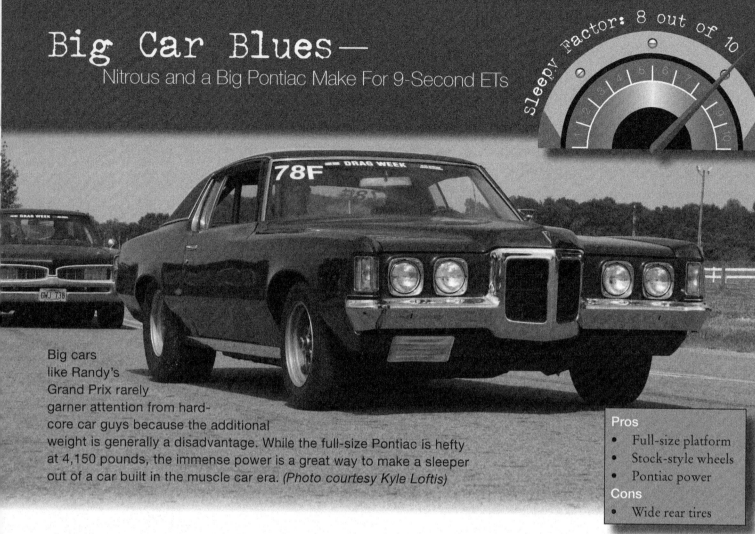

Big cars like Randy's Grand Prix rarely garner attention from hard-core car guys because the additional weight is generally a disadvantage. While the full-size Pontiac is hefty at 4,150 pounds, the immense power is a great way to make a sleeper out of a car built in the muscle car era. *(Photo courtesy Kyle Loftis)*

Pros
- Full-size platform
- Stock-style wheels
- Pontiac power

Cons
- Wide rear tires

If you bought a new Pontiac Grand Prix in 1970, you probably didn't take it to the drag strip that often. You could get one of these cars with a 370-hp Pontiac block under the hood, but when you consider the 4,150-pound curb weight, the combination didn't equate to very quick elapsed times at the track. The rather large platform never lent itself well to the performance-minded fellow, so it's a great sleeper platform, even though it was introduced at the peak of muscle car performance. Randy Belehar of Detroit Lakes, Minnesota, owns this particular car and it bears a completely stock appearance, down to the Pontiac Rallye II steel wheels. It does, however, boast a pair of Mickey Thompson 315/60R15s, but that's the only sign of this car's potential.

Randy bought the Grand Prix in 1996, and it was actually his first car. He was 17, and drove the car to his Senior Prom, never dreaming it would turn out the way it did. He raced it for nearly a decade, running it in total beater form, with primer and rust taking over the car's original paint job. Randy says, "I tore it apart in 2007 to fix the rust in the floor, and it snowballed into completely redoing the whole car." He did an awesome job with it, while keeping it very clean and simple—a perfect combination for a quality sleeper.

Since the rebuild, Randy has competed in *Hot Rod* magazine's Drag Week competition, a week-long, 1,000-mile journey to various drag strips. The car has never gained a ton of recognition because of its tame looks, but it's a great car that exemplifies the full-size sleeper look. The source for horsepower is a 1975 Pontiac 455 block that now comes in at 467 ci, thanks to a slightly longer stroke and a .030-inch overbore. It's a healthy combination that looks relatively mild mannered, so it certainly works with the sleeper theme.

The 467-ci block features an Ohio billet crankshaft, which slings a set of Eagle 6.8-inch connecting rods and Ross pistons to a maximum RPM of 6,700. Atop the forged short-block is a pair of Kauffman aluminum cylinder heads that flow 325 cfm, thanks to the very efficient D-port design, which sends a perfect mixture of fuel and air into the combustion chambers. The valves measure 2.11 inches on the intake side and 1.77 inches on the exhaust, while a set of Crane 1.65:1 roller rockers keeps the valvetrain moving smoothly. The camshaft is from Comp and it's a solid roller, which features 254 degrees of duration on the intake and 260 degrees on the exhaust—both measured at .050-inch lift. Max lift on the camshaft is .669 inch, and it was ground on a 110-degree lobe separation angle.

A port-matched Edelbrock Victor Jr. intake manifold rests on top of the big-block Pontiac, and is finished off with a Proform 850-cfm carburetor. Although the 467-ci engine proved its potential by making 460 hp and 580 ft-lbs of torque to the rear wheels on the motor alone, Randy's secret weapon is a two-stage Big Shot nitrous system from NOS. The car features a separate fuel system, which consists of a 1-gallon fuel cell filled with 110-octane race gas, to feed the nitrous system, while the engine is fed with 91-octane pump gas. After pouring the coals to it on the dyno, the result was 642 hp and 660 ft-lbs of torque to the rear wheels. That means the Poncho big-block is making around 800 hp at the flywheel. To support all this power, Randy relies on a Summit 140-gallon-per-hour fuel pump and an Accel HEI (high energy ignition) distributor, which is assisted by an MSD Digital-6 ignition box. Randy isn't trying to hide anything, in terms of the car's exhaust note, as it beats the ground with Pypes race mufflers and 3½-inch pipes.

Behind the block is a Cottman Transmission–prepped TH400 automatic, which is outfitted with a Continental 10-inch torque converter and a host of bulletproof components to keep it together for long trips like Drag Week. Another part that plays into the long trip aspect of this car is the Gear Vendors overdrive, which makes the 3.73:1 rear end gears seem a little less aggressive at highway speeds. The rear end is a GM 12-bolt, packed with an Eaton Posi unit from Tom's Differentials and Mark Williams 30-spline axles. Rear suspension is the stock triangulated four-link design, fit with adjustable upper and lower control arms, as well as 14-inch 130-pound springs and QA1 single adjustable shocks. The only modification to the front suspension is the 260-pound Moroso springs and QA1 shocks. Randy equipped the Grand Prix with a set of Rallye II wheels, measuring 15x7 inches up front and 15x10 inches out back. The rears are wrapped with Mickey Thompson 315/60R15 drag radials, which required Randy to notch the rear frame rails for clearance.

Shayne Laske installed the 10-point chrome-moly roll cage, and did an awesome job hiding it by tucking the tubes very close to the body structure. The interior is all stock with the exception of RJS harnesses and a B&M shifter. The green exterior is just right for the sleeper look, and the vinyl top adds a luxurious touch to the full-size two-door. Just about anyone's grandmother would've been proud to drive a 1970 Grand Prix, and Randy is proud to leave many cars in the dust as he makes a 9-second pass in the quarter-mile. So far, his best elapsed time is a 9.91 at 133 mph, running 6.26 to the eighth-mile, and the car runs solidly in the low 11s without the nitrous. It's a great looking car, and while it was built in the muscle car era, it's a dead on sleeper, especially on the drag strip.

TOP: Randy's full-size Pontiac is yet another car from the muscle era that would normally be considered a moderate performance car on the street. On the track, however, Randy's stock-appearing Poncho proves it's not a stocker by blasting off high-9-second passes on a regular basis. *(Photo courtesy Kyle Loftis)* MIDDLE: With its stock steel wheels and original body, most folks wouldn't expect this to jerk the wheels off the ground and motor down the track in 9.91 seconds, rolling through the traps at 133 mph. It's big, it's heavy, and it looks stock, so Randy's Grand Prix is a great example of a drag strip sleeper. *(Photo courtesy Kyle Loftis)* BOTTOM: Under the steel hood is true Pontiac power, coming in at 467 ci. A bulletproof rotating assembly is topped off with a set of Kauffman cylinder heads, a port-matched Edelbrock Victor Jr. intake manifold, and a Proform 850-cfm carburetor. The secret weapon is a two-stage nitrous system that helps produce 642 hp at the rear wheels. *(Photo courtesy Kyle Loftis)*

Screamin' Skylark—
This Bare-Bones 1972 Buick Runs 10s
Without a Power Adder

The Buick Skylark was never a huge hit with performance-minded individuals, but Gary used the car's lack of popularity to build a killer sleeper. He didn't take the grandma route with full hubcaps and a flat hood, but the car is still surprisingly fast at the track, running in the 10s with no power adders.

Pros
- Grandma-fresh interior
- Stock body
- Buick power

Cons
- Stage 2 hood scoop
- Two-door muscle car platform

Since its inception, the Buick brand has never been known for its performance, and while Buick had some powerful cars in the muscle car era, it still didn't get much recognition from car guys. Buicks were usually purchased because of their creature comforts or smooth ride, as opposed to horsepower levels, so even the fast cars like the Buick Gran Sport played underdog in the muscle car era. The Skylark pictured here is a special case because it features a bare-bones appearance, but still looks very aggressive to a savvy car guy. It may not fool everyone, but novice car enthusiasts certainly fall for it because it's so plain and simple.

Gary Steele owns the Buick and frequently drives it on the street. He also visits the drag strip with it on occasion, running a best of 10.97 at 123 mph, but feels a few more changes could result in much quicker times. That's not to say the combination doesn't work well together, but every car guy on the planet feels he can squeeze a little more out of his car. Gary bought the car in this configuration, only changing a few things to make it his own. The car features a very slick paint job that is the deepest black you can imagine, and the steel wheels wear a matching hue. It's a combination that is sinister to the right crowd, but a bit tame compared to more well known muscle car trends, which allows it to slip under the radar in most cases.

Underneath, the 1972 Buick is mostly stock, but features QA1 coilovers on all four corners to help weight transfer. Rear suspension consists of Metco upper and lower control arms to help the factory-style four-link suspension plant the rear tires. The rear end housing is a Currie 9-inch, which features a limited slip differential and a 4.11:1 gear set, while the transmission is a GM TH400 3-speed automatic that relies on a 10-inch TCI torque converter (3,500 rpm) to transfer power efficiently. Braking consists of stock discs up front and drums out back, covered with black steel wheels and Dog Dish caps. The original front wheels measure 15x7 inches and wear BFGoodrich 215/70R15 tires, while the Stockton rear wheels come in at 15x8 inches and mount to Mickey Thompson 28x11.50-15 ET Street tires. These tires have the soft rubber compound and thin sidewall of a slick, and they're still street legal.

Power comes from a Buick big-block, which was built by the car's previous owner, Gary Paine. It's a stock 455 block that has been bored to 464 ci, and equipped with a nice combination of speed parts. The bottom end is ready for serious abuse, with a set of forged Ross pistons (11:1 compression) and Howards 6.60-inch aluminum connecting rods. A stock nodular iron crankshaft resides in the big-block, as this is rarely the week link of the rotating assembly. The short block is topped with a pair of aluminum TA Performance cylinder heads, which feature 2.125-inch intake valves and 1.75-inch exhaust valves. Though potent out of the box, the TA Performance Stage 2 heads have been ported to flow 315 cfm, and feature a set of 1.65:1 roller rockers to go with the TA Performance valvesprings and hardware. The camshaft is also from TA Performance and it's a hydraulic flat-tappet stick with 258 degrees of duration on the intake side and 272 degrees on the exhaust, at .050-inch lift. Maximum lift is .595 inch on the intake side and .601 inch on the exhaust. Topping the big-block is a Kenne Bell single-plane intake manifold and Holley 1,050-cfm Dominator carburetor.

The stock fuel tank has been modified to accept a large fuel line and in-tank pump, without the need for a sump and the racy looks of a fuel pump hanging below the bumper.

Lighting the fire is an MSD 7AL ignition box with a matching Pro-Billet distributor and Blaster coil. When the combustion cycle is complete, a set of TA Performance long tube headers provide a smooth path into the 3-inch exhaust system, which features an X-pipe and MagnaFlow mufflers. Gary's Buick has an aggressive exhaust note, but it's still not enough to think this car runs 10s without the assistance of nitrous.

At 3,680 pounds, the Buick has a lot of weight to lug around, but it would be much heavier if it still had the factory power steering, air conditioning, and radio. The car could realistically lose more weight, but that would require lightweight race parts, and that's not what Gary wants. He likes the fact that it can be street-driven, and he loves the car's sleeper status, so he won't be making a race car out of it anytime soon. And with the only signs of speed being the street-legal slicks and Stage 2 hood scoop, the bare-bones Buick still flies under the radar and looks good doing it.

TOP: Gary's Buick sits a little lower than stock and has a wicked appearance with its black steel wheels, but this car is actually so nice that most folks underestimate it at the track. Gary takes great pride in the car, and doesn't want to hurt it, but he doesn't mind romping on the all-motor big-block from time to time. BOTTOM LEFT: The beauty of this sleeper is the great interior. The color combination is spot-on for a vintage Buick, with brown carpet, cream seats, and a green dash and steering wheel. Although it has a few auxiliary gauges, a quick glance doesn't totally ruin the car's sleeper status, thanks to the bench seat and column shifter. BOTTOM MIDDLE LEFT: Traction comes from Mickey Thompson 28x11.50-15 ET Street tires, mounted to a pair of standard steel wheels that measure 15x8 inches. The Buick center caps are the perfect touch to this stock-appearing Skylark, and actually give the car an aggressive look, when combined with the slick coat of black paint on the steelies. BOTTOM MIDDLE RIGHT: Another impressive part of Gary's Skylark is the fact that it's Buick-powered. Most folks would've stuffed a Chevy engine in there, but Gary stayed true to the Buick heritage with a bored 464-ci big-block Buick engine. The engine features a set of TA Performance cylinder heads, a Kenne Bell intake manifold, and a 1,050-cfm Holley Dominator carburetor. BOTTOM RIGHT: Underneath, this Buick uses a Currie 9-inch rear end to send power to the rear wheels, while the stock triangulated four-link suspension keeps the tires planted. Gary didn't want the racecar look of a sumped tank, so he modified the stock tank to accept larger fuel lines, keeping the exterior stock.

The Cream Dream—
A Mercury Zephyr That Just Left the Retirement Home

A crafty car guy may notice the powder-coated Weld Draglite wheels, but there are plenty of instances where slow cars use lightweight wheels, be it for appearance or performance. This 1979 Mercury Zephyr may not look like much, but it's run a best of 8.62 at 159 mph in the quarter-mile. *(Photo courtesy Kevin Stachniak)*

Pros
- Unpopular body style
- Color combination
- Bench seat
- Crazy fast elapsed times

Cons
- Drag wheels and tires
- Racing shifter

Though it has been mentioned several times throughout the book, it bears mentioning again—the Ford Fox platform is the ultimate base for a performance build. Most folks limit this to Mustangs from 1979 to 1993, but Ford built many other cars on the Fox platform, including the Ford Fairmont and its sister car, the Mercury Zephyr, which is the model pictured here. This particular car is a 1979, and it originally had an inline six-cylinder engine. In fact, the Zephyr still had the original engine and transmission when its owner, Neil Richards, bought it. Neil's intentions were to pull the original drivetrain and give it a healthy boost in horsepower, while retaining the car's naturally nondescript appearance.

Taking advantage of the Fox platform meant that Neil could install a host of aftermarket suspension parts that would normally be suited for a Mustang. The parts are cheap, and they all interchange from the more popular Mustang model, so he went to work, along with Matt Kuchn, Bobby Hill, and "Flyin' Ryan" Bell to upgrade the car's suspension. The work started with strengthening the unibody structure with a pair of subframe connectors, which are built from 2x2-inch square tubing, and installed through the floor to increase rigidity and keep them from hanging down in clear sight. With some of the cars in this book, the owners take their chances by not installing a roll cage, but Neil had plans to frequent the drag strip and turn in some serious times, so a cage was mandatory to pass tech and keep him safe behind the wheel. The tubing meets the chassis in 10 points and is constructed with chrome-moly tubing because of its strength and light weight.

From there, Neil outfitted the car with a UPR chrome-moly tubular K-member and a set of UPR tubular control arms. This sheds lots of weight off the nose, and made it easy for him to install an LS1-style engine. The front springs are from QA1 and feature a spring rate of 175 pounds per inch, while the shocks come from Strange and offer 10-way adjustability. Steering is controlled by a manual rack-and-pinion setup and braking consists of discs from a late-model Mustang on all four corners. Out back, Neil didn't spare any expense when it came to beefing up the rear end and suspension to handle big horsepower. He swapped in a Ford 8.8 rear end, packed with a Strange spool, and matching 33-spline axles, which are put into motion by the 3.31:1 gear set. The housing features welded axle tubes and additional bracing to support hard launches, while the rear suspension works hard to keep the rear tires glued to the racing surface.

The Zephyr uses a Team Z rear suspension setup, made up of relocated upper control arms and adjustable lower control arms. Stock rear springs are soft enough to soak up the weight transfer, while Strange 10-way adjustable shocks help the cause. The wheel tubs are stock, and the rear end is the stock width, so the car's suspension is a completely bolt-on setup. Rolling stock is a touchy subject with sleepers, but Neil couldn't resist the temptation to bolt on a set of lightweight racing wheels. The black powder coating helps the aluminum race wheels blend in, but hardcore car guys are going to pick up on this detail and start questioning the car's purpose. Traction comes by way of Mickey Thompson racing rubber on all four corners—Sportsman front runners measuring 26x7.5 inches up front and drag radials measuring 275/60R15 out back.

All of this chassis and suspension work is in preparation for a GM LQ9 truck engine, which originally powered a Cadillac Escalade. The 6.0-liter engine is a popular choice for budget-minded builders, as it is much cheaper than a standard LS1-style engine, but it also proves to be the strongest platform to build upon. The stock block has been bored .030-inch over but it is otherwise stock, aside from the Cadillac CTS-V oil pan, which was necessary for fitment into the Zephyr's engine bay. Flyin's Pro Street Engines performed the engine build, using the stock crankshaft, but upgraded to Compstar 6.125-inch connecting rods and Diamond forged pistons, creating a final compression ratio of 8.9:1. The cylinder heads are stock 317 castings from the 6.0 truck engine, ported by "Flyin' Ryan" Bell, and fit with Manley 2.02-inch intake valves and 1.70-inch Yella Terra Ultralite exhaust valves. Camshaft selection is key with a boosted application, so Neil uses a custom grind from Comp Cams, which features 242 degrees of duration on the intake lobes and 238 degrees of duration on the exhaust side, both measured at .050-inch lift. Maximum lift is .610 inch on the intake and .605 inch on the exhaust, while the lobe separation angle is 115 degrees.

The custom camshaft works in conjunction with the twin Master Power turbochargers to create tons of power without the need for exotic components or lots of maintenance. The turbochargers measure 70 mm, and are fed by flipped truck exhaust manifolds, while forced air from the turbos enters the air-to-air intercooler before it hits the LS2 intake manifold. Fuel system upgrades consist of a 16-gallon aluminum fuel cell, an Aeromotive Eliminator fuel pump, and a set of 80-pound fuel injectors. Neil tuned the car using EFILive and made 780 hp at the rear wheels on pump gas, which required him to keep boost levels at 13 psi. When using C16 racing fuel, Neil turns up the boost to 20 psi, which results in well over 1,000 hp at the wheels. Behind the twin turbo truck engine is a well-built TH400 automatic transmission, which features a trans brake and plenty of bulletproof goodies inside. Power application is handled by a PTC 9.5-inch torque converter, which stalls to 4,400 rpm on the line.

Neil didn't have to make much effort to give his car a sleeper look—he took advantage of the Zephyr's natural ability to look slow, and that's all it took. Aside from the racing wheels and tires, the car has a stock outward appearance, right down to the original two-tone paint. Inside, much of the same

With its outdated styling and equally horrendous color combination, this is a great sleeper, and Neil wouldn't have it any other way. He enjoys driving the Zephyr on the street, and doesn't mind lighting them off on a back road if the opportunity arises. *(Photo courtesy Kevin Stachniak)*

The Mercury Zephyr was built on Ford's Fox platform, which has proven to be the most popular drag racing setup on the outlaw street car scene. Most chassis and suspension parts interchange from a Fox-Body Mustang, so Neil outfitted his Zephyr with all sorts of aftermarket suspension goodies to increase traction and reduce weight. *(Photo courtesy Kevin Stachniak)*

styling can be found, with its brown and beige interior. Neil retained the original seats, door panels, and dash, but added a few gauges to keep an eye on the boosted LS engine and installed RCI five-point harnesses to keep him pinned in the bench seat. The column shifter is still in place, but it's just for looks, as the B&M Pro Stick is used to select the gears in the 3-speed transmission.

There's no doubt that Neil's Zephyr is a sleeper, when you consider the horsepower it produces, but the real surprise comes when it hits the track. The car isn't all that light, weighing in at 3,350 pounds, but it still managed to blast through the quarter-mile in 8.62 seconds at 159 mph! There are plenty of cars that make four-digit horsepower and struggle to make it into the 9s, but the Zephyr proves the potency of Ford's Fox platform by turning horsepower into super-quick elapsed times, thanks to an efficient suspension design and great weight balance. Don't be fooled by the track times—Neil still drives the Zephyr on the street frequently, and loves to pick on unsuspecting traffic light racers. His car is super stealthy and extremely fast—a great combination of traits that results in one great sleeper.

Wide-open throttle almost always results in tire smoke, and the evidence is splattered on the lower portion of the quarter panel. Neil doesn't mind toasting the drag radials when he's having fun on the street, but he'd rather it hook up at the track and lay down a good number. *(Photo courtesy Kevin Stachniak)*

TOP: It's old and outdated, so the Zephyr doesn't get much attention, until on-lookers catch a glimpse of it in action. With more than 1,000 hp at the rear wheels, the Mickey Thompson 275/60R15 drag radials fight for traction, while the Sportsman front runner tires skim across the pavement en route to an 8-second pass. *(Photo courtesy Kevin Stachniak)* BOTTOM LEFT: Cross breeding is a very effective way to go fast, especially when you consider the combination of a Fox-Body car and an LS-style engine. Neil's engine is an LQ9, 6.0-liter truck engine, built by Flyin's Pro Street Engines and fit with ported 317 cylinder heads. A stock LS2 intake manifold tops it off. *(Photo courtesy Kevin Stachniak)* BOTTOM MIDDLE: Feeding the engine is a pair of Master Power T-70 turbochargers, which are plumbed into an air-to-air intercooler. The engine has produced a best recorded figure of 780 hp at the rear wheels, with only 13 pounds of boost on pump gas. Swapping to high-octane C16 racing fuel, boost can be increased to 20 psi, resulting in more than 1,000 hp. *(Photo courtesy Kevin Stachniak)* BOTTOM RIGHT: Peeking in the window you see a ten-point cage and five-point safety harnesses, but when you consider the car's performance, it is surprisingly fast. The stock bench seat is still in use, while a custom gauge cluster houses Race Data instrumentation, a digital boost gauge, and an Innovative Turbo Systems multi-stage boost controller. *(Photo courtesy Kevin Stachniak)*

The Super Sleeper—
A Killer Creation That is More Sophisticated Than it Appears

It may look like a worn and weathered car that reached its prime more than 30 years ago, but this Chevy Nova is one of the most sophisticated cars out there. Extensive chassis strengthening and a well-crafted engine setup make this flawless piece of engineering genius one of the best sleepers around. *(Photo courtesy Dominick Damato)*

Pros
- Rough and faded paint
- Hidden roll cage
- Ratty interior
- Column shifter
- Quiet superchargers

Cons
- Very large rear tires with rim screws
- Lowered stance

Let's be honest, a late 1960s or early 1970s Nova doesn't make the best sleeper platform because these cars have been used for countless drag cars and serious street machines. However, that doesn't mean it can't be done. Kurt Urban, owner of Kurt Urban Performance, set out to build the ultimate sleeper and did just that with this 1972 Chevrolet Nova. At the time of the build, he was the director of operations at Wheel to Wheel Powertrain, a shop that specialized in high-end, high-performance builds. Since this was Kurt's personal car, he went all out when it came to fabrication and sneaky tricks, holding true to his original plans to build the sleeper that every hardcore car guy has dreamed up at some point in his life.

That dream usually starts with a big engine of some sort, but Kurt went about this build with great patience, starting by strengthening the Nova's chassis and upgrading the suspension system to correlate with the build plans. The front subframe was the first area of focus, as the choice of engine required modifications to the crossmember. Rather than giving it a major notch, Kurt simply removed the crossmember, replacing it with chrome-moly tubing with additional bracing to keep it sturdy. He then fabricated a pair of subframe connectors to tie the front frame rails to the rear rails, and attached the connectors through the floorpan to keep them from hanging down below the rocker panels. Kurt also formed reliefs in the floorpan for the larger-than-stock exhaust piping, so it could be tucked close to the body, instead of hanging down in clear sight.

From there, he formed the roll cage tubing to fit very tightly against the inner panels, making sure to hide the tubing in every way possible. It was time-consuming work that wouldn't be performed on a regular street/strip car, but Kurt wanted this car to be at a whole new level, when it comes to hidden potential. Take the wheel tubs for example: Kurt modified the tubs to accommodate the Mickey Thompson 295/65R15 drag radials, but altered the backseat, so it would look completely stock and fit in the original location.

For suspension, Kurt retained the leaf spring design, but swapped to a pair of Smith Racecraft mono-leaf springs, and used offset shackles from Detroit Speed and Engineering to move the springs inward. Up front, stock control arms are in place, but a pair of Afco double-adjustable shocks takes the place of the original units. Baer Serious-Street single-piston disc brakes ride on all four corners, hiding behind standard steel wheels.

Rolling stock was another important aspect of the build, as the Nova not only needed to appear stock, but it also needed to appear as a base-model, six-cylinder car. For this look, Kurt went with 15x7.5-inch front wheels, and a custom pair of 15x10.5-inch Stockton steel wheels out back. He ordered the wheels with the maximum amount of backspacing, so the wheels would appear stock from the outside. After mounting the rear wheels and drag radials, Kurt installed rim screws to keep the tires in place. If not for this tiny detail and the car's lowered stance, this Nova would look like a complete stocker.

The Nova has no shortage of power, as it is equipped with an all-aluminum LS2 engine, which has been stroked to 402 ci, and fit with a dry-sump oiling system. Again, Kurt didn't cut any corners with this build, so the engine is packed with high-dollar goodies, including a Callies crankshaft, Howards connecting rods, and Mahle pistons. The new bottom end, in combination with the All Pro cylinder heads, creates an 8.5:1 compression ratio, which is much lower than stock and perfect for this boosted application. The LS2 has a solid-roller camshaft with .630 inch of lift and 250 degrees of duration at .050-inch lift, which motivates the titanium intake valves and Iconel exhaust valves. Up top is an Edelbrock intake manifold, with a Wilson 90-degree elbow drawing in air from a 90-mm throttle body, which faces the rear. Kurt then installed twin superchargers from Rotrex, which feature a unique design that is one of the quietest superchargers on the market. Piping from the inlets is capped with K&N air filters, while piping from the outlets is routed to the inner fenders, where twin air-to-water intercoolers reside. From there, the piping runs in the cowl and merges at its exit point, the firewall.

The fuel system consists of a stock fuel tank, which is used for pump gas, and a custom fuel cell, which is filled with high-octane race fuel. With two Bosch fuel pumps and two sets of injectors, Kurt designed an octane-on-demand system that supplies the high-octane fuel when the primary injectors reach a particular duty cycle. A BigStuff3 ECM (electronic control module) controls all this. Kurt designed and built the stainless steel headers as well as the 3.5-inch stainless exhaust system fit with Flowmaster mufflers.

On the dyno, the engine made 1,160 hp and 825 ft-lbs of torque on pump gas. Behind the twin-supercharged LS2 is a trusty Powerglide transmission, equipped with a trans brake and an ATI torque converter that stalls to 5,000 rpm. The 2-speed automatic is set up to shift electronically, when the original horn button is pressed, while the column shifter selects all other gears. When Kurt finished the car he put it to work, driving it on the *Hot Rod* Power Tour and competing in the *Hot Rod* Pump Gas Drags and Drag Week events, where the car ran a best of 9.25 at 148 mph at Cordova

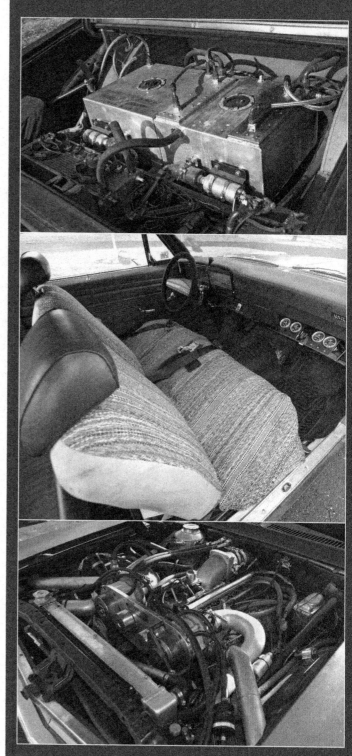

TOP: The stock fuel tank is still in place, and holds pump gas, while the fuel cell on the left is filled with high-octane racing fuel, which is used only when the primary set of fuel injectors reach a particular duty cycle. The other side of the tank is used to cool the transmission and intercoolers. *(Photo courtesy Dominick Damato)* MIDDLE: When Kurt built this Nova, he wanted it to be as sneaky as possible, so he designed the roll cage to fit very tightly against the body, and retained the bench seat. The column shifter is still in use, but the horn button electronically makes the 1-2 shift. Gauges hide in the glove box. *(Photo courtesy Dominick Damato)* BOTTOM: The engine bay leaves little room to spare, but there was just enough real estate to accommodate the dry-sump oiling system. Fuel system upgrades are plentiful, while stainless steel headers and Flowmaster mufflers provide a smooth path for spent gases. The end result is 1,160 hp and 825 ft-lbs of torque at the rear wheels. *(Photo courtesy Dominick Damato)*

Dragway Park in Cordova, Illinois. With more boost, the car is certainly capable of 8s, but the car's weight of 3,800 pounds is a determining factor as well.

The 1968–1972 Nova platform is generally light, but when you consider all of the additional equipment on this car, you begin to see the weight pile on. Also consider the fact that the interior is all there, including two bench seats, full carpeting, and a complete dash. The interior is definitely sleeper-friendly with its column shifter, hidden gauges, and tightly tucked roll cage. Other notable sleeper details include the ratty seat cover and floor mats.

After the car made its rounds in magazines and created plenty of Internet chatter, it was sold to Dru Diesner of northern Illinois, who is the current owner. Dru says he fell in love with the car when he saw it in *Hot Rod*, and was given the opportunity to purchase the highly acclaimed Nova. Since its change of ownership, the car has remained in the same configuration, and mainly serves as a street machine. Dru says, "It's amazing how many people don't know this car is fast. It's been in *Hot Rod* and all over the Internet, but people are still blown away when they look under the hood. It's the ultimate sleeper." With 1,160 hp and low-9-second time slips to its credit, you would be hard pressed to build a better Nova sleeper, especially when you consider the thousands of man-hours and engineering put into the extravagant buildup.

Dented body panels, faded paint, and a general lack of cleanliness make Dru's Nova less than appealing to the average individual, but its performance more than makes up for its lack of style. The best elapsed time for the 1972 Nova is 9.25 at 148 mph, and it was in the midst of an 800-mile round trip! *(Photo courtesy Dominick Damato)*

The Mickey Thompson drag radials are sized at 295/65R15, and fill every square inch of room in the wheel tubs. Power application is handled by a Powerglide automatic transmission and an ATI torque converter, while the Smith Racecraft leaf springs mount to the well-equipped 9-inch rear end to increase traction. *(Photo courtesy Dominick Damato)*

Chapter 8

Grandmas and Groceries

While some sleeper projects require additional effort to hide the car's potential, some cars naturally blend in and rarely grab a car guy's attention. You don't think about your grandmother's daily driver as a performance vehicle, so that's a good way to fool the opposition. A full-size luxury car, or even a station wagon is great for this look, but you can also pull off the look with the right color combination and wheel and tire setup. These cars are generally heavier than other sleeper candidates, so you have to consider that when building the engine, but enough nitrous or boost can fix that problem easily.

Grocery getters can be described in many ways, but the most common definition is a full-size car that is generally occupied by elderly folks—grandmas, specifically. Cars like full-size sedans or station wagons, preferably from the late 1960s and early 1970s, offer the right looks, and actually had options for big engines. This Chevy has a 427-ci big-block.

The advantage to a heavy car is weight transfer. In most cases, a car like a Lincoln or a Caprice station wagon has plenty of weight to begin with, so the years of stress do a number on the springs and shocks. If you see a 1970s or 1980s station wagon on the road these days, you notice they sit a little lower than stock—that's because the springs have settled over the years. The worn-out springs and shocks allow for great initial weight transfer, but you have to mess with it a little to keep the weight where you want it. Usually, cars with worn rear springs rebound and allow the rear tires to break loose, but with full-size cars, like some of the ones showcased in this chapter, it's not as much of an issue since you're tossing around so much weight either way.

Another nice feature of taking the grandma-car or grocery-getter approach is a spacious engine bay and a good rear end. Since these cars had so much weight to pull, they generally had decent rear ends under them, and some of them featured a fairly low gear ratio. Obviously, if you're

Four-door sedans from the 1960s are generally considered cool, but rarely considered fast. This one has the undercover police car look going strong, with the Dog Dish caps and spotlights, and calls upon a Ford FE big-block for power. Cars like this are easily overlooked by today's car-guy generation, making it a great sleeper.

Under the hood of the big green Ford is an FE big-block with an aluminum intake manifold and headers being the only obvious modifications. A closer look reveals head studs, rather than bolts, and a couple of solenoids tucked below the chrome air cleaner.

The Lincoln Town Car is a great grandma car because of its very outdated styling and potential for modifications. These cars came with small-block Ford engines, so the options are endless for big power, as the 5.0-liter platform offers great power per cubic inch. This one features a centrifugal supercharger and makes 500 hp.

making enough horsepower to make one of these hefty machines keep pace with a late-model Corvette, eventually you need to upgrade the rear end. But at that point the weight difference means your 4,000-pound car needs to make 500 hp to keep up with a 3,200-pound car with 400 hp if you're going strictly by power-to-weight ratios. Without question, traction issues can greatly affect this comparison, but the heavy car has the advantage when it comes to hooking up, unless the chap in the Corvette has his traction control turned on. Either way the race goes, if you consider the fact that the average grandma car originally weighed 4,000 pounds and had about 160 hp, the guy in the other lane will be shocked to find that you've even put up a fight against his $60,000 sports car. Try it with a Porsche or a Mercedes and really have some fun!

Depending on your intentions and your budget, some grandma cars and grocery getters are outside the years 1974 to 1986, where most people focus. Some may be older cars, possibly from the muscle car era, and some may be newer, such as those cruising along at 35 mph on the interstate with its blinker on for miles. Late-model Lincolns are great platforms, as they came from the factory with a Ford 4.6-liter modular engine, so the options are endless for horsepower. A turbo would certainly wake up a sleepy Lincoln, but you could also toy with a supercharger, like a Kenne Bell unit, and squeeze some serious power out of it. The earlier modular engines aren't nearly as strong or potent as the DOHC versions that powered 2003 and 2004 SVT Cobras, but 500 hp wouldn't be out of reason. A 500-hp Lincoln? That's a sleeper, no matter how you look at it.

At the other end of the grandma-car spectrum, you find plenty of candidates from the late 1960s and early 1970s, even though these were years when performance was at an all-time high. Back then, elderly folks still drove full-size cars, but many resorted to economy cars in the early 1970s. Cars like the Chevy Vega, or Ford's Maverick or Pinto, offered a much cheaper alternative for the older crowd. (See Chapter 10 for more on domestic and imported economy cars.)

Whether you go for the old grandma look or something a little newer, you're likely to pull off the sleeper look without an extraordinary amount of effort. Large cars are the easiest to deal with, in terms of fitting a large engine and pretty much any power adder under the hood, as well as hooking up. Smaller, lightweight cars are more efficient, since you don't have to make a ton of power to go fast, but hiding the potential is tough, unless you take a few extra steps to make sure it flies under the grandma radar.

Would you believe this minty-fresh 1965 Chevelle has run a best of 11.53 at 117 mph? It certainly has, even with its bench seat, rubber floor mat, and column shifter. Power for the 300 Deluxe sedan comes from a naturally aspirated, iron-headed, 396-ci big-block backed by a TH400 automatic transmission. Z-16 guys, eat your hearts out.

Mean Green—
A Killer 1972 Chevelle That Hides in Grandma's Clothing

Sleepy Factor: 7 out of 10

There's no doubt that a muscle car can be transformed into a grandma car, and Shannon's Chevelle is proof. The car certainly doesn't look like it's capable of running 6-second elapsed times in the eighth-mile. Swapping tires and wheels kills the sleeper look, but Shannon gained nearly a half second!

Pros
- Whitewalls and hubcaps
- Green on green
- Low-budget power
- Hidden roll bar

Cons
- Muscle car roots
- Ratchet shifter

Sometimes, simplicity is the best way to win someone over, in terms of a sleeper. A car that looks simple and stock usually garners very little attention, and that's how Shannon Medley pulls off the sleeper look with his 1972 Chevelle. It's totally stock on the outside, but it doesn't take long for folks to figure out how quickly this car can get from point A to point B. Even after figuring out the car's secrets, it's still unbelievably fast, considering the extremely simple combination. Not to discredit the work that went into it, but an LT1 with nitrous does very little to impress most car guys. This one does just that inside a bone stock Chevelle that rolls on the stock 14s with hubcaps and whitewalls.

The grandma look is hard to pull off with a car like a Chevelle, as it was originally intended for performance, but Shannon has certainly fooled his share of die-hard car guys when the car consistently dips into the 6s in the eighth-mile, even with its tiny rear tires. Shannon has toyed with several different wheel and tire combinations on the Chevelle, and has run a best of 6.32 at 106 mph in the eighth-mile on a set of Weld Draglite wheels and Mickey Thompson slicks. This combination totally ruins the sleeper look, so he rarely runs it, even though it's a half-second faster than the sleeper setup. He's also worked hard to get the car to perform well on regular street radials. He's tested numerous times with the

car, and has learned the proper launch technique and the right moment to lay the nitrous to it. His best effort on hard street radials (275/60R15 Futuras) has been a 7.10 at 102 mph.

Shannon bought the car a few years ago and didn't waste any time sticking the LT1 under the hood. He got it running and driving, and preceded to force tons of nitrous through it, before killing some parts that necessitated a complete rebuild. He sent the block and bottom end to Lance Fugate to prepare it for a rebuild, one that would increase the cubic inches from 350 to 383. The 4.030-inch cylinders are stuffed with Speed-Pro forged pistons, which are connected to a set of Scat forged 5.7-inch connecting rods and a Scat cast steel crankshaft. This combination of components, when combined with the stock cylinder heads, creates an 11.3:1 compression ratio. Shannon felt confident in the stock oiling system, so he simply installed new replacement parts.

While the cylinder heads are the stock castings, with the original 1.94-inch intake valves and 1.50-inch exhaust valves, Shannon had Steve Chapman perform some additional massaging. This allows the heads to flow 262 cfm at .600 inch of lift. Shannon then installed a Comp Cams 292XFI hydraulic roller camshaft, and a set of Comp 1.6 roller rockers before port-matching the original LT1 intake manifold and placing it atop the engine. The original intake manifold proves to be a limiting factor in most LT1 applications, but Shannon seems to have great success with it after installing a 58-mm throttle body and a set of 36-pound injectors. The secret to the combination resides in a blue bottle that rides in the trunk—Shannon sprays the Chevelle with a 175-hp dry shot of nitrous. That's generally way too much nitrous for a dry shot, but Shannon tunes the car to provide an adequate amount of fuel when the nitrous is activated.

Ignition is controlled by an MSD 6AL, while outgoing air passes through a set of Summit 1.625-inch headers before entering the Flowmaster two-chamber mufflers. Though it's loud when the throttle is wide open, the car sounds rather tame at idle, compared to most low-6-second, stock-suspension cars. Behind the stroked LT1 is a TCI TH350 transmission, which features a manual valve body and a PTC 10-inch torque converter, which allows the car to leave the line at 3,600 rpm. Moving farther back, you find a GM 12-bolt rear end, which features a "Lincoln Locker" and a 3.55:1 gear set. The rear suspension is all stock, aside from the adjustable shocks and a set of Jegs control arms, but the car launches nicely no matter the tire choice. The front suspension is completely stock, down to the drum brakes and manual steering, so Shannon obviously hasn't tried to lighten this car in the least. Surprisingly, it weighs 3,280 pounds without a driver, which is fairly light, considering the full-frame design and lack of weight reduction.

For aesthetics, Shannon gave his Chevelle the least desired color for most muscle cars—green. His friend Michael Hudgins did the bodywork on it and then laid down a few coats of the original grandma green and followed that with clear coat. The interior is equally green, with a vinyl-covered bench seat and virtually no factory accessories. It's a plain-Jane car but local tracks didn't like seeing the car run deep into the 6s with no roll cage so Shannon had Sam Daffron build a custom five-point roll bar that is tucked tightly to the inner structure, with enough room for the headliner and interior panels, of course. Sam built the roll cage as a bolt-in unit so Shannon can take it out when he's in all-out sleeper mode.

The only giveaway to this car's potential is the B&M Ratchet shifter, but Shannon gave it some personality with a "custom" console. And though his car had options for go-fast material from the factory, Shannon pulled off the sleeper look with stock hubcaps and whitewalls, and a grandma-fresh color selection.

Stock hubcaps and whitewall tires do a great job of disguising this Chevelle, until it's time to hit the track. Cars from the muscle car era generally don't double as grandma cars, but the color combination, as well as the wheels and tires, give this one just the right amount of old-lady flavor.

Shannon has experimented with different wheel and tire combinations, and even tried his hand at hard street radials. The best he got out of hard radials was a 7.10 at 102 mph, while the car's overall best time is 6.32 at 106 mph. Shannon leaves the line on the motor and hits the nitrous as soon as the rear suspension settles.

Facing Page

TOP: Shannon had Sam Daffron build a bolt-in roll cage for the Chevelle, so he could remove it when it was time for some fun on the street. Sam tucked the tubing tightly against the interior panels to keep it hidden well, but legal for racing at most tracks. MIDDLE TOP: Power is applied with a pair of tiny Mickey Thompson drag radials. Sized at 215/60R14, the drag radials feature a painted-on whitewall and mount to a pair of 14x6-inch steel wheels. Stock hubcaps are bolted into place to keep it legal at the local tracks. MIDDLE BOTTOM: One of the most impressive aspects of Shannon's Chevelle is the nearly stock LT1 powerplant. It's been stroked to 383 ci and the heads have been ported. Shannon also installed a Comp Cams hydraulic roller camshaft to work in conjunction with his secret weapon, a 175-hp dry nitrous system. BOTTOM: If the green paint and hubcaps weren't enough, Shannon's Chevelle features an all-green vinyl interior that would've never been popular with hardcore car guys back in the day. Shannon has fun with his sleeper, using a tissue box as a shifter boot, but that's the only obvious clue to this car's potential.

The Volvette—
550 hp, 28 mpg, and All the Groceries You Can Handle

Sleepy Factor: 7 out of 10

Volvo is known for building safe and reliable cars, so it's a popular car for soccer moms and older folks. This one, however, packs a serious punch with its twin-turbocharged LS1 engine, which makes for a smoke show on the street and 11-second passes at the track. *(Photo courtesy Dan Jenkins)*

Pros
- Soccer mom appeal
- Big power
- No cage

Cons
- Aftermarket wheels
- Lowered stance

Enthusiasts have been building sleepers out of grocery getters for years, and while the popular choice is a full-size car from the 1970s, a late-model rendition can be an exceptional sleeper if the right steps are taken. To pull off the sleeper theme with a late-model grocery getter, or "grandma car," it's important to start with a good vehicle. A Volvo station wagon is a prime example, with its soccer-mom qualities and overall unsuspecting appearance. Spacious interiors make these cars popular with families of all sizes, and Volvo's reputation for crash safety is another high mark for a quality family car. The fact that they are well-built cars helps matters even more, but Dug Strickler didn't mind taking his apart to create an awesome sleeper.

Dug started with a 1989 Volvo 740 wagon, which was actually given to him when his father (Dale) passed away. Dale was passionate about Volvos and that same passion was passed to his son, who exemplifies his love for the car by thrashing on it! When Dug acquired the car, a four-cylinder engine powered it, and even though it was eventually turbocharged, it wasn't exactly fun to drive. Dug changed that by ditching the original engine and fabricating the custom mounts and crossmembers to install a late-model GM engine. The choice was

a good one, as the stock LS1 engine would've been plenty of power for the wagon, but Dug upped his game by installing a twin turbo system, which transformed this family wagon into a high-winding, tire-destroying machine.

The LS1 engine is from a 1999 Chevy, and would've come from the factory with horsepower in the low 300s, which is still tripling the output of the Volvo's original four-cylinder engine. It was no easy task to swap in the new engine, but the fact that the Volvo is a rear-wheel-drive car helped a lot, as Dug could retain the stock rear end for the time being. Dug also chose to keep the LS1 engine in stock form, which doesn't necessarily lend itself well to turbochargers, but the current setup seems to be making plenty of power. Dug admits he could make much more power with a different rotating assembly and a better set of cylinder heads, so there's no doubt that he'll step up the power eventually. For now, the stock long block is outfitted with a custom set of stainless steel headers that lead to a pair of Garrett T4 turbochargers. Twin Tial 38-mm wastegates regulate maximum boost pressure, while a custom air-to-air intercooler allows for more boost by cooling the intake charge before it reaches the engine. Custom piping connects it all, and looks great under the hood.

Turbocharging the LS1 engine wasn't easy, considering the tight confines of the Volvo's engine bay, but physically fitting the turbo system wasn't the end of the process. Dug then had to prepare the engine for the additional stresses, and did so by installing a Walbro electric fuel pump and Aeromotive boost-referenced fuel pressure regulator. Custom fuel rails and 42-pound injectors are the final steps before fuel enters the engine, and a Carolina Auto Masters ECU tune keeps it all running efficiently. After driving the car for a bit and getting it tuned to his liking, he strapped it to a dyno and put down 470 hp to the rear wheels on 7 pounds of boost. He then cranked up the boost to 10 pounds, and put down 544 hp and 567 ft-lbs of torque to the rear wheels. Let's not forget this potent engine is in a Volvo station wagon.

Behind the twin-turbo LS1 is a Tremec T-56, 6-speed manual transmission, which features a Textralia clutch set and a short-throw shifter. The car proves to be very entertaining to drive, as it absolutely roasts the tires through the first few gears. Dug's Volvo is featured in many videos on the Internet and it's always a favorite because of its sleeper qualities and Dug's wild driving. Burnouts, donuts, and top-speed runs are not uncommon for this grocery getter, so it's no wonder the car has quickly gained notoriety on the Internet, as well as in print media with a few magazine features.

Underneath, the Volvo features a set of lowering springs and hefty sway bars from IPD, while the shocks are from Bilstein. These modifications greatly increased the car's handling capabilities, but once the boost comes in, there's no chance of keeping the car glued to the pavement. The rear subframe assembly is a custom unit from Kaplhenke Racing and it's built to handle all of the abuse Dug can throw at it. The stock rear end is no longer in service, as Dug swapped it for a Ford 8.8, which gets the job done. Dug's 740 rolls on a set of BBS LM wheels, which measure 18x8 inches up front and 18x10.5

TOP: There is a lot of action under the hood of Dug's Volvo wagon, but the root of it is a 1999 Chevrolet LS1 engine, which features a stock bottom end and cylinder heads. Even at a moderate 10 pounds of boost, the Volvo put down 544 hp and 567 ft-lbs of torque to the rear wheels. *(Photo courtesy Dan Jenkins)* BOTTOM: The wow factor in this engine bay is certainly the custom headers, which lead to a pair of Garrett T4 turbochargers fit with Tial 38-mm wastegates. To help the engine withstand the additional stress of boost, Dug installed a larger fuel pump, larger injectors, and an aftermarket ECU, tuned appropriately. *(Photo courtesy Dan Jenkins)*

TOP: Up front, the Volvo's interior looks close to stock, but the shifter poking through the console is a tipoff to this car's fun factor—the T-56 6-speed manual transmission. While it doesn't work all that well at the track, the 6-speed creates lots of hairy situations on the street as Dug feathers the throttle and fights for control. *(Photo courtesy Dan Jenkins)*
BOTTOM: The backseat is still intact, so this car is great transportation for Dug's motorcycle stunt crew, known as the Anti-Team. These guys do crazy stunts on sport bikes, and Dug is equally courageous behind the wheel of his 740 station wagon. Gotta love those big Volvo headrests! *(Photo courtesy Dan Jenkins)*

inches out back and hide a set of brakes from a Volvo 960. And while they give the car a modified look, they do very little to take away from the sleeper appeal of this car. The lowered stance is barely noticeable, but the four stainless steel pipes that exit just below the rear end hint at the car's power.

Any doubt of the car's potential is removed when Dug fires it up, dumps the clutch, and fights to keep control as the car skids sideways with smoke billowing from the tires. It's definitely fun to watch, and Dug has shown exactly how fun it is to drive in his Internet videos. One such video is an on-board shot from a Yamaha R1 motorcycle, during a street race/top speed run, where the Volvette outruns the bike and pulls away as the bike tops out at 184 mph. Now that is one killer Volvo!

Burnouts are Dug's specialty, and his twin-turbo LS1 Volvo is there to withstand the abuse. The car has run a best of 11.73 in the quarter-mile at 125 mph, but the drag strip isn't where this car performs the best. The car is known for its Internet video, where it outruns a Yamaha R1 sport bike at more than 180 mph! *(Photo courtesy Dan Jenkins)*

Dug drives the wagon frequently, and he went as far as installing a trailer hitch to make it more practical. He's a stunt rider, so the Volvo turned out to be the perfect towing machine for his sport bike. If you're wondering, yes, he's done a burnout with his motorcycle in tow. *(Photo courtesy Dan Jenkins)*

Yerluzin'—
This Grocery Getter Turned Heavy Hitter Surprises Everyone

Sleepy Factor: 10 out of 10

Perhaps the best platform for a grocery getter sleeper is a mid-1970s to early 1980s full-size sedan, such as this 1977 Buick LeSabre. These cars struggled greatly in the horsepower department, but have tons of room under the hood and the ultimate sleeper appearance package. The stock hubcaps finish it off nicely. *(Photo courtesy Mike Thompson)*

Pros
- Completely stock body and interior
- Hubcaps
- Full-size family car
- Column shifter

Cons
- None

Taking the grandma car approach to building a sleeper isn't going to impress the girls, but it will impress car guys, and keep them guessing. You won't find a much better example than David Thompson's 1977 Buick LeSabre shown here. It's a full-size family car from the 1970s, so that means it has a full frame, it has a rear-wheel-drive platform, and it has lots of room under the hood. The cool thing about David's Buick is the fact that he could list the car's modifications, and most folks would still be at least two seconds off. It just doesn't look *that* fast, and it does surprisingly well, considering the simplistic combination, and the 4,100 pounds it has to motivate.

David and his son Mike are diehard drag racing enthusiasts and have built a number of drag cars over the years, but the father and son duo never really intended to turn this Buick into a performer. And to say this is a drag car is totally out of the question—this car is a street car, any way you slice it. All of the factory equipment is still intact, including the power steering, air conditioning, and even the catalytic converters. With an LT1-based small-block Chevy, the Buick has

run a best of 10.42 at 127 mph in the quarter-mile, hooking up on street-legal drag radial tires. And hubcaps—don't forget about the hubcaps. This is the ultimate grocery-getting sleeper.

So, how does a hardcore car guy end up with a 1977 Buick LeSabre that runs 10.40s? David was in the market for a winter beater, as his location in New York makes for harsh conditions, and you don't really want to take a chance with nice vehicles that generally have a payment attached to them. So he wanted a cheap car he could use during the winter and stumbled across the Buick, which had a $1,500 price tag. He gave the car a once-over and quickly realized it was too nice to use as a winter beater, but decided to buy it anyway. Obviously, it was all stock, but he loved that it was in such great shape. The idea to make this car a sleeper didn't take flight until the Thompsons found out that all of the suspension and running gear from their mid-1990s Impala SS would completely interchange.

The Impala SS had been modified, but a crash left it in poor shape, so the father and son decided to swap the suspension goodies and rear end into the Buick, and give it a healthy powerplant. The first step was to get the suspension figured out, which basically meant unbolting it from the Impala a and bolting the components onto the Buick. The 8.5-inch 10-bolt rear end was swapped, as it already had 3.73:1 gears, a Detroit differential, and Strange axles in place. Rear suspension modifications consist of tubular upper and lower control arms, as well as a pair of Calvert Racing shocks and a BMR anti-roll bar. The Impala had disc brakes on all four corners, so the Thompsons swapped all of that equipment as well. Up front, they left it completely stock, aside from the Calvert Racing shocks, which help transfer weight to the rear end. Traction comes by way of Mickey Thompson drag radials sized at 275/60R15, and wrapped around the original steel wheels, which have been widened to 15x10 inches. Rolling stock up front consists of the original 15x6-inch steel wheels and regular radial tires. All four corners are outfitted with stock hubcaps, which is a great way to finish the exterior for the perfect sleeper look.

Horsepower comes from an LT1-based small-block Chevy, which now displaces 385 ci, but still relies on the stock two-bolt main block. Bill Trovato of BTR Performance in Rochester, New York, handled the engine's machine work and cylinder head work, as well as the dyno tuning after the engine was assembled, while Eric Vanberkum helped Mike choose the right combination of components. The small-block features an Eagle crankshaft, Scat I-beam connecting rods, and a set of custom SRP forged pistons, which are built with a small dish to work better with the LT1 cylinder heads. Final compression ratio for the stroked small-block is 11.5:1, which is tame enough to run on 93-octane pump gas. The cylinder heads are stock LT1 aluminum castings, with custom port work by BTR Performance. Nothing exotic here—just a good port job and a set of Crane roller rocker arms. The camshaft is a hydraulic roller and induction consists of an Edelbrock Victor Jr. intake manifold topped with a 750-cfm Holley from Cubic Flow Modifications (C.F.M.).

The engine breathes through a pair of stock Impala exhaust manifolds, which lead to the Impala catalytic converters and a full exhaust system composed of 2.5-inch piping. It's unbelievable how quick this car has run,

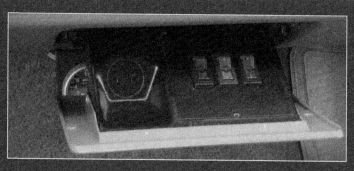

TOP: Although engine bay room isn't an issue with this car, David and Mike Thompson decided to swap the engine from another project. The small-block began life as a fuel-injected LT1, but currently displaces 385 ci and relies on stock cylinder head castings, ported by BTR Performance. Up top is an Edelbrock Victor Jr. intake manifold and a C.F.M. carburetor. (Photo courtesy Mike Thompson) LEFT: While the engine proved its potential by cranking out 435 hp on the dyno, all motor passes have only produced times in the mid-12s for this 4,100-pound sedan. The NOS Big Shot plate nitrous system really wakes up the LT1-based small-block, giving it enough power to gain two full seconds in the quarter-mile. (Photo courtesy Mike Thompson)

TOP: Although David needs to keep his auxiliary gauges visible at all times, he has hidden the activation switches for the nitrous system, the nitrous bottle heater, and the line lock system in the ashtray. He also rewired the cruise control switch to activate the nitrous purge. (Photo courtesy Mike Thompson) BOTTOM: There aren't many tell-tale signs of this car's potential, so opening the door reveals a completely stock interior. There is no roll bar, no aftermarket safety harnesses, and no fancy shifter to control the full-built TH400 automatic transmission. The interior is in very good shape, leading most folks to believe this is simply a well-kept grocery getter. (Photo courtesy Mike Thompson)

considering the tame setup, but the secret weapon is a nitrous system from NOS. The Big Shot plate mounts beneath the carburetor and adds a great deal of power to the engine, which makes 435 hp without any nitrous assistance. Modifying the fuel system is essential for the engine to keep up when the nitrous is in full force, so Mike installed a MagnaFuel 350 fuel pump and plumbed it into the original gas tank. An MSD Digital-7 (7531) box is used to control the ignition.

Behind the small-block is a TH400 transmission that has been heavily modified to withstand the big power and weight. Mike got a lot of tips and assistance from Hutch's Transmission Service when it came time to build the 3-speed automatic for his father's Buick. He wanted it to hold up to the abuse, but also wanted it to be a fully automatic transmission, unlike most racers, who would rather have a manual valve body. The main reason for this was to retain the original column shifter, and the end result is a very easy-to-drive car. Simply put it in drive, and it knows what to do from there. The torque converter is a Transmission Specialties unit, which measures 9 inches in diameter and allows David to leave the line hard and apply every ounce of power as the big Buick motors down the quarter-mile.

The car is very deceptive to the average car guy, but even the folks who knew about the car's potential didn't believe it would run 10.40s at full weight on the small radial. The car certainly turns heads when it hits the track, and it's a legitimate street car that has all of its factory amenities. It doesn't have a roll cage or any type of safety gear, so it's not technically allowed to run at its full potential, so the Thompsons run it in the 11.50 index class, which doesn't require a cage. The only modification that would lead someone to believe this car isn't totally stock is the three-gauge pod that rides below the dash. The Thompsons hid the switches for the nitrous activation, nitrous bottle heater, and line lock in the ashtray, and David uses the cruise control switch to purge the nitrous system. It's a sneaky setup that proves to be one of the best sleepers on the planet. This would be a great sleeper if it only ran 12s, but it manages to bust off 10-second passes with little effort, so it definitely ranks highly.

Because the Buick lacks many of the safety features required to pass technical inspection, David generally runs it in an index class such as 11.50, which doesn't require a roll bar. However, with the track crew "looking the other way" David has run a best of 10.42 at 127 mph in testing. *(Photo courtesy Tracy Smith of TRS Photography)*

On the track, David's Buick looks out of place, but grabs everyone's attention with its surprising performance, whether it's on a motor pass or a nitrous pass. The car hooks up on Mickey Thompson drag radials sized at 275/60R15, and its best 60-foot time is 1.45 seconds. *(Photo courtesy Tracy Smith of TRS Photography)*

Diesel Weasels

Generally, Diesel trucks are used for the sole purpose of doing work. Whether that means hauling a load of gravel or towing your racecar, Diesel trucks have never gotten much credit for the amount of horsepower and torque they make. However, within the past few years, the Diesel craze has hit full force, with folks taking mildly modified full-size trucks and making more than 1,000 ft-lbs of torque without breaking a sweat. In fact, most modern Diesels can make that much torque by only upgrading the turbo and tuning the fuel mixture with an aftermarket programmer. This trend has exploded into a major industry, with folks going all out on Diesel builds in an effort to push the limits of their 5,000-pound pickups. It's not uncommon to see one of these trucks run 12s in the quarter-mile, which is quick enough to outrun a stock Mustang GT.

Dually trucks are particularly sleepy, simply because it adds another layer to the truck's utilitarian purpose, rather than its performance. Even trucks with modified ride height and custom wheels don't stand out as fast trucks, and most folks won't be able to tell until they're left in a plume of black smoke.

Obviously, it takes a lot of power to push a very heavy vehicle down the quarter-mile at such a quick rate, but the sleeper status is undeniable, especially for plain-Jane work trucks. With these cases, the average looks of an all-white, single-cab, long-bed truck is the ultimate platform, and if you leave the dirt and mud stains, that makes it even better. And while the work truck is a viable option to really fool a bunch of people, it's not difficult to surprise savvy car guys with a highly modified truck. Even a truck that's lifted and outfitted with enormous tires doesn't scream "performance," so you can still pull off the look, and add your custom flair to a run-of-the-mill truck. Crazy paint jobs, custom wheels, and extremely large exhaust pipes would normally take a vehicle out of the sleeper realm, but with Diesel trucks, and more importantly 4x4 trucks, these modifications are all part of the culture and it only does more to help the truck blend in with the rest.

You can't deny the potent power of today's Diesel engines, and it's closely related to modern-day turbocharger technology. As seen with production cars and outlaw street cars, turbochargers have come a long way, and the same can be said for turbos in the Diesel market. Larger, more efficient turbos can be used on these engines, without the drawbacks of turbo lag. And with stronger engines in general, you can really crank up the boost without worrying about hurting parts along the way. For most custom Diesel trucks, 50 pounds of boost is very common, and some radical setups produce upward of 100 pounds of boost. Of course, that much boost is hard on parts, and is only used in full race applications.

GM's Duramax Diesel engine is a turbocharged V-8 that produces plenty of power and proves to be a favorite for towing and pulling. There are plenty of performance options for these engines, but high-end builds rarely use a Duramax for a starting point. GM's latest Duramax offering is a 6.6-liter V-8 known as the LMM, which pumps out 397 hp and 765 ft-lbs of torque right off the showroom floor. Add more boost and more fuel, and you have four-digit torque numbers. Gale Banks Engineering (commonly referred to simply as "Banks") specializes in Duramax performance and uses this platform in its all-out racing vehicles that make more than 1,200 hp. Banks also makes parts for the other big Diesel platforms.

Ford seems to have a strong following of Diesel enthusiasts with its lineup of Power Stroke V-8 engines, which are fed by a turbocharger. These engines seem to make great power, but the general consensus leads most enthusiasts to believe they are unreliable, especially when power levels

Taking a stock Diesel truck to the drag strip won't get you very far unless you've upgraded the fuel system and turned up the boost. Stock turbochargers can produce lots of power, but it takes a bigger turbo to make really big power. Wouldn't it stink to be outrun by a crew-cab 4x4 truck with a camper?

increase. The level of unreliability varies between the different sizes, which consist of 6.0-, 6.4-, 6.7-, and 7.3-liter displacements. The highest performance ratings come from the brand-new 6.7-liter Scorpion engine, which produces 390 hp and 735 ft-lbs of torque from the factory, very close to Chevy's Duramax offering. And while Ford's engine makes good power and torque from the factory, when enthusiasts begin looking for increased power, they often resort to an engine swap. This is obviously a big project for a modern Diesel-powered vehicle, but it's common in the industry. When engine swaps do take place, the Cummins Diesel is always the transplant, as it is currently the king of the Diesels.

A quick glance at the stock specs will encourage some head scratching as to why the Cummins is the most popular

Diesel trucks are some of the sneakiest sleepers out there, since most folks don't automatically assume that every obviously modified Diesel truck is fast. This one is lifted with oversized tires, but you'd never guess there's a compound turbo setup on the Cummins engine, creating all sorts of horsepower and torque.

Under the hood is a 5.9-liter Cummins engine, which is essentially stock, aside from the compound turbocharger system and fuel system upgrades. Diesel engines are notorious for their ability to choke down massive quantities of air and fuel, and this example does it with no cylinder head or valvetrain modifications.

Known simply as Camo Truck, this Ford Super Duty is powered by a twin turbocharged Cummins Diesel and makes more than 1,000 hp and more than 1,800 ft-lbs of torque! This truck has run very low 7s in the eighth-mile and makes it look easy. The camouflage paint job, if anything, lessens the chances of assuming this truck is fast.

Diesel platform. The highest production figures out there are 350 hp and 650 ft-lbs of torque; approximately 100 pounds lower than its direct competition. The even more strange part about the fascination with Cummins Diesel engines is the fact that folks revert to the older engines in the search for serious horsepower and torque. The most popular platform is the 5.9-liter inline six-cylinder configuration, which features a singular turbocharger. There are two basic versions of the 5.9, the earlier being the 12-valve and the later being the 24-valve. Many folks believe that the 12-valve is the simplest, and most reliable platform out there, so it's often used in high-performance applications. The 24-valve is a common choice as well, and the newest offering, displacing 6.7 liters, is playing catch-up when it comes to supporting elaborate modifications.

As mentioned, most Cummins powerplants feature a single-turbo setup, but a great way to add horsepower is to add another turbocharger. Some go with two turbochargers, also referred to as a compound setup, where a smaller turbo is used to help spool a massive turbo. This allows for quick response because of the smaller turbo, and amazing top end power because of the larger turbo. It's a great way to make power, but with the elevated boost levels, it's important to make sure the cylinder head seals to the block. At this point in the game, most owners install head studs and an aftermarket head gasket to keep the incredible boost pressure from lifting the head off the block's surface.

The Diesel market is similar to the gas-powered arena, in that singular-power adders are great, but multiple-power adders are better. Nitrous is often used in conjunction with turbochargers on Diesel engines. With lots of boost and massive quantities of nitrous, this is a volatile combination, but it makes big power, and allows these 5,000-pound pickups to run as fast as 9s in the quarter-mile.

While the featured engines in this chapter are on work trucks and lifted 4x4 pickups, Diesel engines are also being transplanted into passenger cars for a whole different approach. So far, there haven't been any real sleepers built out of Diesel-powered passenger cars, but that day is coming with the increased turbo and Diesel technology. Stuff a Cummins in a full-size family car from the 1980s and you have an unsuspecting car that is close to 1,000 pounds lighter than a heavy-duty pickup. With four-wheel-drive Diesel trucks running well into the 9s in the quarter-mile, there's no reason why you couldn't put the same effort into a passenger car and get some pretty staggering results. Another engine swap option is to transplant a modern turbocharged Diesel engine into a 1/2-ton pickup to knock the total weight down by several hundred pounds.

Many high-performance Diesel trucks have four-wheel-drive underpinnings, but this one is doing a smoky two-wheel-drive burnout for the fun of it. Diesel trucks can get away with crazy paint schemes and custom wheels, and still fly under the radar. This Dodge quad cab runs high 6s in the eighth-mile.

White Lightning—
This isn't Your Average 3/4-Ton Work Truck

Sleepy Factor: 8 out of 10

Jonathan's 2002 Chevrolet 2500 HD pickup is the perfect color for a sleeper—white. This color makes it look more like a work truck, helping it blend into society. The truck puts down 575 hp and 1,170 ft-lbs of torque, which translates to very low 8s in the eighth-mile and mid-12s in the quarter.

Pros
- Stock wheels
- Stock body
- Stock interior

Cons
- Limited by stock turbocharger

You probably see one every day—an all-white, heavy-duty pickup, hauling a load of materials to a job site or perhaps towing a trailer. When it comes to building a sleeper from a Diesel truck, there's no better way than going with the work truck look, because it'll look like every other work truck in the United States. The example shown here only displays a few minor exterior modifications, but boasts well over 1,000 ft-lbs of torque at the rear wheels and elapsed times that are in Corvette territory—not quite Z06 territory but a street race would certainly surprise the guy in the other lane. There's no denying the stock appeal of this particular truck and that's exactly how its owner Jonathan Gudel wanted it. No frills, stock wheels, and tons of power!

In reality, Jonathan's truck isn't a miraculous feat of engineering. It simply has the necessary modifications to perform very well and doesn't have the obligatory lift kit and aftermarket wheel and tire combination that most Diesel owners install within the first few months of ownership. With a stock outward appearance, there's no doubt this Duramax-powered Chevrolet sneaks under the radar, so when someone lines up against it at the track, or happens to pull alongside it at a traffic light, the end result is usually a hurt ego when the smoke clears.

Underneath, Jonathan's 2500 pickup is equipped with 3.73:1 gears, which work out well for his tire size and overall setup. The truck rolls on stock Silverado HD wheels, wrapped with Nitto Terra Grappler all-terrain tires, sized at 285/75R16, which is only a couple of sizes up from factory. The larger tires don't give away the truck's performance, and neither does the 2-inch drop in the rear—in fact, the truck sits level now that the rear has been lowered.

The truck's motivation comes from a Duramax Diesel engine, which displaces 6.6 liters (402.7 ci) and is commonly known as the LB7 engine. This engine is a V-8 Diesel, which features four valves per cylinder. It features a cast-iron block with a 3.90-inch stroke and 4.06-inch bore from the factory, while the cast aluminum cylinder heads lower the engine's overall weight. Diesel engines are known for being heavy and bulky, but the Duramax is efficiently designed and makes plenty of power in stock form, coming in at 300 hp and 520 ft-lbs of torque. The fuel system consists of a common rail, direct-injection setup from the factory, while a turbocharger and intercooler are also original equipment from Chevrolet. Jonathan's Duramax is very close to stock, as it was only a matter of allowing more boost to enter the engine to make much more power and torque than the factory claims.

The safest way to add boost in either a gas or Diesel application is to provide additional fuel to prevent a lean condition, which is an engine killer. Running lean means the engine is starving for fuel, and since the turbocharger creates heat when it multiplies the air, the chance of literally melting parts becomes much higher. Other worries with a boosted application are how well the cylinder head seals off against the block. To fix this, most folks replace the original head bolts with studs and nuts, as this is a much better way to apply clamping force and get an accurate reading for torque specifications. Jonathan's Duramax is very simple in that it uses the stock turbocharger, and an all-stock engine to get the job done. He simply added more fuel to the fire, and increased the boost to create most of his power.

Jonathan runs approximately 40 pounds of boost through his Duramax and this normally wouldn't be possible with the stock turbo, but he installed an ATS Water Boy water/methanol injection system to cool the intake charge significantly. Acting as a secondary intercooler, the water/methanol injection makes cranking up the boost easier on the engine, and opens the door for more power. When all was said and done, the truck put down 575 hp and 1,170 ft-lbs of torque to the rear wheels through a 5-inch exhaust system. Jonathan says the truck still manages to get 20 mpg, and current maximum RPM is 3,000 because of the stock bottom end and turbo.

Behind the Duramax is an Allison automatic transmission, which comes stock in Chevrolet's Diesel-powered pickups. Obviously, a stock transmission and torque converter isn't built for abuse on the drag strip, so Jonathan relies on a fully built piece from Goerend Transmission in Saint Lucas, Iowa, to put the power to the ground. At 7,200 pounds, the truck needs a lot of steam just to get going, compared to regular passenger cars, but boasts a best 60-foot time of 1.62 seconds. That's an impressive time, considering the weight, but the four-wheel drive certainly helps Jonathan get rolling without tire spin. It's also interesting to note that Jonathan bolted on a different set of tires and wheels when he hit the track. He used a set of M&H Racemaster drag radials on all four corners, but plans to try it again with a set of DOT-legal slicks, like a Mickey Thompson ET Street tire. The radial is a stiff tire, compared to the somewhat flimsy sidewalls on an ET Street, so he hopes the truck will bite a little harder off the line with the new tires.

His best elapsed time so far with the truck is an 8.02 in the eighth-mile and a 12.62 in the quarter, which is pretty strong for a completely stock-appearing truck. At double the weight of a late-model Mustang GT, it can still walk away from it with little effort, which is an impressive feat for any four-door, 3/4-ton truck. Jonathan has more modifications planned, including twin turbochargers, but the truck definitely has the sleeper look going for it in this configuration. The all-white appearance makes you think of an average work truck, but when the skinny pedal hits the rug, there's no denying the Chevrolet's true purpose.

TOP LEFT: The crew-cab pickup rolls on stock HD wheels with slightly larger Nitto Terra Grappler tires, sized at 285/75R16. These are great for the street, but they're not the ideal choice for the track. Currently, Jonathan uses M&H drag radials for the track, but wants to step up to a set of DOT slicks, like the Mickey Thompson ET Street tire. TOP RIGHT: It's bone-stock on the inside and the stock column shifter controls the fully built Allison automatic transmission. Two gauges in a pillar-mounted pod allow Jonathan to keep track of boost levels and exhaust temperatures. Jonathan uses this truck as his daily driver, so the interior remains complete and original. MIDDLE: Looking under the hood, there isn't much excitement, but Diesel engines don't need a bunch of flashy parts to perform well. The Duramax LB7 engine is mildly modified, but Jonathan plans to completely go through the engine and eventually install twin turbochargers, which will greatly increase the power and decrease track times. BOTTOM: While Jonathan uses the Chevy as a daily driver, he also likes to have fun at the track. After bolting on a set of drag radials, Jonathan managed to motivate the 7,200-pound truck through the quarter-mile in 12.62 seconds. Pictured is an eighth-mile track, where he ran a best of 8.02 with a 1.62 60-foot time.

Cummins Goin'—
This Quad Cab Dodge Ram Dominates at the Track

This bright red pickup is a little less conservative than the other Diesel-powered vehicles in this chapter, but it's surprisingly fast, nonetheless. It is a 2007 Dodge Ram 2500 quad cab with four-wheel drive, and features a Cummins 6.7-liter engine, modified by the crew at Black's Diesel Performance in Adairsville, Georgia.

Pros
- Stock ride height
- Big power and torque
- Quad cab design

Cons
- Custom hood
- Aftermarket wheels

In the world of Diesel performance, at least on the average consumer level, the Cummins engine is the ideal platform to build upon because of its very strong bottom end and unbelievable horsepower and torque capabilities. The Cummins engine is a staple in the Dodge Ram dynasty, as it has powered a great number of these full-size trucks, dating to 1989 when a Diesel engine became an option. Although displacement and valve configuration has changed over the years, the Cummins engine is still an inline six-cylinder setup, which has proven to be a dependable design that can withstand lots and lots of boost. The 2007 Dodge Ram 2500 pictured here features a 6.7-liter Cummins, which came from the factory with more than 600 ft-lbs of torque. The truck's weight kept it from being a strong performer out of the box, but its owner Aron Nick woke the truck up with a lot more airflow.

Originally equipped with a single Holset turbocharger, the straight six-cylinder Diesel engine was efficient and perfect for towing and hauling—the truck's main purpose. How-ever, Aron had other things in mind, like beating up on sports car owners in Saturday night traffic light battles. The goal was to greatly increase the power and torque, as reducing the truck's weight isn't the easiest of tasks, although he shaved a few pounds here and there. Aron's 2500 Quad Cab is a four-wheel-drive model, which uses a solid axle in the back and independent suspension up front. He retained the stock suspension on all four corners, including the stock differentials with 3.73:1 gears. Black's Diesel Performance played a major role in the build and helped Aron get the suspension dialed in.

Aron wanted his truck to have a unique look, so he kept the original bright red paint scheme, and painted the hood, front bumper, grille, and tailgate black. This does draw more attention to the truck, compared to a truck with a stock paint scheme and original hood, but Diesel trucks are rarely considered fast, even with exterior modifications. He also installed a set of 20-inch

Fuel wheels and Nitto 305/50R20 tires to match his taste for style. And while installing aftermarket wheels and tires on a regular passenger car would completely ruin its sleeper status, Diesel trucks can get away with it, so Aron's truck still keeps a fairly low profile on the street and especially at the drag strip.

This truck looks mean with its custom wheels and two-tone paint job, but a quick glance may not provoke a muscle car owner to try his luck. And though it has a rather large exhaust stack exiting the bed floor, it's not an uncommon modification for the Diesel crowd, so it's not necessarily a red flag. Aron didn't make any real efforts to keep his truck's potential a secret, but it definitely blends in with the Diesel truck group, which is not known for quick elapsed times at the track. The secret to the Ram's motivation is a turbocharger system that feeds the relatively tame Cummins engine with massive quantities of air. The bottom end of the 6.7-liter Cummins is stock, consisting of a 4.21-inch bore and 4.88-inch stroke, resulting in a final displacement of 408 ci.

In high-boost applications, such as this engine, head studs are necessary, so Aron had the folks at Black's Diesel Performance install a set of ARP 625 head studs while the head was removed during the buildup. Many Diesel trucks perform well, even with a stock cylinder head, but Aron wanted more out of his Cummins, so Black's performed extensive port work to increase airflow dramatically. The reason behind custom port work is to allow the turbocharged Diesel engine to use the forced air more efficiently, thus making more power. During reassembly, Black's torqued the cylinder head to spec, and then installed a B&B Tooling billet aluminum side-mount intake manifold, which makes for a smooth path from the turbocharger to the cylinder head.

Speaking of the turbocharger, Aron's 6.7 came from the factory with a variable geometry unit, which allows the turbocharger's aspect ratio (A/R) to change as conditions and RPM change. This made for an efficient system, but the size of the turbocharger couldn't support the desired power levels. To meet his needs, Aron bought a custom BorgWarner S478 turbocharger, which features 83-mm turbine wheel and a housing with a 1.00 A/R. He later changed to a custom Bullseye turbo.

Additional fuel is a huge part of making big power in a Diesel application, so Aron outfitted the Cummins with Flux 3.5 injectors to provide the right amount of fuel. On the dyno, Aron's pickup put down 722 hp and 1,200 ft-lbs of torque to the rear wheels, which are impressive numbers for any application, especially a single-turbo Diesel setup. The 6.7-liter Cummins is also equipped with a Nitrous Express NDX4000 system, which is a two-stage system with a progressive controller. The engine is tuned with MADS Electronics. Sending 1,200 ft-lbs of torque to the ground is the responsibility of a very strong transmission and a torque converter that provides

TOP LEFT: Spent gasses exit the cylinder head through an ATS exhaust manifold and into a custom S478 turbocharger, based on a BorgWarner unit. The turbo features an 83-mm wheel and a 1.00 A/R exhaust housing, and it works alone—there are no twins in this engine bay. Custom piping and exhaust tie it all together. TOP RIGHT: As mentioned earlier fuel supply is imperative for a Diesel application, and one of the aspects of its importance is purity. That's why performance-minded folks install a FASS Fuel Air Separator System, like the one in Aron's truck. It makes sure every ounce of fuel is clean, which promotes efficiency in combustion of the fuel. MIDDLE: Underneath, Aron removed a few of the leaves from the rear springs, which allows the truck to transfer weight to the rear tires. Stock 3.73:1 gear sets offer a good ratio for eighth-mile racing, but it's not quite tall enough for the quarter, considering the Cummins' maximum RPM. BOTTOM LEFT: Also onboard Aron's truck is a Nitrous Express system, but it wasn't used during his dyno pulls or best elapsed times to date. Diesel enthusiasts refer to these runs as "fuel only," which means that no additional power adders, aside from the turbocharger, were used. It's the Diesel enthusiast's equivalent to the term "all motor." BOTTOM RIGHT: Seating for Aron's truck consists of racing buckets, but oddly enough, they don't look out of place in a four-wheel-drive pickup. Also, how often do you see a roll cage in a Diesel truck? Aron means business and regularly outruns the roll cage limit of 11.50, so he had Black's install an S&W cage.

the desired amount of slip to allow for optimal turbo spool on the line. At the same time, the converter must apply every ounce of power, so Aron chose Goerend for his transmission and torque converter needs. The Goerend 48RE automatic transmission is packed with billet internals, and uses a stand-alone controller, which is tuned by Injected Engineering. A B&M ratchet shifter selects the gears.

There's no question that the Cummins Diesel engine is a potent design that is very popular with truck enthusiasts. With extremely strong internals and a cylinder head that can handle a ridiculous amount of air, it's no wonder the Cummins engine is being swapped into all sorts of vehicles, including competing brands, like Ford and Chevrolet trucks. Aron's truck is a prime example of a machine that doesn't necessarily try to be a sleeper, but succeeds because of its original purpose and very high level of performance. No one expects a Dodge 2500 pickup to put down more than 700 hp and 1,200 ft-lbs of torque, so even when you consider the truck's hefty weight of 7,200 pounds, elapsed times are remarkably low.

Aron has run his truck at a variety of tracks, and his best elapsed time is 6.93 at 100 mph in the eighth and 10.90 at 122 mph.

By running elapsed times quicker than 11.50, Aron is required to run a roll cage, which is not the average Diesel truck modification. Black's Diesel Performance installed the

S&W roll cage, which essentially offsets Aron's efforts to shed weight from the truck. Although Aron's Dodge Ram has a host of modifications, both inside and out, it proves to be a killer sleeper, as on-lookers don't give it much credit from first glance. When the smoke clears and the ET boards light up with low-10-second times, jaws drop and people begin to take notice. That's what Diesel sleepers are all about, and Aron's Dodge is a fine example.

So what if it has an aggressive look and a big exhaust stack coming out of the bed? It looks like many other Diesel trucks on the road, but makes 722 hp and 1,200 ft-lbs of torque, which is double the stock output. Even at 7,200 pounds, this quad cab has incredible acceleration thanks to four-wheel drive.

At the track, the big red Dodge launches hard, thanks to the softened rear suspension, and has run a best of 6.93 at 100 mph in the eighth, and 10.90 at 122 mph in the quarter-mile.

Out in the sticks—

No One Expects This Country Boy's Truck
to Lay Down a Number

Many Diesel performance trucks rely on a four-wheel-drive platform to hook up off the line, since these heavy-duty trucks suffer from poor weight transfer by design. Garland has it figured out, as his truck makes lots of power and uses it efficiently at the track.

Pros
- Stock body and paint
- Stock wheels and tires
- Two-wheel-drive platform

Cons
- Nitrous bottle in bed

When you live in a small town in the South it's common to see more trucks than regular passenger cars on an average day. Many are work trucks—for the most part, everyone loves a good pickup because of its practicality—but it's also simply part of the culture to have a truck or two at your disposal, even if your line of work doesn't require it. The 1997 Ford F-250 on these pages fits in this segment of society, as its location in middle Tennessee makes it just another truck on the road, on first glance. Closer inspection reveals a laundry list of modifications made by Swamp's Diesel Performance, which specializes in Ford Power Stroke applications.

Garland Scott owns the extended-cab Ford, and this is one of many configurations the truck has been through over the past few years. He's happy with the current setup, as it certainly performs at the track, but still offers plenty of street-friendly qualities, such as averaging an adequate 13 mpg on an 800-mile road trip. It's dependable and strong, thanks to the custom 7.3-liter Power Stroke Diesel engine under the hood, which is a product of many hours from the entire crew at Swamp's. There's no question as to the truck's horsepower, even with no dyno-proven figures. Garland believes in using the blacktop dyno as his guide, and judging by the truck's 7.51-second blast through the eighth-mile, it's making nearly 800 hp and well over 1,000 ft-lbs of torque at the rear wheels.

This particular truck is unique because of its driveline, as most Diesel trucks that frequent the drag strip feature four-wheel drive, which enables a quicker launch, with less chance of tire spin. Garland doesn't mind the two-wheel-drive platform, as it greatly reduces rolling resistance and overall weight, even though the estimated weight of his truck is 6,700 pounds. He has great success with the stock rear leaf springs, only adding a pair of Edelbrock shock absorbers to the original setup. Swamp's installed a pair of custom traction bars to eliminate axle wrap, a common problem with nearly every leaf-spring-equipped vehicle out there.

The front suspension is completely stock, as is the original braking system, which consists of discs up front and drums out back. Rolling stock for the street consists of aluminum eight-lug wheels, wrapped in Michelin rubber, sized at 235/85R16,

TOP LEFT: When it's time to hit the track, Garland bolts this pair of massive Hoosier slicks to the rear of his truck. The race rubber measures 32 inches tall and 14½ inches wide, and mounts to a set of custom Bart steel wheels. This is one of the secrets behind this truck's performance at the track. TOP RIGHT: Mounted atop the engine with a HyperMax H2E turbo mounting kit is a Schwitzer S400 turbocharger, which uses a 74-mm wheel and 1.15 A/R exhaust housing to send massive quantities of air into the Power Stroke V-8 engine. Judging by the eighth-mile times, horsepower levels are close to the 800 mark. MIDDLE: The stock Ford 10¼-inch rear end is suspended by the stock leaf springs and cushioned by a set of Edelbrock shock absorbers. The only real modification to increase traction is the custom traction bars, which prevent axle wrap—a common problem with leaf-spring rear suspension. Also notice the driveshaft safety loop. BOTTOM: Under the hood is a 7.3-liter Power Stroke Diesel engine, built by the folks at Swamp's Diesel Performance. It features custom pistons, ported heads with larger valves, and stiffer valvesprings, so it's a considerably high-end build in the Diesel realm. Fuel system upgrades are plentiful to support the larger turbocharger.

but at the track, Garland relies on a pair of massive Hoosier slicks. The sticky slicks measure 32 inches tall and 14½-inches wide, and mount to a set of custom Bart Wheels. Thanks to a trusty Lincoln locker and a 3.55:1 gear set, the Ford 10¼-inch rear end sends equal power to each rear tire and sends this hefty pickup into motion.

Providing motivation for Garland's Ford truck is a 7.3-liter Power Stroke Diesel engine. Johnny Farrow of Swamp's performed the engine build, fitting the filled block with a balanced rotating assembly, which consists of a stock crankshaft, stock rods, and a set of ceramic-coated Mahle pistons. Johnny used ARP main studs to keep the crankshaft snug, and also installed a set of A1 Technologies alloy cylinder head studs. The cylinder heads are ported, and feature a multi-angle valve job with larger valves, stiffer valvesprings from Comp Cams, and a set of Smith Brothers pushrods. The camshaft is stock, as are the exhaust manifolds.

Big power comes from the custom Schwitzer S400 turbocharger, which features a 74-mm inducer, an 88-mm exducer, and a 1.15 A/R exhaust housing. Swamp's used a HyperMax H2E turbo mounting kit to make easy work of the larger turbocharger, and routed the custom piping to a stock intercooler from a 2000 Ford Super Duty pickup. A maximum boost number is unknown for Garland's truck, but he knows it pegs a 60-psi gauge at full boost, so that tells you something about the amount of air being forced down the engine's throat. With great quantities of air comes lots of fuel, and Swamp's fitted Garland's truck with a sumped fuel tank from a Ford Lightning, and added an Aeromotive A1000 fuel pump. Other fuel system upgrades consist of a Donaldson 2-micron filter, 300-cc injectors with twin high-pressure pumps to drive the injectors. The fuel injector drive module has been modified by increasing voltage from 115 to 140, and increasing the output from 8 to 12 amps.

Jonathan Ryan at Swamp's tuned the 7.3 using Minotaur software from Power Hungry Performance, while most of the driving duties have been left up to another Swamp's employee, Dan Morin. The automatic transmission is a 4R100 unit, built by Brian's Truck Shop in Lead Hill, Arkansas, and equipped with bulletproof internals. Power application is handled by a Precision Industries triple-disc torque converter, which stalls to 3,000 rpm on the line. The stock column shifter controls the transmission and retains the truck's stock appearance. Other notable details are the completely stock body and paint job, as well as the stock cloth interior. The only real signs of speed are the dash-mounted three-gauge pod, and the nitrous bottle, mounted in the bed.

The nitrous system is from Nitrous Express but it was not in use during this truck's fastest run. Dan's best pass in Garland's truck resulted in a 7.51-second elapsed time at 91.8

mph at a local eighth-mile drag strip. Just for reference, a mid-7-second pass generally equates to 11.70s or so in the quarter-mile. Much of the credit for getting this truck off the line without leaving a plume of white smoke behind it goes to the big Hoosier slicks, as regular radials would never stand a chance of hooking. If Garland drove his truck on the street with his drag tires, some folks would assume this truck means business, but when the stock wheels and tires go on, there's no way to tell this truck is any different than your average 1997 Ford. It certainly doesn't look like a mid-7-second eighth-mile truck, which means Garland doesn't have any trouble finding a race. Corvettes and Cobras beware, because this country boy doesn't mind showing you his taillights in a light-hearted traffic light showdown. Just because Garland is from a small town in Tennessee doesn't mean his truck is used for hauling manure—it hauls something else these days...

An open door reveals a stock-appearing interior, complete with a column shifter and all of the truck's stock equipment. It does have a three-gauge pod mounted to the dash, but that's the end of the line when it comes to interior modifications. This truck slips under the radar very easily with its all-stock look.

In Garland's hometown of Woodbury, Tennessee, it's not uncommon to have a Diesel truck at your disposal, whether it's strictly for work or for pleasure. His 1997 F-250 blends in with the crowd, but doesn't disappoint in the horsepower department. With eighth-mile elapsed times in the mid 7s at more than 90 mph, it certainly under promises and over delivers.

Economics 101

In the 1950s and 1960s, the majority of cars in the United States were domestically built, but it was quickly apparent that imported makes and models were growing in popularity due to their outstanding efficiency. This led American auto manufacturers to follow suit, building economically minded cars and trucks to compete with foreign manufacturers like Honda, Toyota, and Datsun. Though many of the cars featured in this book are built from full-size domestic cars, there's something to be said about a great economy car sleeper, since these cars are a huge percentage of cars on the road today. When most folks modify economy cars, they add a body kit, large-diameter wheels, and colorful graphics making it stand out from the crowd, which works directly in favor of the sleeper enthusiasts out there because even the most savvy car guys wouldn't think twice about a stock-appearing Honda Accord.

Economy car sleepers are easy to come by, since you start with an average, everyday car, like a Honda Accord. This Acura is a prime example of a great sleeper platform, as it can be outfitted with the power adder of your choice or possibly an engine swap.

Keep in mind that foreign auto manufacturers build sports cars, like the Nissan 370Z, so these types of cars are generally out of the question when it comes to using them for a sleeper build. However, there are millions of average, everyday cars out there that have the potential to be fast and still blend in. Successfully building a sleeper out of an import or even a domestic economy car can be challenging, but it's the absolute best way to get under a car guy's skin. Even if your car is decked out in gaudy body modifications, outrunning a domestic car is always a huge accomplishment, and a huge embarrassment for the guy in the other lane. Try it with a totally stock-looking econo-box and it's even more fun!

There's no doubt that it's best to go with the lightest combination possible, since you're dealing with smaller engines than most full-size cars, and you need all the help you can get with the power-to-weight ratio. The advantage to most economy cars is the fact that they're naturally smaller (and therefore lighter) than the larger and more luxurious models. Let's face it—today's muscle cars are toting around 4,000 pounds of mass, so if you take a 2,000-pound Honda and drop in a 200-hp engine, you're in the hunt. Add a nitrous system or a turbocharger and you have a Mustang-killing machine. And

the great thing about building a sleeper from an economy car platform is the lack of memorable details, which translates to the opponent forgetting about your car and falling for it again. Some of the cars in this book would fool someone once, but a red flag would go up on the second go 'round. However, with an import or basic economy car, it's not going to stick in the brain of most car guys, especially if you go the extra mile and get rid of any items (such as decals or other modifications) that would refresh his memory from a quick glance at your car.

Finding horsepower in an import or domestic economy car isn't all that hard, and many engine platforms work really well in combination with turbochargers or nitrous injection. Honda is the most notable manufacturer when it comes to average automobiles, and it also has a great number of potent four-cylinder engines that have been hurting the feelings of muscle car owners for the past 15 years or so.

It all started in the mid 1990s with its series of engines that were very popular from the factory, but easily gained horsepower with the right modifications. One of those is the H22, a DOHC four-cylinder engine that originally came in the Honda Prelude and some Accord models. Depending on the year and model, you're looking at roughly 200 hp, and

It may not have been marketed as an economy car, but the Pontiac Grand Prix had a front-wheel-drive design that is very similar to many other economy cars and imports. Pontiac released a great number of supercharged V-6 models, such as this GTP, which are capable of making 400 hp and running well into the 11s.

the benefits of variable valve timing and lift electronic control (VTEC). Most domestic car owners poke fun at VTEC, but it's honestly one of the greatest innovations in the automotive industry, as it allows the car to run efficiently during regular driving, but the system advances the timing and increases valve lift under hard acceleration. It's the best of both worlds, but it's proven to be difficult to deal with, when you start adding boost or nitrous into the equation.

Other manufacturers have potent engines of their own, and one of the most popular platforms has proven to be the Mitsubishi Eclipse and Eagle Talon from the 1990s. These sister cars were built by Diamond-Star Motors (DSM), and they are a great source for horsepower, as some of the models came with turbocharged engines. With the potential for 300 hp without much effort, the DSM engines are still popular with the import crowd. Add to that the fact that some DSMs featured all-wheel drive, and you have a serious combination that hooks hard off the line and keeps pulling on the big end. These cars are a little more recognizable, even in stock form, but still sneaky enough to stay under the radar if they appear to be stock. Folks still use these cars as everyday drivers, so they blend in, and they're old enough to look slightly run-

down in terms of paint condition, which works in the favor of a sleeper enthusiast. Sometimes, a rough-looking driver is the best way to build a sleeper, especially if you'd rather spend money on speed parts instead of bodywork and paint.

Speaking of rough-looking drivers, you can't go wrong with an older economy car, like the Chevy Vega or Ford Pinto. These platforms are super light, and feature a rear-wheel-drive design, so all it takes to stuff a V-8 under the hood is a torch and a welder. Other economy cars, such as the Ford Maverick work well in this situation because of the slightly healthier underpinnings, which reduce the chances of driveline breakage, and help in the traction department. You quickly find that with a lightweight car, traction is your biggest obstacle, so it doesn't hurt to use a heavier platform like the Maverick or possibly an early Falcon or Chevy II. The best way to pull off the look if you opt for a car from the 1960s is to use a four-door platform or a station wagon, as opposed to the more popular two-door hardtop models, which were commonly used for racing. Domestic economy cars are certainly trickier when it comes to fooling the opposition, so stock hubcaps are a must, and rough, original paint helps keep the car off the average car guy's radar.

Don't think that economy cars are strictly imports, as American auto manufacturers played a big part in the econobox trend. And though drag racers have used the Chevrolet Vega for years, the compact, rear-wheel-drive cars make great sleepers if you can find an all-original survivor and stuff a big engine in it.

No matter which platform you choose, an economy car sleeper is a great entry-level project car, as it gives you the option to keep power levels low, since most cars of this nature are light. As mentioned earlier, it's easier to fool someone with a car that looks like it should have never been fast, than a car that is simply "faster than it looks." For instance, a stock-appearing Mustang GT with a supercharger may be faster than it looks, but it's nowhere near as great of a sleeper as a rusty and ragged Ford Pinto with a small-block Ford and nitrous.

You have to consider the car's original purpose and determine the severity of your build from there. If the car originally came with 87 hp, then a 200-hp engine will make it feel like a rocket ship and it will definitely surprise your opponent. You won't get the same result with a car that is regularly considered a fast car from the factory, so economy cars make sense as potent street sleeper candidates.

Ford had its own economy cars, which have great potential for a sleeper build. The general public never considered the Pinto a great-looking car, but the indestructible 2.3-liter, four-cylinder engine is very capable of big power, when combined with a turbocharger. You can go 11s with a stock block and cylinder head with the right amount of boost.

The Chrysler Corporation's offerings to the economy car market were plentiful, and it outfitted several of its models with turbochargers in the 1980s and 1990s, giving them a sliver of hope in the performance world. This example is a Dodge Omni GLH, which produced nearly 200 hp in stock form.

Almost Antique—
A 20-Year-Old Economy Car Makes a Good Sleeper

First-generation Eagle Talons are rather outdated in terms of style, but make plenty of power, making them perfect for a quality sleeper buildup. This one rolls on stock wheels and tires, and doesn't give you any reason to believe it's not completely stock, aside from the front-mount intercooler.

Pros
- Outdated styling
- All-wheel drive
- No cage

Cons
- Common performance platform

If there's one thing that's certain about the endless argument between domestic car owners and import car owners, it's that domestic cars eventually grow into valuable pieces of automotive history. Most people don't consider imports to be classic cars, unless you consider the world of European sports cars, but the subject at hand is a bit of a hybrid—it was offered by an American auto manufacturer, but had a parent company of Japanese descent. Known as Diamond-Star Motors, this company was a joint venture from the Chrysler Corporation and Mitsubishi, and the vehicles were actually manufactured in the United States. The three Diamond-Star offerings were the Mitsubishi Eclipse, the Plymouth Laser, and this car—the Eagle Talon.

At the time, these three offerings were stylish, but the appearance package does little to please the eye these days. Originally sporty, these cars just don't fit in with modern-day styling, but actually had a fair amount of horsepower for the early 1990s. The base-model cars were never equipped with high-horsepower engines, but the Eagle Talon pictured here is a TSI model, which means it featured a turbocharged engine from the factory. Some TSI models had the conventional front-wheel-drive setup, but this one is a highly desirable AWD (all-wheel-drive) edition, which proves to be hard to find. It's a great advantage when racing from a dead stop, as the all-wheel drive keeps both ends digging, while front-wheel-drive models lose traction or wheel-hop under hard acceleration, even

with stock boost. Tom Tharp knows DSMs well, and has a pretty cool sleeper with this 1991 Eagle Talon TSI.

The car is simple and clean, wearing its original coat of white paint and rolling on a set of 16x7-inch aluminum wheels from a 1996 Eclipse. Tom admits that steelies and hubcaps would've added to the sleeper appeal, but he stuck with the stock Eclipse wheels because the car still tends to slip beneath the radar in its current state. Tom bought the car in the summer of 2005 for $1,000 and didn't waste any time digging into it. The car makes a lot of horsepower these days, and it doesn't do much to stir the pot within the racing crowd with its stock appearance. However, as soon as Tom makes a pass, all bets are off, as the Talon generally traps 100 mph in the eighth-mile, which equates to a wickedly fast car on the street.

Originally, horsepower levels came in just under 200, which is a respectable figure for an economy car. However, the AWD versions were fairly hefty, in comparison to other compact cars of the early 1990s, so the power-to-weight ratio wasn't exactly optimal in stock form. The turbocharged 2.0-liter, four-cylinder engine, commonly known as the 4G63t, is a strong foundation for horsepower, as it responds very well to boost, especially when a larger turbo is installed. To prepare for big power, Tom sent the engine to Buschur Racing in Wakeman, Ohio, where the bottom end was treated to a set of JE forged pistons that resulted in a 9.0:1 static compression ratio. The stock crankshaft and connecting rods are still in use, as is the stock cylinder head, but it received custom porting to the intake runners and exhaust ports to greatly increase airflow. The valves are Ferrea titanium units, motivated by a pair of HKS 272 camshafts that feature 195 degrees of duration at .050-inch lift.

Outgoing air flows into the stock Evo III exhaust manifold, and then into a Forced Performance 68HTA turbocharger, which is a Mitsubishi/Garrett hybrid. The turbo is suited specifically to the 4G63t engine to create quick spool times and big power and torque numbers throughout the RPM range. An air-to-air intercooler rides behind the front bumper to cool the intake charge, while an owner-built water/methanol injection system further decreases air intake temperatures, allowing for more boost. A MagnaFlow muffler rides out back to keep noise levels to a minimum, and the car's fuel system consists of a Walbro 255-liter-per-hour pump and an Aeromotive fuel regulator, which feeds a set of 880-cc fuel injectors. The stock intake manifold has been swapped for a Magnus Motorsports sheet metal unit, which sends massive amounts of air into the ported head. It runs on 93-octane pump gas and is very efficient, with fuel mileage in the high 20s.

Tom has never strapped the car to a dyno, but he estimates 525 hp, using calculations from the car's weight and trap speed in the eighth-mile. Sending the power to all four wheels is a stock-style Mitsubishi 5-speed manual transmission, modified by Shepherd Transmission to withstand the upgraded power. Internal modifications include upgraded synchronizers, shifting forks, and first and second gears. The gears and forks are cryo-treated for durability. Tom uses an ACT 2600 pressure plate in combination with a stock Mitsubishi clutch disc to connect the engine and transmission.

Since AWD cars hook up well from the factory, the need for serious suspension modifications was minimal, but Tom still upgraded the struts and springs to increase the car's handling capabilities and help keep the BFGoodrich G-Force Sport radials (215/55ZR16) glued to the pavement. Gear ratios are stock at 3.73:1, but the stock rear differential didn't hold up to a hard launch, and gave up on him. He upgraded it from a stock three-bolt design to a stronger four-bolt rear end.

The car relies mostly on its stock appearance to fly under the radar, but savvy car guys are well aware of the potency of these AWD cars. Tom's Talon is just old enough to be considered outdated by the younger crowd, and plain enough to stay out of the muscle car guys' line of vision. Tom enjoys driving the car on the street, but isn't afraid to abuse it on the track. He competed in a local "import vs. domestic" event at an eighth-mile track, and got kicked out after one pass because the car doesn't have a cage. He ran a 7.41 with a slow 60-foot time, and trapped 101 mph, so the track crew knew it had 6s in it if he could get it hooked up. They didn't give him another chance, so speculation of its potential is the only real proof of the car's performance. Judging by the car's trap speed, when translated to the quarter-mile, Tom's Talon is very capable of running high 10s.

Having owned the car for more than five years, Tom is accustomed to upgrading parts and pieces as he goes, but a roll cage would certainly decrease the car's sleepiness, so he's unsure about future plans. He could put a cage in it and turn up the wick, or keep it stock and retain the car's awesome sleeper status. Stock and simple, the car doesn't get a lot of attention, until it lights up all four BFGs as boost levels rise. That's what the sleeper game is all about, and Tom's car is a great example.

Under the hood is a turbocharged 2.0-liter, four-cylinder engine that is commonly called the 4G63t. It's widely known that these engines love boost, so Tom outfitted it with a Forced Performance 68HTA turbocharger and upgraded the fuel system accordingly to produce approximately 525 hp and run on 93-octane pump gas.

Inside, the Talon is completely stock, with the original cloth interior. There are no obvious modifications, which is another key element for economy car sleepers, because owners who modify these cars tend to get carried away. The whole "ricer" movement gave imports and tuner cars a bad name, but they're undeniably impressive on the street and at the track.

Bait and Switch—
An Already Sneaky Maverick Gets Even Faster

The Ford Maverick has been used in drag racing for years, but finding a survivor like this one makes for a great sleeper. This example has an interesting story, as its owner first installed a turbocharged 2.3-liter engine, only to swap it for a turbocharged 460-ci big-block Ford engine without changing the car's outward appearance.

Pros
- Stock body and ratty paint
- Small tires
- No cage or visible safety equipment

Cons
- Common platform for performance builds
- Aggressive stance

It's always important to keep your sleeper fresh, because eventually, most local guys become wise to your tactics. When you feel like everyone knows that your car is pretty fast, even though it looks stock, that's when you should switch things up a bit. In the case of this Ford Maverick, its owner, Josh Dillon, decided to up the game big time, going from 140 ci to a whopping 460, without changing the looks of his car. The plan was to retain the car's appearance, so the folks that thought they knew the car would be drastically surprised the second time around.

Josh's first buildup was fairly simple, as he jerked the 2.3-liter four-cylinder engine out of a 1988 Ford Thunderbird Turbo Coupe and stuffed it between the shock towers of his 1973 Maverick. Although it required lots of homework to get the fuel system and computer to keep up with the new setup, Josh built the car in a matter of months and drove it to and from work, getting 29 mpg along the way. The setup was straightforward, and very budget friendly. It involved a bone-stock, 250,000-mile four-cylinder engine, and 26 pounds of boost from a Holset HE351CW turbocharger, which originally assisted a Cummins Diesel inside a 2005 Dodge Ram pickup.

In this configuration, the car weighed 2,725 pounds, so the horsepower-to-weight ratio was on target for an efficient and sneaky sleeper. The first street kill consisted of outrunning a Fox-Body Mustang coupe, which had normal bolt-on modifications and 4.11:1 gears. The second was a modified Honda S2000, but an encounter with local law enforcement took a bit of the glory out of the win. Josh's street racing days may be over, but he still doesn't mind having a little fun on the back roads. In this configuration, the car sounded rough, because any four-cylinder with an open down pipe takes on a certain tractor exhaust note, but it worked to his advantage when it came to surprising the opposition.

And just because the engine had lots of miles on it didn't mean Josh would cut it any slack. His driving technique at the drag strip consisted of 6,500-rpm clutch dumps, which still only resulted in a best of 1.89-second 60-foot times because of the lack of boost in first gear. The car ran a best of 8.000 at 89 mph in the eighth-mile with this setup, which equates to mid 12s in the quarter. Josh could've greatly improved his track times with an automatic transmission, among other modifications, but he didn't want to exceed the limits of the 2.3 in an effort to gain a tenth or so. He wanted way more power, and knew the only way to get it was to spend thousands of dollars on the 140-ci four-cylinder, or start over with a new setup. It made the most sense to swap to a turbocharged V-8, and Josh took the same budget-friendly, junkyard approach.

Like many car guys, Josh bases his fun factor on many things, one of which is money. His mindset is to build what he wants without breaking the bank. This means he fabricates pretty much every aspect of the project, only forking out cash for the important stuff, like turbocharger equipment. With the four-cylinder, Josh had a total investment of $3,000, so to say he got his money's worth out of that combination would be an understatement. Swinging for the fence, Josh went for a big-block Ford, and knew that it would involve a little more money and a lot more time. When all was said and done with the new setup, he still had less than $5,000 tied up in the car because he built it all at home.

Now the car weighs 3,000 pounds and has an estimated 600 hp—a combination that is a terror on the street. Rolling into the throttle at nearly any speed results in tire spin on the street, which is good because hooking hard would destroy the stock 8-inch rear end. The drag strip isn't this car's strongest area, due to several factors, including the torque converter, the rear end, and the limits of the stock head castings. It works well on the street, and the end result is a very-low-budget car that provides the same thrill as a big-buck, high-end car.

When Josh swapped the 2.3-liter four-cylinder for the 460-ci big-block, it was no easy task. Mavericks are known for their cramped engine bay, thanks to the large shock towers, so he knew those two pesky details would have to go. This meant he'd completely do away with the stock front suspension and utilize a Mustang II setup instead. The new front suspension required lots of fabrication, but Josh handled every bit of it in his home garage, with very limited tools. He made good use of a cutting torch, a MIG welder, and a grinder, and had the car back on its wheels in a couple of weeks. The change in suspension also meant a change in the

LEFT: When the car was first completed, this was its powerplant, a mildly modified 2.3-liter, four-cylinder engine from a 1988 Thunderbird Turbo Coupe. Josh ditched the original turbo for a Holset HE351CW unit, which made 26 pounds of boost in this application. This combination was a great conversation piece, but didn't make enough power for Josh's tastes. RIGHT: In order to make the power Josh wanted, and keep the junkyard theme, he needed to make some room in the engine bay. He used a 460-ci big-block from a 1970s Ford pickup, and completely redid the front suspension, swapping to a Mustang II setup. This required lots of cutting, grinding, and welding, but it was worth the effort.

LEFT: After installing a new crossmember, spring perches, and control arm mounts, Josh needed to test fit the engine to check oil pan clearance and see if the firewall needed any modification. Luckily, the firewall only needed minor persuasion, but the oil pan and oil pickup tube had to be changed to fit. RIGHT: With the engine assembled and almost ready for installation, you can see that Josh took the minimalist route when it came to accessories. He eventually swapped the cast-iron intake for an Edelbrock Performer to save several pounds and reap the benefits of much better airflow than the stock casting.

Installing the engine was not the end of the fabrication process, as Josh then needed to build the turbo system around the big-block Ford. He cut up a set of headers and turned them around to exit at the front, and then fabricated the piping that leads to and from the turbocharger and intercooler.

With loads of torque, burnouts are a common practice for Josh's Maverick. The really fun part is when he's rolling along at 45 mph, and rolls into the throttle. The boost hits like a freight train and creates quite a struggle for the rear tires to stay glued to the pavement. Cheap thrills are the best kind.

This car and its owner certainly give you the street racer vibe, with no dyno numbers and no track times to speak of with the new combination. The fact that the car looks exactly the same as it did when it had the four-cylinder will ultimately fool a lot of people and it's already proven to be a fun ride.

steering system, as he swapped the original box and linkage for a less intrusive rack-and-pinion. The additional engine bay room allowed Josh to lower the engine into place and fabricate new mounts without any issues. The C6 automatic transmission required a different crossmember than the old 5-speed, so he took care of that with a piece of square tubing.

With the engine and transmission mounted, he began fabricating the turbo system, and implemented a BorgWarner S475 turbocharger. The compressor side inducer is 75 mm in diameter, while the exhaust housing features an 87-mm wheel with a 1.32 A/R. Since the turbo features a divided T6 housing, Josh was able to block off one side of the exhaust inlet, which makes for a quicker spool time on a stock engine, such as his big-block. The wastegate is a Chinese eBay special, as is the blow-off valve, so he didn't lay down too much cash to get the turbo system up and running.

The engine is from a mid-1970s Ford pickup, so it was no powerhouse from the factory, but Josh rebuilt it with a slightly larger camshaft to move the power band to his liking. He then opened up the exhaust ports in an effort to increase outgoing airflow, while leaving the intake runners in stock form. The intake is an Edelbrock Performer cast aluminum piece, which is only 1 inch higher than the stock cast-iron manifold. Hood clearance is very important, as Josh didn't want to put a scoop on the car. Atop the intake is a Holley carburetor that Josh disassembled and modified to handle blow-through boost. Josh equipped the Maverick with a Walbro 255-gph fuel pump and an Aeromotive fuel pressure regulator to keep the big-block from leaning out under boost and then upgraded the ignition with a Mallory control unit, which also includes a two-step and timing-retard feature.

Most folks think he's crazy, but he left the stock 8-inch rear end under the car for the time being, and plans to upgrade when it breaks. This isn't always the right approach but it works for Josh, as the stock torque converter keeps the car from boosting on the starting line, which gives the driveline much less stress than most turbo combinations. The key to hiding the car's horsepower has been retaining the stock wheels and hubcaps, as well as resisting the urge to fix the body's problem areas and repaint it. The car grabs a surprising amount of attention, despite its granny-like flavor, but it often surprises folks when Josh rolls into the throttle.

Obviously, going from a turbocharged four-cylinder backed by a 5-speed manual transmission, to a turbocharged big-block and automatic is a big change, in terms of driving habits, and Josh learned a lot during the switch. The car certainly doesn't get 29 mpg anymore, but it has a lot more power, and even more potential if Josh wants to upgrade the big-block with aftermarket cylinder heads or possibly set up the rear suspension for serious drag strip use.

Ego Killer—
This Average-Looking Honda Accord Hurts Feelings on a Regular Basis

Sleepy Factor: 10 out of 10

Driving or walking past this Honda Accord on a street corner would be quite the norm. It's a four-door sedan, and it's more than 15 years old, so there really isn't any interest in a stock-appearing 1994 Honda Accord, which is exactly what Brian wants. Being noticed wasn't part of the idea behind this ego-killing sleeper. *(Photo courtesy Josh Mackey)*

Pros
- Stock wheels and hubcaps
- No cage
- No body modifications
- Blacked-out intercooler

Cons
- None

By now, you understand that a proper sleeper must look completely stock, or at least look like an average vehicle, even if it has minor exterior modifications. Sometimes, a diehard sleeper enthusiast chooses a totally unsuspecting vehicle to build, and then goes the extra mile to keep the vehicle's original appearance. You've seen muscle cars with this treatment, and cars that might normally raise a question in a car guy's mind, but the 1994 Honda Accord on these pages is not this type of sleeper. It's a super sleeper with its econo-box flavor and original exterior details from front to back. The fact of the matter is that this Accord would be considered a sleeper, even if it only made 200 hp, yet it has put down 750 hp to the front wheels, which takes it to a whole new level of sleepiness.

Brian Spiker set out to build the ultimate Honda sleeper when he grew tired of the constant bother from thieves who are attracted to obviously modified performance cars. He also did a little street racing on the side, so the stock appearance would help his car blend into society if law enforcement got involved. The fact that millions of similar-looking Honda Accords roam the highways in the United States proves that Brian's efforts were well worth the time, money, and work. An impressive list of components and a highly talented group of individuals made the build a reality, and Brian's willingness to give up his speed secrets made it a perfect fit for this chapter on economy cars.

It all starts with a potent engine combination, which is based on the popular H22A4 engine, which originally came in the Honda Prelude and produced 197 hp and 156 ft-lbs of torque from the factory. The engine is one of many Honda four-cylinder engines that feature VTEC technology, which is a variable timing system that helps the engine's efficiency at low speeds, and gives it great power when the skinny pedal hits the floor. With this as his base, Brian sent the H22 to D&G Machine to have the block bored and new GE HD sleeves installed. The final bore size is 90 mm, up from the original 87 mm, which brings total displacement to 2.3 liters.

Other bottom end modifications are the Kaizenspeed balance shaft eliminator kit, Eagle connecting rods, and CP pistons. ARP fasteners were used throughout, including the head studs. Fastened to the block is a stock cylinder head casting, with mild port work from Mike Dope at D&G Machine. The valves are from Ferrea, with Supertech valvesprings, and titanium retainers, while the camshafts are stock JDM units.

TOP: Sitting in traffic among other economy cars, this Honda doesn't reveal any signs of speed. It has stock steel wheels and hubcaps, and the body is completely original, front to back. The only aspects you may spot are the M&H tires, which are heftier than the OEMs. *(Photo courtesy Josh Mackey)* MIDDLE: Under the hood is an H22A4 engine, which has been bored to 2.3 liters and fit with a ported cylinder head. The car didn't originally come with this engine, so Brian used an engine conversion kit from Explicit Speed Performance to make easy work of the swap. Stock JDM-spec camshafts motivate the aftermarket valves. *(Photo courtesy Josh Mackey)* BOTTOM LEFT: Like many sleepers, the secret to power lies in the turbocharger system. Brian's Accord features a Tial T04ZR 67-mm ball bearing turbocharger, fit with twin Tial 44-mm wastegates. The header is hand built from stainless steel, and the intake piping is made from aluminum. Total horsepower and torque is 750 and 575, respectively. *(Photo courtesy Josh Mackey)* BOTTOM RIGHT: You're looking at the only serious red flag on this entire car—a large tachometer with a shift light. It's a common part on performance cars of any kind, and it's necessary to keep the RPM in check, so Brian let it slide. Even if someone spotted the tach, no one would assume this car makes 750 hp. *(Photo courtesy Josh Mackey)*

There's no question that the engine alone would handle itself well in Brian's Accord, but the secret to his big horsepower is a Tial T04ZR ball-bearing turbocharger. This turbocharger features a 67-mm inducer, which is the optimal size for Brain's H22 engine and uses twin Tial 44-mm wastegates to control boost. An equal-length header is constructed from stainless steel and feeds the turbo, while owner-made 3-inch aluminum piping goes to and from the blacked-out intercooler. All this piping leads to a BDL 68-mm billet throttle body, which mounts to the Skunk2 Pro Series intake manifold. Exhaust from the turbo consists of a 4-inch stainless steel down pipe that meets an aluminum exhaust system, fit with a MagnaFlow race core muffler. The fuel system features a Walbro 255 in-tank fuel pump as well as a Bosch 044 inline pump, which feature upgraded wiring and dedicated relays to make sure the H22 doesn't lean out. The fuel pressure regulator is from SX Automotive, which feeds the Golden Eagle Pro fuel rails and FIC/Bosch 1100 injectors. Lighting the fire is an MSD 7AL-2 ignition box and an MSD Blaster SS coil.

When all was said and done, the H22 engine had taken on a new attitude, so engine management duties were handed over to an eCtune system. On the dyno, the stock-appearing Accord put down 520 hp and 380 ft-lbs of torque to the wheels on 92-octane pump gas with a maximum of 17 pounds of boost. By draining the pump gas, and adding a few gallons of C16 racing fuel, Brian was able to run 35 pounds of boost, which netted a total of 750 hp and 575 ft-lbs of torque to the wheels. Obviously, with this kind of power, there's no need in becoming attached to your transmission, as it's bound to self-destruct if left stock. Brian's solution is a custom-forged, straight-cut Saenz gear set, among many other internal modifications. A Competition Clutch twin-disc clutch set applies the power, while an OBX limited slip differential disperses it to the OEM Prelude axles, which are under lots of pressure when boost hits.

To keep the sleeper theme going, Brian resisted the temptation to install lightweight racing wheels and retained the stock Accord steel wheels, and popped a set of 1998 Accord hubcaps into place. For the street, he uses M&H Racemaster DOT tires sized at 235/50-15, while track time requires the use of M&H 26x8.5-inch slicks. Suspension modifications consist of Skunk2 coilovers and an Explicit Speed Performance traction bar, but the car doesn't sit incredibly low, or have an aggressive look.

Considering the horsepower and fairly light weight of the Accord, Brian upgraded the braking system to a set of Brembo discs with Hawk pads and Type R calipers.

Inside, the Accord looks very tame, aside from the tachometer and auxiliary gauges. The seats are stock, and Brian hasn't made any efforts to gut the interior for weight savings, which retains much of the car's "regular daily driver" appearance. With elapsed times in the mid 10s and trap speeds at 145 mph in the quarter-mile, the lack of safety equipment is certainly a concern, so going faster requires a roll cage, safety harnesses, and a few other details to please the tech officials.

Whether Brian is hurting the feelings of an arrogant sports car owner in a heated traffic light battle, or laying down serious numbers on the drag strip, his Accord is a wicked sleeper. He chose the right car from the get-go, gave it tons of power, and retained the stock appearance, which is a rare combination in the world of import performance. The finished product is a perfect 10 on the sleeper scale, and you can bet Brian has used the car's appearance to kill a few egos and prove that Honda performance can be deadly if it's wrapped in the right package.

There's no doubt that Brian's Honda looks stock, but it has run well into the 10-second range in the quarter-mile, meaning that it needs a roll cage to pass tech for the next go-round. M&H DOT tires hook up on the street, while M&H 26x8.5-inch slicks do the job at the track. *(Photo courtesy Josh Mackey)*

No spoiler, no body kit, no stickers—this isn't your average Honda. Brian built it for racing, and he kept the stock appearance to help blend into society. The end result is big power in a nondescript package, which is what street sleepers are all about. The stock hubcaps finish it off nicely. *(Photo courtesy Josh Mackey)*

Modern Muscle

The sleeper genre usually doesn't include that many muscle cars, as these types of machines are generally considered fast, straight from the factory. Any car that is described as muscular is considerably powerful, and features capable underpinnings that help it perform well in regular driving situations, as well as harsh abuse on the street or at the track. It worked this way in the real muscle car era (1964–1972) and it's the same these days with a number of choices of high-performance automobiles on the market. Auto manufacturers keep raising the bar, in terms of horsepower, with models hitting the streets with 500 hp or more, in stock form.

Chrysler Corporation has produced a number of great cars in the past decade, most of which call upon the modern Hemi for power. Late-model performance shops commonly modify, tune, and dyno-test family cars like this Dodge Magnum. Modifying a base-model car to perform as good as or better than an SRT8 edition makes for a cool sleeper.

There's no doubt that modern technology has helped the horsepower department, as it would've taken well over 450 ci, 12:1 compression, and a radical solid-lift camshaft to create that kind of power. Now, it all seems pretty simple, and the fact that you can get more than 20 mpg makes it seem like the "good old days" were overrated. Real modern muscle started in the late 1990s, as General Motors perfected the LS1 engine platform and Ford dialed in the modular engine, so you can have a 15-year-old car and still be considered modern in the grand scheme of things. Mustangs, Camaros, and Corvettes are pushing the limits of being a sleeper, even if they are surprisingly fast, because these models have been consistently proving their performance on paper, and in real world driving situations. However, if the power level is high enough and the car retains its stock appearance, it can be pulled off.

The real meat of modern muscle car sleepers is the V-8-powered family sedans that seem to effortlessly slip under the radar and surprise everyone on a regular basis. The Big Three American auto manufacturers have participated in building factory sleepers, but that's not to say there isn't room for improvement. They didn't intentionally hide the horsepower, but stuffing a 400-hp engine in a four-door sedan has the tendency to naturally be a sleeper. Give it a few modifications and you more than make up the weight difference in performance-oriented cars, thus increasing your chances of coming out on top in a traffic light challenge.

The Chrysler Corporation gave sleeper enthusiasts a few choices by adding the SRT option to the 300C, the Charger, the Magnum, and the Jeep Grand Cherokee. All of these SRT8 models feature the 6.1-liter Hemi engine, which pumps out 425 hp at the crankshaft. And while the SRT8 models feature large-diameter wheels, and special appearance packages, it does little to change the four-door family car appeal. The ultimate sleeper would be a base-model Chrysler product with one of the SRT 6.1 Hemi engines under the hood.

General Motors has been exceptionally crafty with these high-horsepower sedans and sport utility vehicles, proving that a 400-hp family car is perfectly acceptable, and that factory-built sleepers are as cool as ever. A model like the Cadillac CTS-V is a great platform for sleeper enthusiasts, as it's a four-door sedan that looks like your average Caddy until a closer inspection reveals larger brakes, larger wheels, and a potent engine under the hood. The CTS-V may not be an incredible sleeper from the factory, but the potential for big power is ever present, as it is with all LS-powered vehicles. Bolt on a supercharger, or give it a shot of nitrous and you have a Z06-killer with the looks of a luxury sedan. Other options for GM loyalists are the Pontiac G8 GT or the Chevrolet TrailBlazer SS, which are both equipped with LS-style engines that are sneaking up on 400 hp. The G8 GT is a rear-wheel-drive sedan that is rather sporty but still has the bland looks of a family sedan, while the TrailBlazer is available in either two-wheel-drive or all-wheel-drive configurations. Both are great platforms for a sleeper buildup.

Ford also jumped on the bandwagon with its own high-power family sedan, the Taurus SHO. A throwback to the old SHO models, the new version is very different than the standard model. It features the all-new EcoBoost engine, which is a 3.5-liter, direct-injected V-6 with twin turbochargers. This high-tech six-cylinder produces 365 hp from the factory and hardcore car guys have already begun toying with higher boost levels and additional fuel supply. At 4,400 pounds, the all-wheel-drive

General Motors stepped up to the plate with a full-size sedan, packed with an LS-series engine, which produces 400 hp from the factory. While the 2004–2007 Cadillac CTS-V is a bit of a sleeper from the factory, bolting on a supercharger makes it even better. This example has a MagnaCharger and makes 440 hp at the rear wheels—a gain of more than 100 hp.

Another GM product that catches the eye of sleeper enthusiasts is the Chevrolet TrailBlazer SS. Available with a 400-hp LS2 and all-wheel drive, these trucks are quite sneaky from the factory. Minor modifications can certainly increase the sleepy factor, but any of the three common power adders put it over the top.

SHO is on the hefty side of the spectrum, but getting one of these cars into the 12s hasn't been that difficult of a task.

Other types of modern muscle sleepers can be cars that would normally be deemed as fast, straight off the showroom floor. Performance cars like the Camaro Z28 or the Pontiac Trans Am can be considered a sleeper, only if the horsepower greatly exceeds the original figures, and if the appearance is completely stock. This is generally accomplished by installing a power adder, be it nitrous, a supercharger, or a turbocharger.

Late-model engines, such as the LS1 or Ford's modular engine, respond well to power adders, making them great for power, but platforms like the Camaro or Mustang are difficult to build as a sleeper. To pull off the look, it needs stock wheels and tires, and a completely stock body, but even then, the car's potential may shine through the original equipment. Also, the level of horsepower is a determining factor on a modern muscle car's sleeper status. You can't just bolt on a nitrous kit and call your late-model Mustang a sleeper—to succeed at making a muscle car surprisingly fast, you need to double or sometimes triple the horsepower.

Other forms of modern muscle car sleepers are similar to this example, a 2000 Pontiac Trans Am. The car is generally accepted as fast, even in stock form, but this owner went all out on the engine, while retaining the stock wheels and tires. The car has run a best of 10.52 at 133 mph in the quarter-mile.

Under the Pontiac's hood is a 408-ci stroker, based on a 6.0-liter truck engine. Hand-ported 317 cylinder heads inhale a forced intake charge, thanks to an 88-mm turbo kit from Kentucky Turbo and Performance. This car put down 785 hp and 710 ft-lbs of torque to the rear wheels on pump gas and survived the entire 2010 Power Tour.

Having produced turbocharged cars in the past, Ford decided to try it again with the 2010 Taurus SHO. Equipped with a twin-turbo, 3.5-liter V-6 engine that Ford calls the EcoBoost, the new SHO produces 365 hp from the factory. With only a few minor upgrades and a custom tune, these cars have already dipped into the 12s. *(Photo courtesy Ford Motor Company)*

Plain White Wrapper—
A Stock Appearing 2002 Camaro That Runs Low 9s at More Than 150 mph

A car like this 2002 Camaro SS produced 325 hp from the factory, which is quite respectable power and puts all LS1-powered F-body cars into the modern muscle car category. This example rolls on stock wheels and tires, but calls upon a twin-turbo LS1-based engine that makes well over 1,000 hp.

Pros
- Completely stock appearance
- Street-friendly combination
- Four-digit horsepower

Cons
- Powerful car from the factory
- Performance background

There's something to be said for a clean coat of white paint when it comes to building a sleeper. If the car on these pages was bright red or black, it wouldn't be nearly as unassuming, but its white paint does little to make it stand out as a performance car. The car is a 2002 Camaro SS, which is a potent car from the factory with its 325-hp LS1 engine and 3,500-pound curb weight. This setup, when combined with a 6-speed manual transmission has produced lots of tire smoke and fun times behind the wheel, but it didn't cut it for owner Chris Hunter. He didn't cut any corners with the build and the end result is a car that makes well over 1,000 hp at the rear wheels and is still capable of occasional driving on the street.

Some people say a Camaro can never be a sleeper because of its performance roots and pedigree for performance, but Chris pulled off the look with his car by retaining the stock SS wheels, resisting the urge to lower the car's ride height, and tinting the windows to hide the roll cage. He also kept the stock seats and most of the stock interior pieces to keep things simple, and made sure to keep the body all original. A close inspection reveals an air-to-air intercooler mounted behind the grille, but that's the only sign of this car's capabilities. Even if you see the intercooler and assume the car is fast, you wouldn't think about a best elapsed time of 9.06 at 151 mph in the quarter-mile. Of course, that run was on slicks instead of the street tires seen here, but still very impressive considering the car's stock appearance.

Chris went about the build in the appropriate manner, by outfitting the car with a strong rear end, and an efficient suspension setup, designed for drag racing. A Moser 9-inch rear end is first on the list, as it withstands a lot of abuse and features a Trac-Loc differential, 3.50:1 gears, and 31-spline axles. The original suspension design is intact out back, but Chris had Atlanta Performance and Fabrication install a Spohn torque arm and BMR control arms to help plant the rear tires, while a pair of Competition Engineering adjustable shocks assist in the traction department. A rear sway bar keeps the car level during the launch. Up front, the Camaro features a PA tubular K-member, which provides attachment points for the BMR tubular control arms. This front suspension

TOP: To hold up to four-digit horsepower, the owner upgraded to a Moser 9-inch rear end, fit with 3.50:1 gears, and a host of aftermarket equipment. The rear suspension is the stock torque arm configuration, upgraded with a combination of components from Spohn, BMR, and Competition Engineering to increase traction off the line. MIDDLE: The folks at Lamar Walden Automotive transformed the 6.0-liter Vortec truck engine into a bulletproof combination set up specifically for forced induction. Cylinder heads are box-stock Air Flow Research castings, while the cam is a custom-grind hydraulic roller from Comp Cams. The twin turbochargers are Turbonetics T60-1 units, plumbed into an air-to-air intercooler. BOTTOM: Inside Chris' Camaro is a clean and simple interior that is stock aside from the shifter and steering wheel. The six-point roll cage is the only obvious sign that this car is faster than your average Camaro SS. Even if you consider the cage, you may assume the car runs 11s, when it actually runs low 9s.

setup is much lighter than the factory equipment, and the QA1 12-way adjustable coilover offers lots of options when it comes time to adjust suspension travel and weight transfer.

Rolling stock consists of regular street radials mounted to stock SS wheels, which have an aggressive appearance from the factory, but the general thought process of a car guy leads him to believe this Camaro is more than likely a 13-second quarter-mile car. And that's not the case at all. The car does look a lot faster when it's in race trim, as it rolls on a set of Weld Prostar wheels, with skinnies up front and 15x10s on the back. Mickey Thompson slicks did the difficult task of hooking up more than 1,000 hp to the surface.

So, what does it take to produce four-digit horsepower numbers and keep it hidden? It all starts with an LQ9 engine, which is a 6.0-liter Vortec truck engine. This seems like a low-buck approach to such a high-end car, but these engines have proven to withstand lots of power, and this particular combination even used the original crankshaft. Lamar Walden Automotive handled the machining and assembly of the truck engine, boring the cylinders .060-inch larger than stock to create a final displacement of 377 ci. The stock crankshaft sends a set of forged H-beam connecting rods and forged Manley pistons into motion, a combination that creates a 9.5:1 compression ratio when the Air Flow Research (AFR) cylinder heads are bolted into place. The aftermarket heads feature 225-cc intake runners, with 2.08- and 1.60-inch valves, so to say they flow better than a stock set of truck cylinder heads would be a major understatement, even though engine builders like using "317" truck heads for boosted applications. In comparison, a stock set of 317 heads flow 184 cfm on the intake side, while the AFR heads flow 315 cfm at the same amount of lift. The new cylinder heads work in conjunction with a Comp Cams hydraulic roller camshaft, which is a custom grind, designed for boost.

There's no denying this car's horsepower, and the twin Turbonetics turbochargers are the starting point. The turbo installation was a joint effort from Kentucky Turbo and Performance and Atlanta Performance and Fabrication, and the final decision involved mounting the turbos directly in front of the engine, which required modifying the radiator support. This allowed the entire turbo system to stay hidden when the hood is closed. The turbos are T60-1 units, which draw plenty of air from a pair of forward-facing truck exhaust manifolds and feed a Bell intercooler with forced air. The twin-turbo setup required lots of fabrication when it came time to mount the turbos and run the ductwork, and Kentucky Turbo did an awesome job with it. Two TiAL 38-mm wastegates regulate boost while two Bosch fuel pumps keep the boosted Vortec engine from leaning out under boost. On Chris' quickest runs with the car, he had the boost set at 18 psi, and the engine was proven to max out at 26 psi, so there's certainly enough steam to get it in the 8s.

Behind all of this power is a Powerglide transmission, which is one of the least street friendly components in the car, but it's the only way to turn 1,000 hp into 9-second elapsed timess without leaving a pile of parts behind. Glenn McCary built the 2-speed automatic transmission and fitted it with a trans brake. The torque converter is a PTC 9.5-inch unit that stalls to 5,000 rpm on the line. He kept the interior close to stock, only changing the steering wheel and shifter, while hiding the auxiliary gauges behind the A/C vents. It's a full-weight car with no serious weight reduction, aside from the suspension components, which are more than likely offset by the additional weight of the turbochargers and related piping.

It's a very potent combination of parts stuffed in an unassuming package, which makes it a great sleeper when it comes to late-model muscle. With most modern muscle cars producing 300 hp or more, it's hard to take them lightly, even in stock form, but this one quadruples that horsepower number, and still looks bone stock. Thanks to a great combination of components, Chris Hunter's Camaro is a great sleeper, proving that it's possible to take a modern-day muscle car and keep its horsepower a secret.

Tinted windows generally make a vehicle look more aggressive, but the tint on this Camaro's windows hides a six-point roll cage, so it's actually making it look closer to stock. The stock ride height, stock body panels, and stock SS wheels seal the deal and make this 1,000 hp Camaro a great sleeper.

The 2002 Camaro has run a best of 9.06 at 151 mph in the quarter-mile, with only a tire and wheel swap. The car honestly looks fast from the factory, but bottom 9s are never someone's first assumption, so this is a perfect example of a modern muscle sleeper.

```
      Silver Dollar Raceway
       Muscle Car Evolution
      Sunday, March 30, 2008
         PA on 91.9 FM

  3:26 PM
  31/MAR/2008


     Mid State RV            CSR


  ------------ LEFT ..... RIGHT

  Car # ...                  39
  Class ...

  DIAL  ...
  R/T   ...                1.659
  60'   ...                1.399
  330   ...                3.794
  1/8   ...                5.818
  MPH   ...              121.59
  1000  ...                7.569
  1/4   ...                9.061
  MPH   ...              151.07

  Right 1st
  Compulink AUTOSTART ON !!

  Rnd # TO  0/1270

  ..... CompuLink StarTRAK 2007
```

Any late-model Camaro is capable of a burnout like this one, but not all of them can do it from a 60-mph rolling start. Chris' car instantly breaks the tires loose at nearly any speed on the street, making it a blast to drive, but quite hard on tires.

King of the Street—
Would You Expect Low 10s Out of This 4x4 Silverado?

Sleepy Factor: 10 out of 10

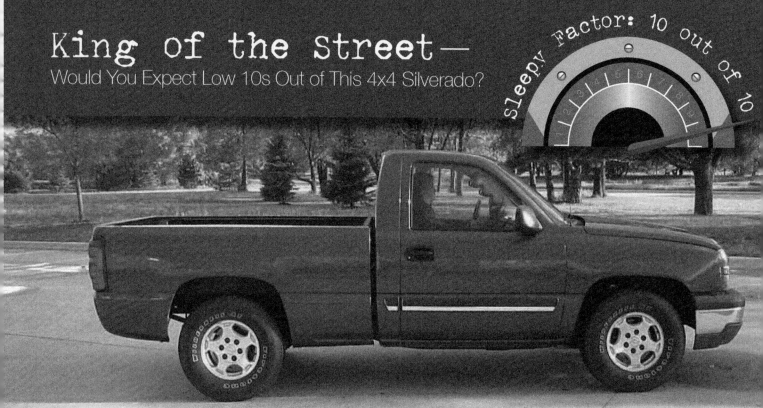

It's a full-size Chevrolet Silverado with four-wheel drive—how fast could it be? Many folks asked themselves this very question moments before being absolutely embarrassed by one of the best sleepers ever built. This Silverado has featured a few engine and turbo combinations, all of which worked well on the street. *(Photo courtesy Kyle Loftis)*

Pros
- Totally blends in
- 1/2-ton 4x4 platform isn't known for performance
- Everything appears to be stock

Cons
- None

As you've learned, the key to building a good sleeper is taking an ordinary vehicle and stuffing lots of power under the hood. Without question, you can't get much more ordinary than a Chevrolet pickup, especially one that is fairly modern, like the thousands that roam the roads in any town every day. And if it's a four-wheel-drive model, it blends into society even better, because most car guys don't give it a second look, unless they're thinking about a potential vehicle to use for towing. This particular truck is very well known, as it's graced the pages of *Hot Rod* magazine multiple times, and spent plenty of time in Internet videos.

The truck was an Internet sensation, and its owner Jim "Parish" Neuenfeldt had a blast, outrunning everything in sight. He fooled just about everyone, and even after the videos reached the Internet, it was still unreal to see a bone stock Silverado outrun supercharged Cobras on the street. It had the stock wheels and all-terrain tires on it, for goodness sake. It caught hundreds of unsuspecting opponents off guard, which led to all sorts of publicity, which usually ruins a vehicle's sleeper status. That's not the case with Parish's truck, since it was such an average-looking daily driver.

Parish says, "I bought the truck in September of 2003 and immediately ripped into it." He started with a single 76-mm turbo setup, and a larger camshaft, which was enough to put the Vortec V-8 into 12-second territory. The "shift-on-the-fly" four-wheel-drive feature made for very hard launches, and he could shift into two-wheel drive down track to reduce rolling resistance. Even on the stock 265/75R16 Firestone tires, he managed 60-foot times in the 1.60s, a marvelous feat for a 5,000-pound pickup truck. The truck's success quickly led to more modifications but Parish retained the stock wheels and tires for quite some time. Eventually, he utilized stickier tires and lighter wheels, but the truck's sleepiest moments occurred during its serious street racing days.

As the setup evolved, Parish had CMotorsports build a 408-ci stroker, which is comprised of a Callies crankshaft, Oliver connecting rods, and JE pistons. Obviously, the rotating assembly is high-end forged equipment to withstand lots of boost, but the block is a stock cast-iron Vortec core. At one point he used stock cylinder heads, but later swapped to a set of Air Flow Research 225 units, which flow tremendous amounts of air, compared to the stockers. Considering the amount of boost he'd be dumping into the engine,

Parish outfitted it with a pair of SCE Titan head gaskets, as well as ARP head studs to keep a good block-to-head seal. Parish retained a very similar camshaft from the other combination—it's a Comp Cams stick with 234 degrees of duration on the intake side and 232 degrees on the exhaust side, measured at .050-inch lift. The hydraulic roller camshaft is ground on a 114-degree lobe separation angle and features a maximum lift of .595-inch intake and .590-inch exhaust. Other valvetrain upgrades consist of Patriot Gold valvesprings and retainers, and hardened pushrods, which ride on Comp Cams lifters.

For a while, Parish used a stock truck intake manifold topped by the original engine cover. It had the stock look, but didn't perform up to his expectations. He eventually used an Edelbrock Victor Jr. intake manifold to draw air through an LS2 90-mm throttle body and an aluminum intake elbow, which are the final links in the turbo system, before the forced air enters the engine.

The first setup used a single turbocharger, but the most recent setup features twin Precision GTS 70-mm turbochargers. The turbo system also features twin Tial 44-mm wastegates to control boost, while twin Turbonetics Raptor blow-off valves keep boost from entering the engine when it isn't needed. Twin air-to-water intercoolers keep the intake charge at a reasonable temperature, while custom headers and ductwork tie it all together.

Fuel system upgrades consist of a Racetronics twin-pump in-tank kit, as well as 96-pound injectors. While the truck's primary fuel source is race gas, Parish also added a methanol injection system, which features a separate 4-gallon fuel cell. In addition to this, the Silverado has a dry nitrous system on it, so the amount of stress on the engine is substantial.

On the chassis dyno, Parish's pickup put down 767 hp and 1,000 ft-lbs of torque to the rear wheels with the old configuration. After rebuilding and installing twin turbos, it put down more than 1,000 hp to the wheels! If you consider parasitic loss of the automatic transmission and torque converter, 1,200 hp is a close estimate, and the turbos are plenty capable of more. However, the stock block won't support much more power, so Parish doesn't want to push it.

Behind the twin-turbo Vortec engine is a 4L80E automatic transmission, built by Finish Line Transmissions. The torque converter is a Precision triple-disc unit, which stalls to 2,800 rpm on the line. The driveline was the weakest link in the setup, so Parish installed a 3.5-inch Dynotech chromemoly driveshaft, which connects the 3/4-ton transfer case to the Eaton carrier. As for suspension, Parish kept it stock for a while, but eventually lowered the front 1 inch and the rear 3 inches. He also bolted on a pair of CalTracs to prevent axle wrap on the line.

TOP: Parish's truck went through a number of changes, but the first turbo setup is pictured here. It consisted of a single turbocharger, and made great power, but he eventually stepped up to a twin-turbo setup, feeding into a CMotorsports-built 408-ci stroker. Final horsepower numbers for the twin turbo setup is just north of 1,000. *(Photo courtesy Kyle Loftis)* MIDDLE: The final engine configuration calls upon twin Precision GTS 70-mm turbochargers, which use twin Tial 44-mm wastegates to control boost. Custom headers and ductwork were required to link the system together, while dual air-to-water intercoolers and a methanol injection system keep intake temperatures at a minimum. *(Photo courtesy Kyle Loftis)* BOTTOM: When the truck had the single 76-mm turbocharger on it, and a 100-hp shot of nitrous, it made 767 hp and a tick more than 1,000 ft-lbs of torque, as shown here. When the twin turbos came into the picture, Parish outdid himself with 1,065 hp and 1,025 ft-lbs of torque, putting his Silverado into legendary sleeper status. *(Photo courtesy Kyle Loftis)*

With four-digit horsepower and four-wheel drive, the truck is a handful if it doesn't hook off the line, but when it's straight, it's unbelievably fast. Parish consistently bettered his elapsed times and mph at the track with an overall best of 10.08 at 136 mph with a 1.55 60-foot time. He certainly has the horsepower for 9s, but aerodynamics and suspension were the limiting factors.

Obviously, with these elapsed times, he eventually installed a roll cage and racing harnesses to make it legal at the track, but the configuration you see on these pages is at the height of this truck's sleeper status. Even after the extensive modifications to prepare it for the track, Parish's pickup still did well on the street and still made a fool out of hundreds of vehicles in the other lane, including 1,000-cc sport bikes.

There's no doubt that Parish's truck will go down in history as one of the best sleepers of all time, and he exemplified the mindset every sleeper owner should posses. He wasn't afraid to race for fun, and surprised lots of folks along the way. Reactions were always positive, even though egos were bruised in the process, but it was all in fun. He didn't get too crazy with modifications, and even competed in *Hot Rod* magazine's Drag Week event, which involves driving your vehicle from track to track to see who has the fastest real street car. Generally, these drives were in excess of 1,000 miles and the truck handled the abuse very well, winning its class both times it was entered. The truck has a long list of accomplishments, and even though Parish sold it a few years ago, its legacy will remain intact as long as people are building sleepers.

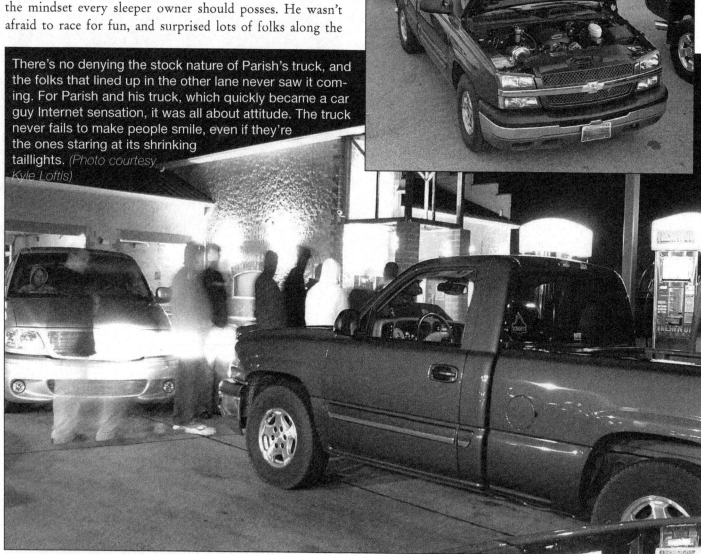

There's no denying the stock nature of Parish's truck, and the folks that lined up in the other lane never saw it coming. For Parish and his truck, which quickly became a car guy Internet sensation, it was all about attitude. The truck never fails to make people smile, even if they're the ones staring at its shrinking taillights. *(Photo courtesy Kyle Loftis)*

With the stock wheels and tires, Parish's Silverado blends into society as "just your average daily-driven 1/2-ton pickup," but when the sun goes down, this truck's true colors show. Even when the truck was solidly in the 12-second range, it was a great sleeper on the street, slaying Cobras and Corvettes on a regular basis. *(Photo courtesy Kyle Loftis)*

Four-door Performer—
This Pontiac G8 GT Puts Down More Than 700 hp

Sleepy Factor: 8 out of 10

Parish built an amazing sleeper out of a Chevy Silverado and did the same with a 2009 Pontiac G8 GT by installing twin turbochargers.

The G8 GT is a bit of a sleeper from the factory, as it's a four-door sedan, available with 361 hp in GT trim and 415 hp in GXP trim. *(Photo courtesy Kyle Loftis)*

Pros
- Four-door family car
- Stock wheels
- No body modifications

Cons
- 13-second car from the factory
- GT body trim designates V-8 power

Just two years before the demise of the entire Pontiac brand in 2010, the company developed a great performance car, based on the Zeta platform, which had previously been used by Holden in Australia. It was to be a rear-wheel-drive car, with the option for a V-8 powerplant, so it caught the attention of performance-minded individuals across the country. Unfortunately, a harsh economy and a steep price tag prevented the Pontiac G8 GT from producing great sales, with fewer than than 50,000 units being built in the two-year production run, and that even includes the V-6-powered base-model sedans. The GT model featured GM's L76 engine, which is a fourth-generation small-block that comes in at 6.0 liters. With 361 hp and 385 ft-lbs of torque, the L76 has plenty of grunt to motivate the 3,950-pound car. Stock G8 GTs do 0-60 in the low-5-second range, with quarter-mile times in the mid 13s.

In stock form, these cars are impressively fast for a four-door sedan, and Jim "Parish" Neuenfeldt couldn't resist the temptation to pick one up at his local dealership. If the name seems familiar, Parish also owns the turbocharged Silverado in this chapter, so you might foresee the theme for his 2009 G8 GT build. If you guessed turbochargers, you are correct, but you'll still be surprised by this car's performance and street-friendly driving characteristics.

Parish kept the combination simple by retaining the stock long block, only opting for a camshaft swap. He modified the fuel system to accommodate the turbo system, and then beefed up the driveline to withstand the abuse. The result of this combination is 717 hp at the rear wheels and 10-second elapsed times in the quarter-mile in a four-door sedan.

While the G8 GT is a rather sporty sedan, it still has an extra pair of doors, which generally doesn't interest a car guy, therefore resulting in the car being ignored. Parish didn't make a huge effort to pull off the sleeper look—the extreme power level keeps everyone guessing either way, so there was no need for intentional sleeper details. Parish started by disassembling the 6.0-liter LS engine and installing a Comp Camps camshaft, which features 216 degrees of duration on the intake side and 224 degrees on the exhaust side, both measured at .050-inch lift. Maximum lift for the camshaft is .561-inch intake and .568-inch exhaust, and lobe separation angle is 115 degrees. Other Comp Cams equipment includes the valvesprings, pushrods, and adjustable timing set, while GM lifters from an LS7 engine link the valvetrain to the new camshaft. The only upgrade to the bottom end is a Melling oil pump.

The secret to Parish's horsepower ride on either side of the engine where the original catalytic converters mounted. Twin Precision 60-mm billet wheel turbochargers are ducted into the stainless exhaust system and stay hidden from sight. Stainless tubing runs from the turbochargers to the custom air-to-air intercooler, and then to the intake manifold, all of which is connected with V-band clamps. Exhaust gases pass through the dual 3-inch, stainless steel exhaust system before entering the atmosphere with an aggressive rumble. Twin Tial 38-mm wastegates and a Tial 50-mm blow-off valve are also on the list of turbo goodies. A Blitz speed-based boost controller allows Parish to dial in the boost pressure on the fly, and it's what C&S Dyno Shop used to tune the twin turbo G8 GT and produce 717 hp at the rear wheels on its Dynojet dynamometer.

C&S also had to deal with an upgraded fuel system, which consists of triple 392 Walbro pumps, -10 AN feed line, Aeromotive fuel rails, and 96-pound injectors. The car is set up to run on E85 and does well on long drives, such as the 2010 *Hot Rod* magazine Drag Week event, where the car consistently ran low 11s and drove 3,200 miles round trip. On Parish's final run of the event, he turned up the wick and ran a 10.82 at 129 mph with a 1.68-second 60-foot time. At this point, he was only a tenth away from the world's fastest G8 at the time, but the stock rear end and driveshaft motivated Parish to save the equipment and make sure he could drive the car home.

Behind the 364-ci engine, which now has twice as much horsepower as cubic inches, is a 6L80E automatic transmission, which is the standard transmission for G8 GT models. The 6-speed automatic didn't stand a chance in stock form, so Parish sent it to Circle D Specialties for a complete build. Before installing the new transmission, he slid a custom Circle D Pro Series Stage III torque converter into place, which is a billet, triple-disc design that measures 245 mm (9.75 inches) and stalls to 3,200 rpm. This allows Parish to build boost on the line and keep it hooked up all the way down the track. The independent rear end and suspension is completely stock.

Traction comes by way of Mickey Thompson drag radials, sized at 295/45R17.

At this point, Parish could easily increase the horsepower and go quicker, but the fact that the car doesn't have a roll bar limits him greatly. He doesn't want to ruin the car with a cage, so he's in a bit of a pickle, unless he resists the urge to run at the track. As noted in the profile on his turbocharged Silverado, Parish has experienced quite a bit of street racing, but that comes with a long list of risks, so time will tell the G8's future. For now, it's a wicked street sleeper, and it certainly turns heads at the track.

These four-door Pontiacs have a slight sleeper vibe straight from the factory, so when you add twin turbos and a host of other goodies, the sleepy factor elevates quickly, and the result is a 10-second street car that still has all of its creature comforts and is fully capable of hauling the kids to school, or picking up groceries on the way home from work. This modern muscle car is very practical and very fast, making a great combination for everyday driving, and plenty of thrashing on the weekends.

You won't find anything exciting under the hood—it looks like a stock G8 GT. However, crawling under the car reveals the twin Precision 60-mm billet wheel turbochargers, mounted where the catalytic converters originally called home. Tucked close to the engine, the turbos are out of sight, but help produce 717 hp at the rear wheels. *(Photo courtesy Kyle Loftis)*

Parish is a fan of *Hot Rod* magazine's Drag Week event, and made the trip in his G8 GT. The car ran low 11s for most of the event, but clicked off a 10.82 on the final day. The potential for quicker times is there, but the stock differential and lack of safety equipment are the limiting factors. *(Photo courtesy Kyle Loftis)*

Mad Marauder—
Four Doors, Leather Seats, and 830 hp at the Wheels

Sleepy Factor: 8 out of 10

When Mercury built the Marauder, it wanted to appeal to the guy who was looking for a luxury sedan with a few custom touches to set it apart from the crowd. The great part about these large sedans is the fact that power comes from Ford's modular engine, which is an ideal platform for performance builds.

Pros
- Full-size platform
- Four-door sedan
- Stock-appearing wheels
- Stock interior

Cons
- Loud supercharger and exhaust

These days, it's not uncommon to see production vehicles eclipse the 300-hp mark from the factory, even with the use of a high-output V-6 engine, rather than relying on the additional weight and lackluster fuel economy of a V-8. In 2003, Ford Motor Company had a leg up on the competition with its SVT models, such as the Cobra and the Ford Lightning, both of which featured supercharged modular engines producing close to 400 hp. In the same year, Mercury released its new Marauder, a performance-oriented rendition of its Grand Marquis sedan. That car also shares traits with Ford's Crown Victoria, but the Marauder was a special, low-production vehicle that packed a little more power than your standard Crown Vic.

The Marauder was only available for two years, and while sales didn't turn the automotive world on its ear, the car's performance was notable, and the potential for modifications was ever present, with the highly acclaimed 4.6-liter DOHC modular motor. The naturally aspirated engine produced a tick over 300 hp in stock form, so it did little to make the 4,400-pound, four-door sedan feel like a sports car, but it's proven to be a great candidate for a sleeper build when you toss a power adder into the equation.

This example, owned by Steve Schingler, is very heavily modified to the tune of 829 hp at the rear wheels and low 10-second passes in the quarter-mile. With stock-appearing wheels and a stock body, the car doesn't garner much attention until it hits the track, which is exactly why Steve built it this way!

The fun starts with the underpinnings, which consist of the original 8.8 rear end housing, which features welded axle tubes, packed with Mark Williams 35-spline axles, attached to a spool and a 4.10:1 gear set. Metco upper and lower rear control arms help the car plant the rear tires, while the stock air-ride suspension provides the necessary squat to keep the car stable as it motors down the track. Front suspension modifications are limited, but include a pair of QA1 springs and Strange struts, along with larger-than-stock Baer brakes.

Rolling stock consists of what appear to be original Marauder wheels—but upon closer inspection, you'll find that the front wheels have been narrowed to 18x4 inches. From the side, you'd never notice the modified front runners, but Steve reaps the benefits of much-needed weight reduction on the front end. Out back, stock wheels are wrapped in 305/45R18

Pro-Line Racing Engines built the 4.6-liter modular engine, while the folks at Injected Engineering handled the fuel system and Vortech YSI supercharger installation. Thanks to the ported cylinder heads, which are equipped with four custom-grind camshafts, the Marauder cranked out 829 hp and 663 ft-lbs of torque to the rear wheels.

Some folks may notice the lowered stance and peek inside to see a roll cage, but the majority of people won't get that far before turning their attention to another car in the pits. Not that Steve's car is unattractive—it just doesn't have the wow factor that grabs the attention of most car guys.

tires for street use, while track days necessitate a pair of bead-locked 16x10-inch Holeshot wheels and Mickey Thompson 295/50R16 drag radials.

Injected Engineering in Kennesaw, Georgia, handled all of the suspension modifications but Steve sent the car to Bell Chassisworks to have the eight-point chrome-moly roll cage installed. Although the Marauder has a full frame, the cage helps to stiffen the structure and it also allows him to pass tech at any track. Other safety features include a driveshaft loop, a push/pull kill switch at the rear bumper, and G-Force five-point harnesses. The weight reduction is canceled out by the additional safety gear, so the car is still at its original 4,400 pounds.

Motivating all that weight is the original 4.6-liter engine, which seems small in terms of displacement, but more than makes up for its small size with lots of airflow and a big power adder. The stock block was bored .020-inch over and assembled by Pro-Line Racing Engines with a stock Cobra crankshaft, a set of Carillo billet connecting rods, and a set of Diamond pistons. The cylinder heads are stock castings that have been ported by Chris Howe and outfitted with larger valves for optimum airflow throughout the RPM band. Injected Engineering developed the ideal camshaft specifications and had four custom-grind cams built to suit Steve's engine. From there, Injected hung the Vortech YSI supercharger onto the front of the engine and plumbed in a custom air-to-air intercooler to cool the intake charge. With plans for big-time boost, the Marauder is outfitted with twin Ford GT fuel pumps, and 80-pound Ford Racing fuel injectors. Fuel delivery and ignition timing is controlled by SCT software, and Injected Engineering performed multiple dyno tests to dial in the horsepower. With a milder tune and a tank of 93-octane pump gas, the Marauder put down 677 hp and 572 ft-lbs of torque to the rear wheels. Swapping fuel to C16 and upping the boost resulted in 829 hp and 663 ft-lbs of torque.

The exhaust system isn't all that sneaky with Kooks headers, 3-inch piping, and MagnaFlow mufflers, but the aggressive exhaust note still isn't enough to ruin the car's sleeper status. Behind the supercharged modular engine is a 4R70W automatic transmission, which is what originally came in the Marauder. Lentech built the current setup and it's a bulletproof design to withstand big power, and the more than 2 tons of mass. A Precision Industries torque converter applies the power and stalls to 2,800 rpm on the line. The shifter is stock, so there aren't many clues to the car's potential on the inside.

Aside from the cage, safety harnesses, and a few auxiliary gauges, the interior is completely stock, right down to the stock leather seats. Steve didn't want to remove any of the stock equipment from the interior or trunk area, so this slick four-door sedan is a legitimate, full weight street car. The Marauder proved its street-worthy characteristics when it made a 90-mile return from Brainerd Optimist Dragstrip after another Injected Engineering customer car had suffered a parts failure. Steve had fun with the unexpected situation, and made the trip back with three passengers aboard. And though he admits that hot rods are never complete, Steve is content with the car's current performance, which has topped out at 10.32 at 136 mph for the time being. With 1.57-second 60-foot times, there's certainly a little more time left on the table, so if the crew at Injected Engineering has anything to do with it, this Marauder will eventually see a 9-second pass. For now, it's still a very genuine modern muscle sleeper, and Steve plans to keep it that way.

TOP LEFT: When Steve Schingler decided to build his Marauder for drag racing, he wanted to retain the looks of the stock five-spoke wheels. To shave weight off the nose and reduce rolling resistance, he had the front wheels narrowed to 4 inches wide. The 16x10-inch Holeshot wheels are wrapped in Mickey Thompson radial tires. TOP MIDDLE: Aside from the roll cage, the Marauder has a completely stock interior, down to the seats, floor mats, and shifter. With the original interior intact, Steve can run 10.30s in the comfort of his heated leather seats, and can accommodate a few passengers on the return trip home. TOP RIGHT: Opening any of the four doors reveals a roll cage, which is a required to pass technical inspection at this Marauder's level of performance. The crew at Bell Chassisworks built and installed the eight-point roll cage to fit closely to the interior panels, without any interior modifications, resulting in a stock-appearing car. BOTTOM: At the track, Steve uses a different rear wheel and tire combination to better apply the power and keep the Marauder glued to the track. The 4,400-pound four-door sedan has run a best of 10.32 at 136 mph with a 1.57-second 60-foot time. There's no question as to this car's sleeper status.

Chapter 12

What, This Old Thing?

Sometimes, to build a good sleeper, you need to make the best use of the car's existing appearance—meaning those less than desirable traits, such as an unpopular body design or a rough and rusty exterior, thanks to years of neglect. This effect can be used for many applications, but it seems to work best on cars and trucks from the 1970s, and it can apply to certain models from the 1960s if the right approach is taken.

What could be a better sleeper than a replica of the famous "Family Truckster" station wagon from the classic movie, *National Lampoon's Summer Vacation*? This replica is a spot-on recreation of the movie car, but power comes from a GM Vortec truck engine, which you have learned is a potent combination, when treated to boost or nitrous.

For instance, a mid-1970s station wagon is naturally ugly and undesirable to most car guys, so put a big engine in it and you're done. Cars from the muscle car era can also be used, but there's a fine line, so the car pretty much needs to be a four-door or have some serious body rot to pass the "clunker" test. If a guy sees an old Chevelle two-door that looks a little rough, he might still have a hunch that the car has a hidden agenda, but choose a four-door or a wagon, and that assumption goes out the window!

It's important to remember what people consider "junky" these days, as the rat rod craze is still a strong force at rod runs across the United States. They are getting wilder by the minute, and some of them are downright unsafe, but the trend does tend to put certain muscle cars into the rat rod category. People used to call them "beaters," but anything with faded paint seems to automatically be classified as a rat rod nowadays. Beaters have always been cool with hot rodders because you could take a rough old car and stick a big engine in it to create an instant sleeper. With the current rat rod trend, the common perception is that the builder doesn't want to go fast—he just wants the car to look bad, which is good in the rat rod world. It's really a confusing segment of the automotive hobby. Make it look worse, so people like it more? Apparently, that's how it works.

Building a junky sleeper is similar to building a rat rod, but a little less animated. Your goal is to distract the eye from speed secrets by relying on the car's natural or sometimes intentional defects to draw the attention. Rusty panels, rough paint, and missing parts are all part of the game, but it doesn't always have to be difficult. Some of the cars in this chapter are rather simple machines, in that the owners took a neglected body and outfitted it with some sort of high-horsepower

engine—end of story. Others were intentionally built to fool the eye, with custom details inside and out to keep folks guessing. It's not always easy to detect the genuine details from the fabricated ones, but if that's the case, the builders who are intentionally modifying their cars to look junky are doing a great job!

This approach to building a sleeper is often used as more of a novelty, rather than being out to trick someone into street racing for money. Street racers are smart enough to know when someone is trying to hustle them, so pulling up in a junker and demanding a race for money blows your cover very quickly.

Again, the goal isn't to make your vehicle downright ugly, rather to make people think, "There's no way that thing can be fast." And yes, there is a fine line between a sleeper and a scabbed-together piece of junk, although some people have been known to go extremely fast in dangerous machines. The owner's mindset needs to be in the right place to build a sleeper of this nature, because a beater never really gets the respect it deserves. A beater does, however, garner much more attention from hardcore car guys. For instance, if you park next to a show queen at a rod run or big-time car event, like the *Hot Rod* Power Tour, your sleeper is going to attract way more attention than a fiberglass street rod or a slammed custom with a slick paint job. This is the beauty of a beater, whether it's a bone-stock barn find, or a stone cold sleeper like some of the cars featured in this chater. Real car guys love beaters, and when they see a major powerplant under the hood, they love it even more, so this type of sleeper lends itself to the more

Station wagons from the 1960s and 1970s are ideal for a sleeper of this nature. Unfortunately, there aren't many of them left, so finding a good starting point is sometimes difficult. If you can't find a well-kept original, simply leave the rust alone and let it add to the car's understated demeanor.

Under the hood of this Chevrolet Kingswood station wagon is a big-block Chevy of unknown specifications. It fits nicely under the hood of the wagon, with plenty of room to spare, and boasts a pair of Edelbrock aluminum cylinder heads, among other speed parts that help lighten the load of this full-size wagon.

hardcore automotive enthusiasts out there, whereas a super-shiny car with super-sized chrome wheels appeals to the novice end of the spectrum.

There's no mistaking the cool factor of a sleeper that truly looks like it doesn't belong on the drag strip, and there isn't a more appropriate candidate than an old truck. Guys have built short-wheelbase trucks for years, and they're often a popular platform for drag racing, but a long-wheelbase truck is seldom considered cool among drag race rs or car guys in general. Considering the lack of appeal, you have an excellent sleeper on your hands, and you rarely have to worry about inadequate engine bay room, or a wimpy rear end when you're dealing with a full-size truck. The fact that many Ford, Chevrolet, and Dodge trucks from the 1970s came from the factory with big-block engines, the options are wide open for engine selection, and you could even do a junkyard buildup with a do-it-yourself turbo system to take advantage of the low-buck nature of an old pickup truck. Nitrous is also a cheap way to make big power, and it's generally easy to hide, as long as you can find a home for the bottle that isn't in the middle of the bed for everyone to see.

The end result of a beater sleeper is a fun machine that still gets a lot of attention, much like a rat rod. On that subject, there are actually some owners stuffing crazy powerplants in

traditional hot rods and cars that most people would consider a rat rod. Generally, these cars aren't considered sleepers, even though they're much faster than they appear. The cars in this chapter are rough around the edges, and lack the show-winning finish qualities that some folks desire, but they're ridiculously fast and they always draw a crowd when the dust settles.

Some folks call them rat rods—others call them beaters, but whatever you call them, just know that a killer engine could be under the hood. For this mid-1950s Ford F-100 pickup, a 500-hp V-10 from a Dodge Viper provides the power, while a rusty patina and whitewalls keep people guessing.

A common trend with rat rods is to take advantage of the vehicles' very light weight and actually put these things to use. This one is heavily chopped and channeled, but uses power from a twin-turbocharged small-block Chevy to motor down the track at alarming speeds. Safe or not, these rat rods are fun to watch!

Honk if Parts Fall Off—
It Might be Rough, But it Sure is Fast!

Sleepy Factor: 9 out of 10

In normal circumstances, a 1967 Chevelle is rarely considered a sleeper. However, add another pair of doors into the mix and give it a rotten, spray-painted body and you have the makings of a classic sleeper combination. The only sign of speed here is the pin-on cowl induction hood. *(Photo courtesy Rick Steinke)*

Pros
- Four door
- Rusty and rough body
- Hidden roll cage
- Big horsepower

Cons
- Cowl induction hood
- Floor-mounted Ratchet shifter

When it comes to sleepers, you'll be hard pressed to find a better candidate than a four-door sedan. Even if you choose a car from the muscle car era, like this 1967 Chevelle, the two extra doors make a huge difference in the perception of your car. This particular car, owned by Rick Steinke, is one of the premier sleepers in the country with its big horsepower and crusty appearance. Most folks won't look twice at this car because, at a glance, it truly looks like a beater that someone picked up for a few hundred bucks. In reality, Rick takes great pride in his car, and puts having fun first on the list of priorities.

Though it's gone through many phases, this Chevelle was actually Rick's first car, given to him by his father in 1994. His dad paid $650 for the car back then, and it was in fair shape for its age. Years of neglect on Rick's part resulted in rusty body panels, which are now covered with a rattle-can paint job, but the car's chassis is still structurally sound. A full-frame car has advantages and disadvantages when it comes to being a sneaky muscle car. A full-frame car provides a stiff platform without the need for extensive bracing, but at the same time, it lugs around a little more weight than a unibody platform. Rick's car weighs 3,622 pounds with him behind the wheel, which isn't excessive for a four-door, full-frame car.

The Chevelle is a popular car on the Internet, as it truly embodies the sleeper theme and surprises folks on a regular basis, whether Rick is driving it on the street or busting off an 8-second pass in the quarter-mile. The car is relatively tame, so Rick can still enjoy it on the street, but it has all of the necessary safety equipment to pass tech at any track. It's a simple combination that has lots of low-budget qualities, and shows the potential of a conventional small-block with a set of Vortec heads on it.

Even if it were in a full-on race car, the engine alone is impressive by sleeper standards, as most folks would never expect a Vortec-headed 355-ci small-block to run 8s. These

incredible times are possible because of a single turbocharger—more specifically a BorgWarner S480 turbocharger, which has an 80-mm inducer and a 1.32 A/R exhaust housing. This turbo was originally designed for a Diesel truck, but is perfectly sized, so it has a quick spool-up time, while also having great top end power. Of course, this turbo sizing is relative to the engine, which is a fairly basic combination.

It all starts with a 1996 Chevy Vortec engine—it's the closest thing to a regular old small-block you can get. The engine was originally a roller, so that knocked one important step out of the way. Rick strengthened the bottom end by filling it to the bottom of the water pump holes with Moroso block fill, and then outfitting it with an Eagle 4130 crankshaft. The rods are Eagle H-beams, which are 6 inches long and connect to a set of dished Wiseco Pro Tru forged pistons. This results in an 8.4:1 compression ratio, when combined with the Vortec cylinder heads. Scott Woodington of Engine Specialties handled machine work, while the head work was performed by Rick, with some guidance from Lorenzo's Fast Flow Cylinder Heads. Rick also ported the Professional Products single-plane intake to match the intake runners, and then bolted on a CSU 850-cfm carburetor, which is prepped for boost and topped off with an Extreme Velocity bonnet.

The camshaft is a Comp Cams hydraulic roller with 230/236 degrees of duration at .050-inch lift, with .551/.554 inch of maximum lift. Lobe separation angle is 114 degrees, which is perfect for a turbo car. To prepare the engine for serious boost, Rick installed an Aeromotive fuel system, which consists of an A1000 pump, an inline fuel filter, and a boost-sensitive pressure regulator. The ignition is fairly simple, compared to most 8-second quarter-mile cars, as it's merely an MSD 6AL box that works in conjunction with a Blaster 3 coil and a single stage timing retard that's wired into an HOB switch. The switch is activated as boost levels rise, and

TOP: Rick ported the Vortec cylinder heads to accommodate the additional airflow created by the single 80-mm turbocharger, but didn't go overboard with the modifications. Rick chose not to run an intercooler, making the turbo system even simpler than most, with the piping running directly from the turbocharger to the 850-cfm CSU blow-through carburetor. *(Photo courtesy Seth Cohen)* MIDDLE TOP: Rolling stock consists of 14x6-inch Chevy Rallye wheels up front and 15x8-inch Rallyes on the back, painted red and outfitted with disc brake center caps. Rick painted the whitewall on the Mickey Thompson drag radials to continue the sleeper theme and keep folks guessing. The rears are sized at 275/60R15. *(Photo courtesy Rick Steinke)* MIDDLE BOTTOM: Inside Rick's Chevelle, you see a bench seat in the front and back, and a roll cage that conforms nicely to the car's inner structure. From a side view, the cage is undetectable, but it is certified by the NHRA and allows Rick to run as fast as 8.50s. *(Photo courtesy Rick Steinke)* BOTTOM: The Chevelle is by no means glamorous on the inside, but it gets the job done, and looks completely stock when the doors are closed. Rick uses a hat to cover the ratchet shifter when it isn't in use, and left the column shifter in place just for the fun of it. *(Photo courtesy Seth Cohen)*

it retards the timing as the car goes down the track—a very important detail for most turbo cars.

According to Rick's math, he says it takes more than 1,000 hp to push 3,622 pounds down the track at 152 mph in the quarter-mile. He's never dyno'd the car, and prefers to show its potential on the track, rather than strapped to a set of rollers. To hook up all that power he uses a modified Powerglide 2-speed automatic transmission. Application of power is handled by an ATI 10-inch torque converter, which stalls from 3,000 to 5,000 rpm, depending on boost levels at launch. Rick uses a trans brake to help get off the line quickly and shifts the 'Glide with a B&M Pro Ratchet.

For suspension, Rick installed a pair of six-cylinder coil springs up front, with the stock, stamped control arms. It's all stock with new bushings, and hardware, and the rear suspension is similar, as it's outfitted with boxed lower control arms with D-M Products adjustable upper arms. A GM 12-bolt

rear end features a Strange spool and Alloy USA axles, along with a 3.73:1 gear set. Rick also installed a D-M Products anti-roll bar, and then gave the Chevelle a pair of QA1 coil springs to keep plenty of weight over the rear tires. Speaking of which, Rick runs a pair of Mickey Thompson drag radials, which are sized at 275/60R15, and feature a painted-on whitewall. The wheels are bright red Rallyes, 14x6 inches up front and 15x8 inches out back.

What makes this car a great sleeper is the fact that it's a four door. Most people automatically disregard four-door sedans as "fast cars," but this one has surprised quite a few in the racing world. Rusty holes, a rattle-can paint job, and painted-on whitewalls add to the sleepy details, while four-digit horsepower is under Rick's right foot. He went the extra mile to hide the roll cage, and keep the car stock, and only slipped up in a few areas. The end result is a best elapsed time of 8.96 at 152 mph, running 5.75 at 125 mph to the eighth-mile. It looks rough, and has a very simple and affordable engine combination, making it one of the best sleepers out there, on the street or at the strip.

Rusty rocker panels and worn-through spray paint give this four-door Chevelle the right amount of beater quality to go along with the big-time horsepower. The stance is a little more aggressive than stock, and that's due to the six-cylinder springs up front and QA1 springs out back. Added traction comes from tubular rear control arms. *(Photo courtesy Seth Cohen)*

On the track, Rick's Chevelle is certainly a standout and surprises everyone, even when he turns the boost down to run in the 10.00 index class, as seen here. Rick has run a best of 8.96 at 152 mph on VP C12 racing fuel. The all-time best on 93-octane pump gas is 9.53 at 147 mph. *(Photo courtesy Seth Cohen)*

Meet Vinny—
A 1963 Pontiac Tempest LeMans That Packs a Punch!

When you have 1,200 hp at the mercy of your right foot, it's not difficult to obliterate a pair of rear tires in an afternoon of spirited driving. This car has run a best elapsed time of 8.92 at 162 mph through the quarter-mile. Rob also competes in standing mile top-speed events, where the car has trapped more than 215 mph! *(Photo courtesy Rich Chenet)*

Pros
- Rough body and paint
- Hidden turbos
- Lots of horsepower

Cons
- Large rear tires and rim screws

A car can sometimes give away its big secret by toting around a big set of rear tires, and it's rare that anyone can get away with it, even at the drag strip. It's common to assume that big sticky tires equate to quick times, but you've more than likely seen some unbelievably slow cars rolling on slicks, so that logic doesn't exactly make sense. For this 1963 Pontiac LeMans, the big rear tires are the only giveaway, but when you figure out how much power it puts down, you won't blame the owner, Rob Freyvogel. His car is an ideal sleeper, and the extremely quick times and big horsepower more than make up for the slightly revealing slicks.

Rob bought the car for $900 a few years ago and built it into one of the best sleepers on the planet, with the help of Tom Napierkowski. The duo tackled every detail with intentions of making this a very sneaky car, and never really planned to participate in organized racing with it. When it was first built, the car didn't have a roll cage or any safety equipment, and that's when it was its sleepiest—it currently has a few more safety details, but the photos you see here are from 2007 to show off the car's true potential as a sleeper.

The car is rough and ragged on the outside, bearing its original paint, which has certainly seen better days. It's not perfectly manicured, or precise on the outside, but everything changes when you look beneath it or check out the engine bay.

Originally, these Pontiac Tempests had a transaxle rear end that severely limited their potential as a performance car. Most folks, including Rob, ditch the original setup for a solid rear—a 1957 Olds for this particular car. The big rear end is narrowed 3/4-inch on each side and features a pair of 35-spline axles, but still utilizes the original 3.08:1 gear set. It's strong enough to hold up to the big-block's torque, and the rear suspension works flawlessly on prepped surfaces, as well as unprepped pavement. It's a custom ladder bar design, with 175-pound-per-inch springs and double adjustable race shocks. The only modification to the front suspension is a pair of QA1 shocks.

Rob says he drives the car on the street at least 1,500 miles a year, and attends the Flashlight Drags as often as he can. The Flashlight Drags events are held at various airstrips in Rob's home state of Pennsylvania, and offer the street-racing feel with an unprepped racing surface, and limited rules. Before Rob installed the chrome-moly roll cage, the Flashlight Drags was the only racing he could participate in, because he'd quickly be run off from local drag strips with the car's lack of safety equipment. Now that he's upgraded the car to pass tech, he's gotten into a new hobby, which is land speed racing. He enjoys running the Maxton Mile events, held in Maxton, North Carolina, where the car has run more than 200 mph in the standing-mile competition—215 mph to be exact! That's an astonishing feat for any car, especially a brick, like Rob's Pontiac. He did fabricate an air dam for the front to help matters, but it definitely surprised the regulars at the Maxton Mile.

Power comes from a 496-ci big-block Chevy, which started life as a basic 454. The big-block features an Ohio billet crankshaft, Oliver 6.385-inch connecting rods, and a set of custom Mahle forged pistons, so it's safe to assume the bottom end is plenty strong. Atop the short block is a set of Brodix Big Brodie cylinder heads, ported by Rob and installed over a set of Fel-Pro MLS head gaskets to create a compression ratio of 8.6:1. Massive Ferrea valves are put into motion by a Bullet camshaft, which is designed specifically for lots of boost. The intake manifold is a Holley Strip Dominator, which has been modified to accept the modern fuel injectors (Bosch 160-pound), and to match the ports on the Brodix cylinder heads.

While the big-block would make plenty of power on its own, Rob relies on a pair of Holset HT3B turbochargers to make insane horsepower and give this Pontiac the edge on any unsuspecting competitor. The fact that Rob and Tom went to the effort to hide the turbochargers makes the car even more cool, and it certainly adds to the sleepy factor. The custom headers lead to the turbo piping, which is eventually routed back toward the engine after passing through an air-to-water intercooler. Again, they could've run the piping anywhere in the engine bay, but chose to route it directly out of the center of the firewall, into a stock Pontiac breather. At a glance, the piping is not visible, and the blue-painted engine tricks the eye into thinking this big-block is really an old Pontiac mill.

TOP: Supporting all this horsepower is a mighty Oldsmobile rear end packed with 3.08:1 gears and 35-spline axles. Ladder bars and coil springs help put the power to the ground, while shaving 3/4-inch from each side of the housing allowed for the 28x11.50-15 street slicks. See anything unusual in this photograph? *(Photo courtesy Rich Chenet)* MIDDLE: Under the hood, you see an engine coated in Pontiac Blue paint, and fit with an original-style air cleaner for a 326-ci Pontiac engine. What you may not notice is the big-block Chevy that hides under the Pontiac hue, and the small pipe that connects the air cleaner to the firewall. *(Photo courtesy Rich Chenet)* BOTTOM LEFT: It has aftermarket gauges and a few switches in the console but you won't find a roll cage or aftermarket safety harnesses in this configuration. Rob eventually installed a roll cage to prepare the car for standing-mile top-speed racing, and the occasional trip to the drag strip. *(Photo courtesy Rich Chenet)* BOTTOM RIGHT: There's not much room left in the trunk by the time Rob installed the air-to-water intercooler, ice chest, aluminum fuel cell, and battery, but sometimes that's what it takes to keep all of your speed parts hidden. The ice chest is used to keep the intercooler fed with cold water, which significantly lowers intake charge temperatures. *(Photo courtesy Rich Chenet)*

Fuel delivery is controlled by an Aeromotive A1000 pump, which draws racing fuel from a 20-gallon aluminum cell. Ignition is controlled by an MSD 7AL box that sends fire to the MSD low-profile Pro-Billet distributor.

Mike Doban of OST Dyno tuned the car on the dyno, using the F.A.S.T. XFI system, and it put down 1,247 hp at the rear wheels. That's more than 1,500 at the flywheel, and it looks bone stock!

Obviously, Rob had to put a serious transmission behind the big-block, but he didn't go for the obvious Powerglide. He installed a TMC-built TH400 transmission, which is a 3-speed automatic. The bulletproof transmission has lots of billet goodies inside, and a TMC electric valve body, which also features a trans brake. The torque converter is a Neal Chance 10-inch unit, which stalls to 3,800 at the line—plenty of RPM for the turbochargers to begin spooling up. Traction comes from street-legal tires, and Rob has switched back and forth between a pair of 325/50R15 Mickey Thompson Drag Radials and a pair of 28x11.50-15 Hoosier Quick Time Pro DOT cheater slicks. These are mounted to a pair of 15x10-inch steel wheels from Stockton Wheel. Stock poverty caps top off the beater look.

The end result of Rob's work is a killer Pontiac that surprises everyone in its path. Whether it's at the drag strip or on an abandoned airstrip making a top speed run, this Pontiac seemingly does the impossible—go fast! It looks like a beater, but has proven to be quite the performer despite its poor aerodynamics. Rob has run a best of 5.85 at 130 mph in the eighth-mile, and a best of 8.92 at 162 mph in the quarter—and don't forget about a top speed of 215 mph. Rob has proven the potency of his Pontiac numerous times, and with quick elapsed times and mind-blowing top speeds, no one can deny this car's ultimate sleeper status.

Rob used regular big-block Chevy headers on his LeMans, which lead to the rear end, where two Holset HT3B turbochargers reside. Rob mounted the turbochargers and intercooler out of sight, which makes maintenance tough, but it's completely worth it when it leaves folks scratching their heads. *(Photo courtesy Rich Chenet)*

A flat hood, no sign of a roll cage, and a well-worn body—this Pontiac looks like a cool beater, but most folks are unaware that it makes more than 1,200 hp at the wheels. In this configuration, the car's only real signs of speed are the large tires and rim screws. *(Photo courtesy Rich Chenet)*

Buck the Buick—
A Hard-Launching 1968 Skylark That Keeps Folks Guessing

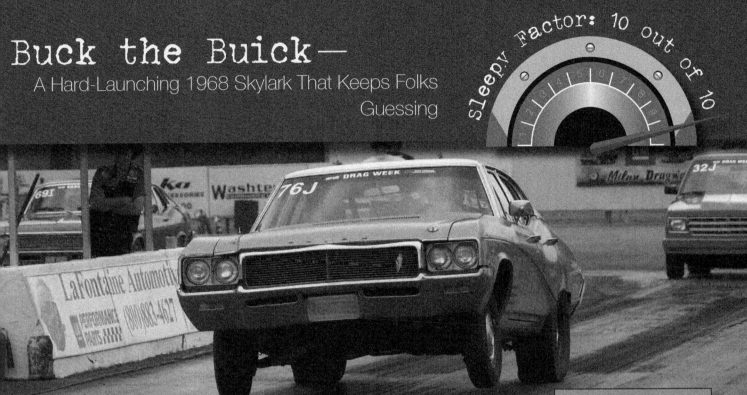

Sleepy Factor: 10 out of 10

A 1968 Buick Skylark four-door doesn't exactly belong on the drag strip, so when bystanders see this crusty example jerking the front wheels off the line, and blasting down the quarter-mile in 10.41 seconds, jaws drop. The owner has the right attitude to go along with the car, and has lots of fun with his sleeper. *(Photo courtesy Kyle Loftis)*

Pros
- Old and dirty four-door family car
- Stock hubcaps
- Owner's attitude
- Weird engine setup keeps people guessing
- Budget built

Cons
- None

When an owner understands what this sleeper thing is all about, it makes a big difference in the overall perception of the vehicle. Brent McCoy gets it. He built this 1968 Buick Skylark four-door on a budget, and has lots of fun, whether he's driving it on the street or hitting the track. The car is remarkably stock underneath, and has an odd combination of parts under the hood, but the result is blazingly fast elapsed times, and the street credibility of a regular street car. It's a great example of a sleeper that falls into the category of "intentionally junky," which keeps it very sneaky.

Brent and his wife, Vera, have a great time with the Buick, and they share driving duties in the four-door family car. The story behind the car is a great one, and it started with a brief sighting, which led to a second visit and a knock on the door to see if the car was for sale. Apparently, it only took $250 to convince the owner to turn it loose, but the man claimed that his grandfather still had the title, so Brent paid him $150 and promised him another $100 when the title turned up. Unfortunately, it never did, and when Brent paid the previous owner a visit, he'd already moved out of the house—if that's what you want to call it. He was actually in jail, so Brent had to spend a little extra dough to get a title for the car. A sum of $295 is Brent's total investment in the body, so to say this is a budget-built sleeper is completely accurate.

Brent may act like he doesn't know much about this "going fast" stuff, but seeing one of his passes quickly removes all doubt that he knows what he's doing with this old car. Brent calls his shop the Hillbilly Garage, but he received help from a number of folks, including Gary Salisbury, Dave Hight, Mike Leighty, Collin Williams, and Larry and Chris McCoy. Each of them helped in various parts of the build, and if they're anything like Brent, they know how to have a good time.

The Buick features a full frame, and the one under Brent's car is completely stock. He removed the original engine mounts and replaced them with Chevrolet mounts, so the small-block would slide in without any problems. The car currently features Moroso trick front springs, and adjustable rear control arms, but these components haven't helped it run any quicker than it did when it was completely stock, mainly because of axle breakage in the stock 8.5-inch 10-bolt. Brent says he tried a pair of Moser 28-spline axles and they broke quicker than the stock ones, so he keeps a pile of stock axles at the shop. The welded spider gears are holding up just fine, and the 4.11:1 gear ratio works out well for this combination, but going faster will more than likely mean swapping rear ends for something a little healthier.

These full-size GM cars had a triangulated four-link rear suspension from the factory, so it made sense to retain this design, as it lends itself well to hard launches. Brent did add an airbag to the passenger side to better support the load, and installed a pair of Rancho shocks, which are painted to look like rusted old shocks. That's all the suspension modifications, and Brent even kept the original drum brakes on all four corners. Rolling stock consists of Center Line racing wheels, but you'd never know it, as they're painted black, and covered with a set of stock hubcaps. To pass tech, the hubcaps have to be securely mounted to the wheel, so Brent screwed them into place. The 15x8-inch rear wheels mount to a pair of Hoosier 295/60R15 drag radials, which fit nicely, thanks to a little bit of persuasion on the inner quarter panel with a bumper jack and a block of wood.

The most interesting part of Brent's Buick is the powerplant. While most would say that a small-block Chevy is anything but interesting, this one has been known to cause some serious head scratching. It all starts with a stock GM block, which was given to Brent by a friend. The block needed a sleeve, but that didn't scare Brent, so he assembled the bottom end with a stock cast crank, a set of Scat connecting rods, and a set of Wiseco forged flat top pistons.

The freebie block has held up well, but it's the cylinder heads that cause the most confusion when Brent opens the hood. One cylinder head is a GM double-hump, which is a rather dated design that was popular many years ago, but is currently way behind the times, unless it is ported profession-

ally. Even then, double-hump heads can't compete with quality aftermarket heads, and that's what rides on the other side of Brent's small-block. That's right, the 355-ci small-block Chevy has a GM cast-iron double-hump head on one side and a Dart aluminum head on the other.

As mentioned before, Brent likes to play dumb and act as if the car is fast by accident, but it's all in good fun. He says it obviously makes more power on the left bank, because the first trip to the track with the new head resulted in a broken left axle. Brent plays the part of a sleeper owner very well.

The cylinder head swap was caused by a crack in one of Brent's double-hump heads, so he trashed it. He didn't want to spend the money to have another one professionally ported, so Dave Hight at VAMP Speed Shop helped him find an aluminum head to replace the double-hump and come close to matching the specs. A used Erson camshaft moves the used stainless steel valves, while 25-year-old Crane rocker arms are still getting the job done. The camshaft is a roller design with .555 inch of lift, and 238 degrees of duration on the intake side and 246 degrees on the exhaust side. The intake is an Edelbrock Victor Jr., and the carburetor is a 750-cfm Holley double pumper, which is on loan from Brent's brother Chris.

Nitrous is the power adder of choice, and Brent sprays the small-block with a 150 shot because any more than that results in the instant death of an axle. The nitrous system is an Edelbrock Performer RPM plate kit, which is combined with a separate fuel system that features a small fuel cell and electric pump. The engine's fuel source is the original gas tank and a stock mechanical fuel pump.

Brent says he skimped on a lot of parts, but never skimps on ignition when he's dealing with nitrous. He outfitted the

The Buick's powerplant is a 355-ci small-block Chevy, outfitted with one GM double-hump head, and one Dart aluminum head. Somehow, these mismatched heads work well, in combination with a 150-hp shot of nitrous. Induction consists of an Edelbrock Victor Jr. intake manifold topped by a 750-cfm Holley carburetor. (Photo courtesy Kyle Loftis)

A pink, fuzzy seat cover is a nice way to take the attention away from the safety harnesses and auxiliary gauges. The roll cage is tucked tightly against the interior panels, and the column shifter is still in use, while the backseat is still functional as well, making for fun road trips. (Photo courtesy Kyle Loftis)

Buick with an MSD 6AL ignition box, an MSD Pro-Billet distributor, and an MSD crank trigger. Outgoing air travels through a set of Hooker headers, which feature 1¾-inch primaries, and 3-inch collectors that lead to a pair of cheapo mufflers. Brent says the car has never been on a dyno, but he thinks it makes at least 300 hp—try doubling that and you'll be a little closer to the real numbers. Backing the small-block is a TH350 transmission, which was modified and rebuilt by Gary Salisbury and Mike Leighty. The torque converter is from TCI and stalls to 2,800 rpm on the line, while the stock column shifter selects the gears in the 3-speed automatic.

Brent drives the car frequently and recently competed in the *Hot Rod* magazine Drag Week event. He runs the car on pump gas and averages 12 mpg, so the car has definitely proven its street worthiness. Brent handled all of the wiring for the nitrous and ignition system, and didn't make much of an effort to hide it, aside from using the horn button for the nitrous purge. The fact that it's a full-size, four-door car is enough to give this car plenty of sleeper points, but Brent takes it to the next level by leaving it dirty, and playing the part wherever he goes.

Inside, only a few details allow the car's potential to shine through, but a few gauges and a well-hidden roll cage are the extent of the interior modifications. Brent's wife, Vera, made the fuzzy, pink seat cover, which adds a little more grandma flavor to the car. So far, the best elapsed time is a 10.41 at 127 mph in the quarter-mile, and there's a lot left in the car if he could turn up the wick and keep it together. It's certainly fast as it sits, and it perfectly represents a quality sleeper. It might be built from what Brent considers junk, but it's no slouch when you consider the wheels-up launches, 10-second time slips, and superb driveability.

With its stock hubcaps, full trim, and interior, Brent's Buick definitely provides the right amount of clunker flavor to pull off the sleeper look. It is seen here, loaded with people, while it made its way to the staging lanes during Hot Rod magazine's Drag Week event. *(Photo courtesy Kyle Loftis)*

Brent plays dumb about his Buick Skylark, but never fails to lay it all down on the track. He retained the stock suspension on all four corners, painting the aftermarket shocks to look like well-worn, original units. Brent built this car on a budget, but didn't cut any corners when it came to hiding its 10-second potential. *(Photo courtesy Kyle Loftis)*

Rolling stock for Brent's Buick consists of Center Line aluminum wheels, which are the standard skinnies up front, and 15x8s out back. Stock hubcaps are bolted to the racing wheels, while Hoosier 295/60R15 drag radials provide the traction. A TH350 transmission and TCI torque converter control power application to the GM 10-bolt rear end. *(Photo courtesy Kyle Loftis)*

Farm Truck—
This Long-Bed Chevy Hauls More Than Hay

Sean built *Farm Truck* for one reason—to fool people into thinking it was an old clunker, when it actually makes more than 800 hp, thanks to a nitrous-assisted big-block Chevy. The long-wheelbase Chevy C-10 is known for its hard launches and undeniable performance. *(Photo courtesy Sherry Driggs)*

Pros
- Long wheelbase truck
- Ratty body and paint
- Camper shell

Cons
- Very large rear tires

There's something to be said for a sleeper that gains national notoriety, and becomes a household name for car guys. Pretty much every car guy with a TV or an Internet connection has seen or at least heard of *Farm Truck,* because it's one of the coolest sleepers on the planet. The truck is beat up, and for goodness sake, it has a camper shell on it, so no one expects it to be fast. And there's no way you'd expect to see this thing jerking the left front wheel a foot off the ground, while motivating to a mid-10-second pass through the quarter-mile. For a machine that tips the scales at nearly 5,000 pounds, *Farm Truck,* which is a 1970 Chevy C-10 pickup, makes tons of power to run that kind of number, and its owner Sean Whitley certainly nailed the sleeper look.

Sean has been working on the truck for more than a decade, perfecting the sleeper look, and constantly making it faster. It's been a group effort from many of his close friends, including Ron Burton, Jimbo Lofgren, Roy Mullenix, Mitchell Perry, Aaron Ratliff, George Ray, Mel Rowe, and Tony Torrez just to name a few. This guy has lots of friends, and lots of Midwest street racers know about the truck, but the fact that it's actually fast comes as a surprise to many people. Although the truck has lots of power, it would be useless without a host of good components to back it up, as well as an efficient suspension setup to keep it hooked up. Also, Sean is the creator of Pimp Juice traction compound, a potion that is often used in the street racing environment. You essentially pour a little out in front of the rear tires, and do your burnout through it to get complete coverage.

While Sean has certainly pleased a great number of folks with his Pimp Juice, he's created thousands, if not millions, of smiles with his super sleeper pickup. He admits that it's a constant work in progress, but the current configuration seems to be treating him well. It all starts with a stock long-wheelbase frame, which is narrowed in the rear and fit with a narrowed Ford 9-inch rear end. The original trailing arms are still in use, but a pair of QA1 drag coilovers replaces the original coil springs and shock absorbers. This allows Sean to dial in the launch, and control how hard the massive Hoosier 32x14-inch slicks have to work. These slicks are big but at first glance seem to blend into the look. The backspacing on the wheels offers a bit of stock-appearing flavor, and the mud flaps add another level of sneaky detail. Measuring 15x14 inches, the steel rear wheels are equipped with stock style hubcaps, and attach to a pair of Moser axles. Moving farther within the 9-inch rear, you find a Strange spool and a 5.13:1 gear set.

Up front, there isn't much to speak of, in terms of modifications, aside from removing the sway bar, and swapping to a pair of drag shocks. The chassis does feature additional bracing, as well as a very tightly tucked roll cage, built by George Ray and Aaron Ratliff. Unless you literally stick your head inside Sean's truck, you'll struggle to find the roll cage, and the camper shell actually does an amazing job of hiding the rear support bars for the cage. The camper shell also hides the enlarged wheel tubs, and further elevates the truck's sleeper status.

For horsepower, *Farm Truck* relies on a big-block Chevy, which comes in at 502 ci and features a laundry list of speed parts that result in 837 dyno-proven horsepower. The bottom end consists of a GM crankshaft, which sends a set of Scat connecting rods and Diamond pistons into motion. A set of ported aluminum GM Performance Parts cylinder heads offers plenty of airflow, while the Comp Cams roller rocker arms keep the Manley valves moving efficiently. The camshaft is also from Comp Cams, and is a custom ground stick, designed for nitrous. Induction consists of an Edelbrock Victor Jr. intake manifold and a Holley 950 HP carburetor, while a two-stage system sends nitrous oxide into the engine through a plate and fogger kit.

A MagnaFuel fuel pump and regulator provides the fuel, while an MSD ignition sends spark to the combustion chambers. Spent gases flow through Hooker headers and into a 3½-inch exhaust system with MagnaFlow mufflers. Marc Brown at Advanced Engine & Machine (AEM) handled the engine build, while Justin Shearer tuned it. Behind the big-block is a TH350 automatic transmission, which was built by Bryan Flippone at A&A Transmission, and features a Neal Chance torque converter.

Though Sean's big-block makes plenty of steam, this truck's biggest appeal is actually its lack of good looks. It's

TOP: Under the stock hood is a 502-ci big-block Chevy engine, fit with GM Performance Parts aluminum cylinder heads. The big-block produces 837 hp thanks to a two-stage nitrous system consisting of a plate and fogger system. Up top is a Holley 950 HP carburetor, mounted to an Edelbrock Victor Jr. intake manifold. *(Photo courtesy Kyle Loftis)* MIDDLE TOP: Traction comes from a set of massive Hoosier tires, which measure 32x14 inches and mount to a pair of 15x14-inch steel wheels. Mud flaps take some of the attention away from the super-wide rubber, while the stock center caps finish off the look. A narrowed Ford 9-inch is suspended by QA1 coilovers. *(Photo courtesy Kyle Loftis)* MIDDLE BOTTOM: Inside is a tightly tucked roll cage that allows Sean to run quicker than 11.50 in the quarter-mile. In this configuration, he's actually run a full second quicker, with his best elapsed time of 10.43 seconds at 129 mph. Louise (the dog) always rides shotgun with Sean, even during races. *(Photo courtesy Sherry Driggs)* BOTTOM: Elk City, Oklahoma, shuts down a street every year for legal street racing, and Sean is a fan favorite. He comes from a street racing background, so he loves to get out on the street and have some fun without the risk of going to jail. Here, he's seen toting the left front wheel on the street. *(Photo courtesy Kyle Loftis)*

This is a common scene wherever Sean goes with *Farm Truck*. Folks don't give it much credit at first, but after one run, the swarm of onlookers is generally quite large. Sean is a diehard racer, and he's been known to partake in a few grudge races, sometimes on the street. *(Photo courtesy Kyle Loftis)*

intentionally rough and ragged to keep folks guessing, and it seems to be working, even though the truck is very well known. The camper shell, the pizza delivery sign, and the "cow catcher" mirrors give the truck an obscure look, but that was the goal. Original orange and white paint rides on the body panels, and an open door reveals a stock interior, right down to the bench seat.

Sean Whitley and Sherry Driggs campaign this truck at all sorts of events from *Pinks All Out* to organized street races. It's a crowd favorite no matter where it goes, and it's brought a whole new meaning to the term sleeper. While it may have big tires and a throaty exhaust note, the truck never fails to surprise onlookers, be it the general public or hardcore car guys. So far, the best run Sean's gotten out of the truck is a 10.43 at 129 mph, so when the boards light up during one of his runs, jaws generally drop. It's not natural for a truck this "ugly" to run this good, but that's what makes it one of the greatest sleepers of all time.

Sean is the man behind Pimp Juice traction compound, so he knows how to make *Farm Truck* hook on the street, which means it hooks really well at the track, as evidenced by this wheels-up start. The 1970 Chevy long wheelbase pickup looks like it belongs on the farm, not on the drag strip. *(Photo courtesy Sherry Driggs)*

CPSIA information can be obtained
at www.ICGtesting.com
Printed in the USA
BVOW04s0843110717

488538BV00024B/82/P

9 781613 252000